HARCOURT SCHOOL PUBLISHERS

Think Math!

Student Handbook

 Developed by Education Development Center, Inc. through National Science Foundation
Grant No. ESI-0099093

 EDC

 Harcourt
SCHOOL PUBLISHERS

Visit *The Learning Site!*
www.harcourtschool.com/thinkmath

This program was funded in part through the National Science Foundation under Grant No. ESI-0099093. Any opinions, findings, and conclusions or recommendations expressed in this program are those of the authors and do not necessarily reflect the views of the National Science Foundation.

Chapter 1

Algebra: Machines and Puzzles

Chapter 2

Multiplication and Large Numbers

Chapter 3

Factoring and Prime Numbers

Chapter 6

Grids and Graphs

Chapter 7

Decimals

Chapter 8

Developing a Division Algorithm

Chapter 9

Attributes of Two-Dimensional Figures

Chapter 10

Area and Perimeter

Chapter 11

Fraction Computation

Chapter 12

Three-Dimensional Geometry

Chapter 13

Fun with Algebra

Chapter 14

Data and Probability

Chapter 15

Graphing

Chapter

1 Algebra: Machines and Puzzles

Dear Student,

When you saw the title of this chapter, "Algebra: Machines and Puzzles," you might have wondered what machines and puzzles have to do with math. You will see a variety of machines, puzzles, and puzzling machines in this program.

Here is an input-output machine that you will see in some of the lessons in this chapter.

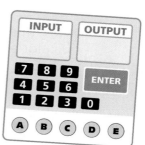

What do you think this machine does? Does it look like anything you have seen before? What do you suppose the five buttons at the bottom of the machine do?

This completed puzzle may look familiar to you.

18	11	29
16	15	31
34	26	60

If you have seen it before, how would you describe how it works to a younger student? If it is new to you, try to figure out how it works.

You already know how to add, subtract, multiply, and divide, but did you know that by the end of this first chapter, you will also be doing some algebra? Mathematicians and high school students use algebra, and you can too!

Mathematically yours,
The authors of *Think Math!*

Food for Thought

Food is like fuel. It stores the energy your body needs to grow, play, and stay healthy. This energy is measured in calories. You need a balance between the number of calories you eat and the energy you use. If you don't get enough calories, you may feel tired. But, eating too many calories can also slow you down.

grilled chicken sandwich: 300 calories

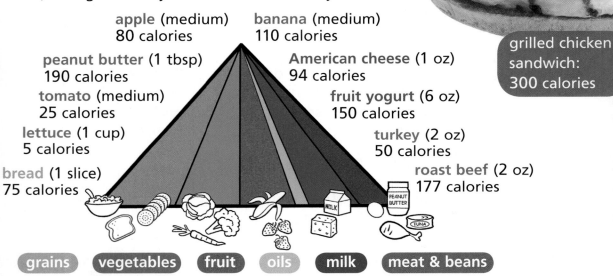

apple (medium)
80 calories

banana (medium)
110 calories

peanut butter (1 tbsp)
190 calories

American cheese (1 oz)
94 calories

tomato (medium)
25 calories

fruit yogurt (6 oz)
150 calories

lettuce (1 cup)
5 calories

turkey (2 oz)
50 calories

bread (1 slice)
75 calories

roast beef (2 oz)
177 calories

grains   vegetables   fruit   oils   milk   meat & beans

FACT·ACTIVITY 1

Use the food pyramid to answer the questions.

1 Plan a sandwich using any of the ingredients shown above. How many calories are in your sandwich?

2 How do the calories in your sandwich compare to the calories in a ready-made grilled chicken sandwich?

3 Michael is a professional soccer player. He can burn about 1,000 calories during a game. What combination of foods on this page could Michael eat that would be burned up during a soccer game? Create two different menus for Michael to eat.

The table below shows the approximate number of calories used in **10 minutes** for different activities. Use the table to answer the questions.

Calories Used in Various Activities			
Calories used in 10 minutes if your weight is...	50 lbs	100 lbs	150 lbs
Activity			
Sleeping	4	8	12
Standing	8	16	24
Raquetball	30	60	90
Running	44	88	132
Rock climbing	30	60	90

1 How many calories would a 150-pound person burn waiting in line for 10 minutes?

2 How many calories would a 100-pound person burn by sleeping for 1 hour? for 8 hours?

3 How many calories would a 150-pound person use playing racquetball for 30 minutes?

CHAPTER PROJECT

Make choices to balance calories and activities.

- Research the number of calories that two other activities use up in 10 minutes.

- Select an activity from this page or from your research that you would like to do. Estimate the number of calories you would use in one hour of that activity.

- Use the food options from Fact Activity 1 or research the calorie content of other foods. Create two different lunch menus that will balance (be about equal to) the calories you use in one hour of the activity you chose.

- Present your choices on a chart or poster.

ALMANAC Fact

When Sir Ranulph Fiennes and Dr. Mike Stroud walked across Antarctica in 1993, they each used about 12,000 calories per day—about as many calories as are found in 200 apples, 24 burritos, or 5 pounds of chocolate.

EXPLORE
Exploring Coin Combinations

1 Here is the kind of question you will not often see in this program.

> **Ashley made a 75¢ purchase.**
> **She paid with a one-dollar bill.**
> **How much change should she get?**

All Ashley needs to know is that she should receive a quarter's worth of change!

2 In this book, you are likely to find questions like this:

> **How many different combinations**
> **of pennies, nickels, and dimes make**
> **a quarter's worth of change?**

3 List four different combinations of coins that make 25¢.
You will list more later.

REVIEW MODEL
Cross Number Puzzles

You can practice computation and learn about equations and properties of addition in Cross Number Puzzles. To complete these puzzles, follow the rule: Amounts on both sides of a thick line must be the same.

Look at the numbers in this Cross Number Puzzle.

25	17	42
15	38	53
40	55	95

You can write addition and subtraction number sentences to go with a puzzle.

Some number sentences you might write for this puzzle are:

$$25 + 17 = 42$$
$$53 - 38 = 15$$
$$40 + 55 = 95$$
$$95 - 53 = 42$$
$$(25 + 17) + (15 + 38) = 42 + 53 = 95$$

Solve this puzzle by choosing numbers to make amounts on both sides of thick lines the same.

Example Find the missing numbers.

In the second row I see 45 on one side of a thick line and 73 on the other side. I need more on the side with 45. How much more? I can think of ■ + 45 = 73 or 73 − 45 = ■

The missing number is 28.

24	51	
	45	73
52	96	148

24 and 51 are on one side of the thick line. What belongs on the other side?

$$24 + 51 = ■$$

75 is the missing number.

✔Check for Understanding

Copy and write the missing numbers in the Cross Number Puzzles.

❶
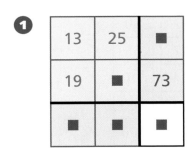

13	25	■
19	■	73
■	■	■

❷
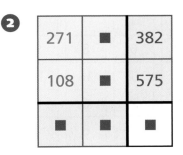

271	■	382
108	■	575
■	■	■

❸

683	■	194
■	100	■
■	■	115

EXPLORE
Exploring Input-Output Machines

If you press Button A, type in these inputs, and press ENTER, you get these outputs.

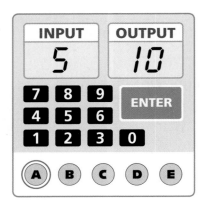
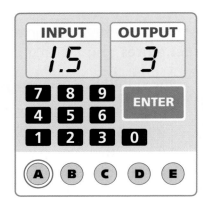
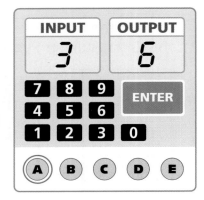

1 Find a rule for what the machine is doing when you press Button A.

---

2 Do the numbers in this table work for your rule?

INPUT	2	5	1	3	0	4	12	50
MACHINE OUTPUT	4	10	2	6	0	8	24	100

---

3 This table shows a three-step rule. What do you notice about each output?

INPUT	2	5	1	3	0	4	12	50
Add 5	7	10	6	8	5	9	17	55
Double	14	20	12	16	10	18	34	110
Subtract 10	4	10	2	6	0	8	24	100
MACHINE OUTPUT	4	10	2	6	0	8	24	100

REVIEW MODEL
Input-Output Tables

To complete an input-output table, you use a rule, or rules, and an input number.

This table shows a 1-step rule. The rule is *add 6*. Sometimes you have to figure out what the rule is by looking for patterns in input-output pairs you know.

INPUT	6	3	10	0	21	7
Add 6	12	9	16	6	27	■
OUTPUT	12	9	16	6	27	■

Think:

$7 + 6 = 13$

So, the output is 13.

This table shows a 3-step rule. The rules are *multiply by 3*, then *subtract the input*, then *add 2*.

INPUT	5	12	0	8	10	9
Multiply by 3	15	36	0	24	30	■
Subtract the input	10	24	0	16	20	■
Add 2	12	26	2	18	22	■
OUTPUT	12	26	2	18	22	■

Think:

$9 \times 3 = 27$

$27 - 9 = 18$

$18 + 2 = 20$

So, the output is 20.

✔ Check for Understanding

Copy and complete the input-output tables.

1

INPUT	8	0	10	12
Multiply by 4	32	0	■	■
OUTPUT	32	0	■	■

2

INPUT	10	20	30	40
Subtract 8	2	■	■	■
OUTPUT	2	■	■	■

3

INPUT	5	1	11	8
Multiply by 2	10	■	■	■
Add 4	14	■	■	■
Subtract 2	12	■	■	■
OUTPUT	12	■	■	■

4

INPUT	10	9	8	7
Multiply by 3	■	■	■	■
Divide by 3	■	■	■	■
Add 10	■	■	■	■
OUTPUT	■	■	■	■

EXPLORE
Exploring Button B and Button C on the Machine

This is what happens to 6, 10, and 7 when Button B on the machine is pressed.

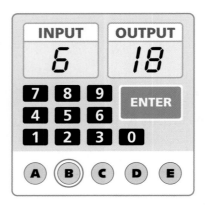 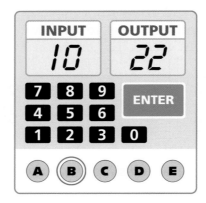 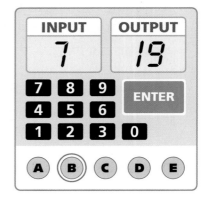

1 What is a rule for Button B?

_____

2 How would you make bag-and-dot drawings for your rule?

_____

This is what happens to three inputs when Button C on the machine is pressed.

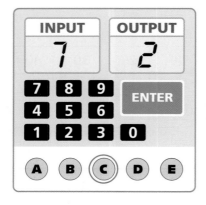 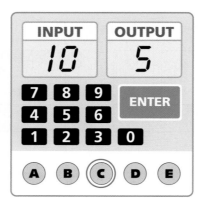 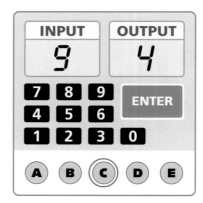

3 What is a rule for Button C?

_____

4 What will the OUTPUT be if the INPUT is 4?

REVIEW MODEL
Negative Numbers

You can use a thermometer or a number line to help you think about negative numbers.

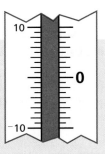

On a thermometer, positive temperatures are above 0. Negative, or minus, temperatures are below 0.

On a number line, positive numbers are to the right of 0. Negative numbers are to the left of 0. 0 is neither positive nor negative.

Negative Numbers   **Positive Numbers**

⁻10 ⁻9 ⁻8 ⁻7 ⁻6 ⁻5 ⁻4 ⁻3 ⁻2 ⁻1 0 1 2 3 4 5 6 7 8 9 10

Negative numbers are always written with a negative sign.
⁻6 is read "negative 6."

You can use a thermometer or a number line to help you subtract.

Example
Rule: Subtract 4 or − 4.

INPUT	7	6	5	4	3	2	1	0
OUTPUT	3	2	1	0	⁻1	⁻2	⁻3	⁻4

Think: Start at 3. Move 4 spaces left on the number line. End at ⁻1.

✔Check for Understanding

Copy and complete the input-output tables for the subtraction rules.

1 Rule: Subtract 2, or − 2.

INPUT	4	3	2	1
OUTPUT	2	1	■	■

2 Rule: Subtract 5, or − 5.

INPUT	6	4	2	0
OUTPUT	1	■	■	■

3 Rule: Subtract 8, or − 8.

INPUT	12	10	8	6
OUTPUT	4	■	■	■

4 Rule: Subtract 10, or − 10.

INPUT	20	10	5	0
OUTPUT	■	■	■	■

EXPLORE
Exploring Button D on the Machine

If you press Button D, type in these inputs, and press ENTER, you get these outputs.

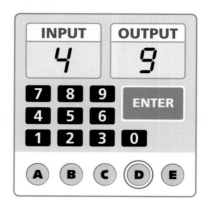

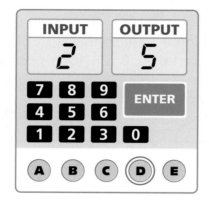

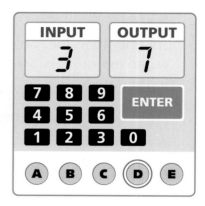

1 Find a rule for what the machine is doing.
Try combining operations.

2 Do the numbers in this table work for your rule?

INPUT	6	8	5	10	25	12
OUTPUT	13	17	11	21	51	25

REVIEW MODEL
Multiplying Cross Number Puzzles

You can practice multiplication in Cross Number Puzzles. Remember the Cross Number Puzzle rule: Amounts on both sides of a thick line must be the same.

Look at the numbers in Puzzle A and in Puzzle A × 5.

- Each number in Puzzle A × 5 is 5 times the matching number in Puzzle A.

- The new puzzle still works—the amounts on both sides of a thick line are the same.

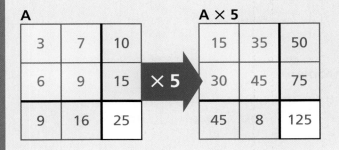

Here are some matching addition and subtraction sentences for these puzzles.

Puzzle A	Puzzle A × 5
3 + 7 = 10	15 + 35 = 50
15 − 9 = 6	75 − 45 = 30

When multiplying a puzzle by a number, you multiply all the numbers in that puzzle by the number.

(3 × 5) + (7 × 5) = 10 × 5, or 15 + 35 = 50

(15 × 5) − (9 × 5) = 6 × 5, or 75 − 45 = 30

✔Check for Understanding

Copy and write the missing numbers in the Cross Number Puzzles.

1

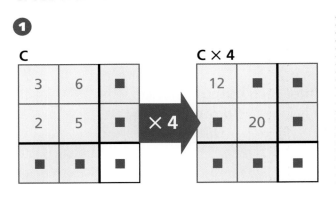

2

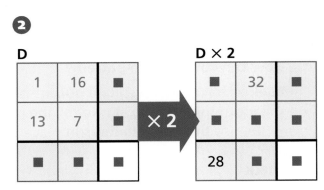

REVIEW MODEL
Problem Solving Strategy
Look for a Pattern

Hailey is making a design with squares. She started at the top and kept adding rows of squares to the bottom.

Complete the table to show the number of squares there will be in rows 5, 6, and 7. Write a rule.

Row 1
Row 2
Row 3
Row 4

Row	1	2	3	4	5	6	7	r
Number of Squares	1	3	5	7	■	■	■	■

Strategy: Look for a Pattern

Read to Understand

What do you know from reading the problem?

Hailey made a design with squares. The design shows 1 square in Row 1, 3 squares in Row 2, 5 squares in Row 3, and 7 squares in Row 4.

Plan

How can you solve this problem?

You can look for a pattern in the table that tells you how to find the number of squares, if you know the number of rows. Then you can use the pattern to complete the table and to help you write the rule.

Solve

How can you find the pattern?

Look at how the input- and output-pairs relate. Each output is twice the input minus 1. So, a rule for the pattern is $2r - 1$. To complete the table, use the Row numbers in place of r. $(2 \times 5) - 1 = 9$.

Check

Look back at the problem. Did you answer the questions that were asked? Do the answers make sense?

Problem Solving Practice

Look for a pattern to solve these problems.

① Mike saves 4 pennies on Day 1, 8 pennies on Day 2, 12 pennies on Day 3, and 16 pennies on Day 4. If the pattern continues, how many pennies will he save on Day 8? What is a rule for the pattern?

② Monica is making picture frames where the length and width are related by a rule. Sizes are shown in inches in the table. What is the length when the width is 8 inches? What is a rule for the pattern?

Width	2	3	5	8	x
Length	4	5	7	■	■

Problem Solving Strategies

- ✔ Act It Out
- ✔ Draw a Picture
- ✔ Guess and Check
- ✔ **Look for a Pattern**
- ✔ Make a Graph
- ✔ Make a Model
- ✔ Make an Organized List
- ✔ Make a Table
- ✔ Solve a Simpler Problem
- ✔ Use Logical Reasoning
- ✔ Work Backward
- ✔ Write an Equation

Mixed Strategy Practice

Use any strategy to solve. Explain.

③ Anthony had 4 boxes with 6 erasers in each box. He gave 2 erasers to each of 3 friends. How many erasers does he have left?

④ Madison earns $10 each week walking a neighbor's dog. She saves half the money she earns. How long will it take her to save $50?

⑤ In the morning Thomas spent 15 minutes raking and 20 minutes mowing the lawn. In the afternoon, he spent twice as much time raking and twice as much time mowing. How much time did Thomas spend raking and mowing?

⑥ Jasmine bought a notebook for $5, a ruler for $2, and a set of markers for $4. Heather bought a book bag for $8 and some pencils. They both spent the same amount of money. How much did Heather pay for the pencils she bought?

For 7–9, use the table.

⑦ How much farther is it from Dallas to New York than from Dallas to Chicago?

⑧ How far is a round trip between Dallas and Atlanta?

⑨ Carla made a round trip between Dallas and one of the cities listed in the table. She drove 2,722 miles in all. To which city did Carla drive?

Distance Between Dallas and Some United States Cities	
City	**Number of Miles to Dallas**
Atlanta	782
Chicago	967
Miami	1,361
New York	1,550
San Francisco	1,732

Vocabulary

Choose the best vocabulary term from Word List A for each definition.

1 Division is a(n) ___?___.

2 Numbers to the right of zero on a number line are ___?___ numbers.

3 Numbers to the left of zero on a number line are ___?___ numbers.

4 To ___?___ a number, just multiply it by 2.

5 An algebraic expression is ___?___ for a rule in a function machine.

6 If two values are the same, then one value ___?___ the other.

7 If the input of an input-output table is 8 and the ___?___ is subtract 2, then the output is 6.

8 One way to solve a problem involving groups of numbers is to make a(n) ___?___.

Word List A

algebra
double
equals
function
negative
operation
organized list
output
positive
rule
shorthand
zero

Complete each analogy using the best term from Word List B.

9 Addend is to sum as ___?___ is to product.

10 Input is to rule as ___?___ is to algebraic expression.

Word List B

combination
factor
inverse
variable

Talk Math

Use the vocabulary terms *operation, rule,* and *inverse* to discuss with a partner what you have just learned about algebra.

11 How can you identify a rule to complete an input-output table?

12 If you know the output of a function machine, how can you find the input?

13 Create a Venn diagram for the words *addend, algebraic expression, factor, input, output, product, rule, sum,* and *variable.*

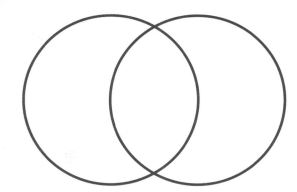

Tree Diagram

14 Create a tree diagram using the word *function.* Use what you know and what you have learned about algebra and rules.

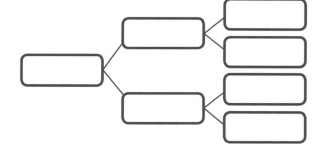

What's in a Word?

COMBINATION The word *combination* has different meanings in the English language. The root of the word *combination* is *combine* which means "to put together." The combination for a combination lock is put together in only one way. If you try other arrangements of the group of numbers, they won't open the lock. In mathematics, however, a *combination* is simply a group of numbers in any arrangement or order. For example, the list of the numbers 5, 13, and 22 is considered to be the same combination as the numbers 22, 5, and 13.

GO ONLINE Technology
Multimedia Math Glossary
www.harcourtschool.com/thinkmath

GAME

Find a Rule

> **Game Purpose**
> To practice finding rules for pairs of input-output numbers

How To Play The Game

1 Play the game with a small group of students. The group will need pencil and paper or space at the board with chalk or a marker.

2 Decide who will be the rule-maker. The rule-maker draws an input-output table and chooses a secret rule. The rule can use addition, subtraction, multiplication, or division.

Examples of rules: + 9, − 8, × 4, ÷ 3

3 The other players take turns writing input numbers in the input-output table. The rule-maker writes the output for each input number using the secret rule.
- If the output is not a whole number, the rule-maker writes an X in the box. This might happen if the rule-maker chooses a division rule or a subtraction rule whose output will be less than zero.

4 When a player thinks he or she knows the secret rule, that player asks the rule-maker to give an input.
- If the player gives the correct output, he or she wins that round. The winner becomes the next rule-maker and chooses a new secret rule.
- If the player is not correct, the game continues until another player determines the secret rule and wins the round.

5 Play as many rounds as time allows.

GAME

Fact Builder

Game Purpose
To practice multiplication facts up to 12 × 12

Materials
- number cube (numbered 1–6)

Fact Builder

$2 \times 4 = 8$

| Sam | ||||| | |
| Luca | ||| |

How To Play The Game

1 Two, three, or four players can play. Each player needs a pencil and paper.

2 The first player tosses the number cube twice to get two factors and writes the multiplication fact.
- Players must agree that the product is correct. To check the product, draw an array or use counters.
- If the product is correct, the player receives 1 point.

3 The next player tosses the number cube once and adds the outcome to the lesser number to make a new multiplication fact.

4 Continue taking turns, adding the number tossed to the lesser factor, and writing the product.
- If the toss of the cube causes one factor to be greater than 12, start again by tossing two cubes.

Example of play:

Roll	Outcome	Multiplication Fact
First	3	
Second	5	$3 \times 5 = 15$
Third	4	$5 \times (3 + 4) = 5 \times 7 = 35$
Fourth	6	$7 \times (5 + 6) = 77 \times 11 = 77$

5 The first player to score **10** points wins the round. Play as many rounds as time allows.

CHALLENGE

What's Going On Here?

Derrick and Lea like to make up codes to try to stump one another. After a lesson on input-output tables and rules, they decided to make up their own math codes. Try these math codes to see whether you can keep up with Derrick and Lea.

Write a rule for each symbol.

1 What does the ♥ mean?

INPUT	2	3	4	3	1	4	3	3	0	1
Code	♥		♥		♥		♥		♥	
OUTPUT	7		13		5		10		1	

2 What does the ⚡ mean?

INPUT	8	2	10	5	4	4	9	3	2	1
Code	⚡		⚡		⚡		⚡		⚡	
OUTPUT	3		1		0		2		1	

3 What does the ♪ mean?

INPUT	3	2	1	6	0	2	5	3	1	11
Code	♪		♪		♪		♪		♪	
OUTPUT	10		14		4		16		24	

4 What does the ● mean?

INPUT	6	2	8	4	1	7	12	8	0	8
Code	●		●		●		●		●	
OUTPUT	2		3		2		5		2	

5 Create your own math code. Write some examples using the code. Then challenge a classmate to determine the meaning of your code.

Chapter

2 Multiplication and Large Numbers

Dear Student,

This chapter is titled **"Multiplication and Large Numbers"** because you already know quite a bit about multiplication and are ready for some new ideas that will help you to multiply large numbers.

We begin by looking for patterns in a multiplication table. Noticing patterns in columns and rows can help you develop new strategies for multiplying larger numbers.

There are many ways to solve a problem such as **24 × 29.**

One way is to think about it as an area model with 29 rows and 24 columns and draw a quick sketch.

By splitting up the area model into smaller parts, we can use four simpler multiplications to solve the one harder one. Here's one way:

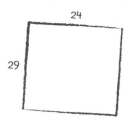

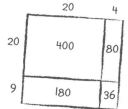

Or we can split up the numbers and multiply simpler ones in a puzzle like this.

We hope that by the end of this chapter you will have seen how patterns, pictures, and puzzles can help you use simpler multiplication problems to do more difficult ones.

Mathematically yours,
The authors of *Think Math!*

×	12	12	24
20	240	240	480
9	108	108	216
29	348	348	696

Watt's That?

FACT·ACTIVITY 1

Solar energy is a renewable resource. One way to collect and use the energy in sunlight is to place large arrays of solar modules (called photoelectric cells) on rooftops. Photoelectric cells change light directly into electricity. The graph below shows the approximate potential amount of solar energy that reaches Houston, Texas, each month of the year as measured in watts per square meter.

1 About how many watts per square meter of solar power does Houston receive in January?

2 Write a number sentence to show about how much solar power a 10-square meter solar module will receive in January.

3 About how many watts of solar power would an 8-square meter solar module receive during October?

4 During which month(s) does Houston receive about 2 times as much solar power as in December? Explain.

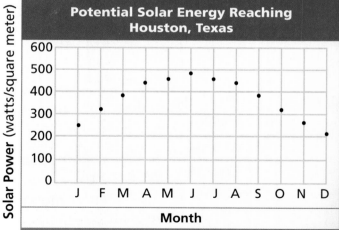

Potential Solar Energy Reaching Houston, Texas

5 If a solar module receives a total of 75,000 watts of solar energy in January, what could be the area of the solar module? First, write a multiplication sentence that will help you figure out the area of the solar module. Then find the area.

Photoelectric solar modules generate electricity when struck by sunlight. These modules may be grouped into an array that covers most of a home's roof. Homes use energy to heat air and water, for air conditioning and refrigeration, and for lights and other appliances. The picture below is a representation of how solar energy might be used in a typical house.

1. Write multiplication number sentences to show how many modules are in each of the four sections (each home use.)

2. Each module generates 90 watts of electricity. How many watts are used for heating water? How many watts are generated by all the solar modules?

3. How many modules would be needed to build 6 of these arrays?

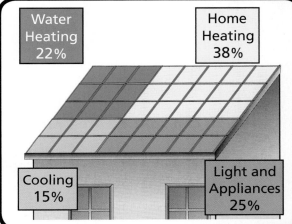

Water Heating 22%

Home Heating 38%

Cooling 15%

Light and Appliances 25%

CHAPTER PROJECT

You can cook with solar power, too. Get a pot (preferably black) and a box that the pot can fit into with room to spare. Line the inside of all 6 sides of the box with aluminum foil to make them reflective. Put some water in the pot, and leave it outside for about an hour. Use a thermometer to test the temperature. Now, put the pot inside the box and place it in a spot where there is sunlight. Check the temperature after another hour to see if the water heats up.

- Write multiplication sentences to help you find the area of each reflective side of your cooker.

- Find the total reflective surface.

- Suppose you built a larger or smaller cooker. Research some home-made solar cookers and explain how they differ from the one you built.

- Do you think more reflective surface will cook the same food faster? Work with your class to select two solar cookers with different total reflective surfaces. Experiment to see which heats the water faster.

ALMANAC
Fact

The Earth is about 93 million miles from the sun. Light travels about 183,000 miles per second. It takes about 8 minutes and 20 seconds for light from the sun to reach Earth.

EXPLORE
Splitting Area Models

You can split an area model and use simpler multiplication problems to solve more difficult ones.

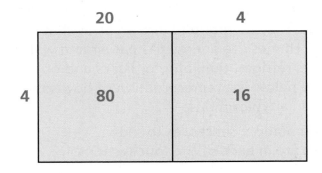

$$24 \times 4 = (20 \times 4) + (4 \times 4) = 80 + 16 = 96$$

Or, you can split an area model more than once.

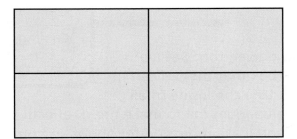

PROBLEM: With a partner, draw and split an area model to show 18 × 22. Find the product.

REVIEW MODEL
Splitting an Area Model to Multiply

You can split an area model, write new factors, and then complete a matching puzzle to help you multiply.

Example: Find 27 × 33.

Step 1 Draw an area model.

Split the area model to show factors that are easier to multiply.

	30	3
20		
7		

Step 2 Write the partial products in the sections of the area model.

	30	3
20	600	60
7	210	21

Step 3 Complete a Cross Number Puzzle to match.

So, 27 × 33 = 891

×	30	3	33
20	600	60	660
7	210	21	231
27	810	81	891

✔ Check for Understanding

Draw and split an area model and then complete a matching Cross Number Puzzle to multiply.

1 14 × 16   **2** 21 × 18   **3** 38 × 22   **4** 13 × 47

REVIEW MODEL
Doubling and Adding to Multiply

You can use the strategy doubling and adding to help find products.

Think about the products in a row of a multiplication table.

First, fill in the products for 17×1, 17×2, 17×3, 17×4, and 17×10.

×	1	2	3	4	5	6	7	8	9	10
17	17	34	51	68						170

You know ↑ | Double 17 ↑ | Add 17 + 34 ↑ | Double 34 ↑ | Multiply by 10 ↑

Then, use those products to fill in the other products.

×	1	2	3	4	5	6	7	8	9	10
17	17	34	51	68	85	102	119	136	153	170

Halve 170 ↑ | Double 51 ↑ | Add 51 + 68 ↑ | Double 68 ↑ | Add 68 + 85 ↑

You can use these same ideas to multiply some two-digit numbers.

Example 1 Find 13×16.
A Think: $10 \times 16 = 160$
B Think: $1 \times 16 = 16$ and $2 \times 16 = 32$, so $3 \times 16 = 16 + 32$, or 48.
C Add: $160 + 48 = 208$
So, $13 \times 16 = 208$.

Example 2 Find 21×43.
A Think: $10 \times 43 = 430$
B **Double** 430 to get 20×43. $2 \times 430 = 860$
C **Add** one more 43. $860 + 43 = 903$
So, $21 \times 43 = 903$.

✔Check for Understanding

Use the strategy doubling and adding to find the products.

❶
×	1	2	3	4	5	6	7	8	9	10
24	■	■	■	■	■	■	■	■	■	■

❷ 24×16 ❸ 12×24 ❹ 15×8 ❺ 14×16

EXPLORE
Greater Multiples

Find these products.

1
10
10 [?]

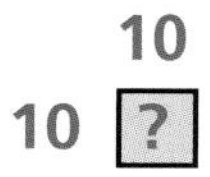

2
100
10 [?]

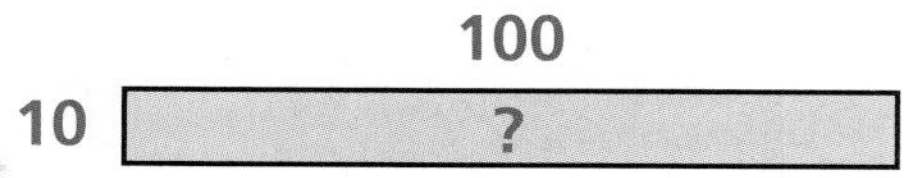

3
100
100 [?]

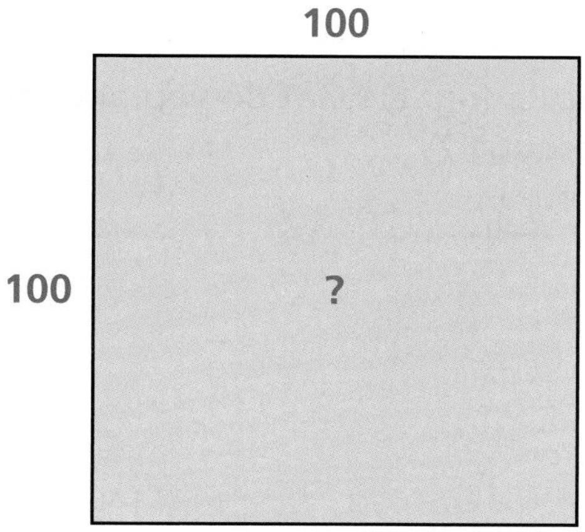

Solve this problem with a partner.

4 Patrick and Jaimee want to estimate **4,162 × 3,321** by multiplying 4,000 and 3,000. Patrick thinks that **4,162 × 3,321** is about 12,000. Jaimee thinks that this product is a lot larger—about 12,000,000!

What do you think and why?

EXPLORE

A Huge Number of Marbles

Jorge counted all the marbles in his collection and found he had **151**. He thought that if all **211** fifth graders in his school had the same number of marbles that he had, that would be a huge number of marbles!

Without calculating it, what do you already know about the product?

REVIEW MODEL
Estimating Products

You can estimate products of whole numbers by rounding the factors or by using compatible numbers for the factors. In multiplication, compatible numbers are factors that are easy to multiply.

Here are four different ways to estimate 23×38.

1 Round both factors up. . . . . $23 \times 38 \rightarrow 30 \times 40 \rightarrow 1,200$

2 Round both factors down . . . . $23 \times 38 \rightarrow 20 \times 30 \rightarrow 600$

3 Round each factor to the nearest ten . . $23 \times 38 \rightarrow 20 \times 40 \rightarrow 800$

4 Use factors that are close to 27 and
38 and are easy to multiply. . . . . $23 \times 38 \rightarrow 25 \times 40 \rightarrow 1,000$

The way you adjust the factors should be tied to the type of estimate you need.

- A way to find an estimate that is greater than the actual product is to round both factors up.

- A way to find an estimate that is less than the actual product is to round both factors down.

- A way to find an estimate that is close to the actual product is to round each factor to the nearest ten or to use factors that are close to the factors and easy to multiply.

✔ Check for Understanding

Estimate each product two ways.

1 62×24

2 52×35

3 127×98

4 77×42

5 17×221

6 119×988

EXPLORE
Bigger Steps Away from Square Numbers

Your teacher will tell you which steps to investigate.

If investigating 2 Steps Away you might try something like this:

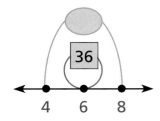

If investigating 3 Steps Away you might try something like this:

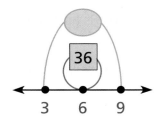

If investigating 4 Steps Away you might try something like this:

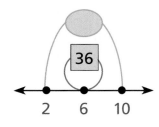

---

1 Try some different numbers and see if you find a pattern.

2 Pick a 2-digit number.

- You may use a calculator to square the number.

- Use your pattern to predict the product for your number of steps away.

3 Did it work? You may check with a calculator.

REVIEW MODEL
Using a Pattern to Multiply

You can use the pattern shown below to help you to find the product of factors that are 1, 2, 3, and 4 steps away from a square number.

In the diagram below, the number squared is 7: $7 \times 7 = 49$.

Look at the products for the pairs of factors that are 1, 2, 3, and 4 steps away from 7. Do you see a pattern?

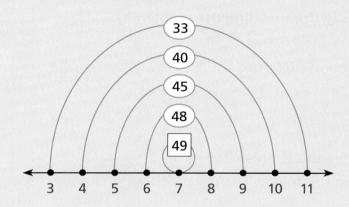

Square number. 49

- **1 step away** → $6 \times 8 = 49 - (1 \times 1) = 49 - 1 = 48$

- **2 steps away** → $5 \times 9 = 49 - (2 \times 2) = 49 - 4 = 45$

- **3 steps away** → $4 \times 10 = 49 - (3 \times 3) = 49 - 9 = 40$

- **4 steps away** → $3 \times 11 = 49 - (4 \times 4) = 49 - 16 = 33$

✔Check for Understanding

Use a pattern to complete these related number sentences.

1 $10 \times 10 = \blacksquare$

$9 \times 11 = \blacksquare$

$8 \times 12 = \blacksquare$

$7 \times 13 = \blacksquare$

$6 \times 14 = \blacksquare$

2 $12 \times 12 = \blacksquare$

$11 \times 13 = \blacksquare$

$10 \times 14 = \blacksquare$

$9 \times 15 = \blacksquare$

$8 \times 16 = \blacksquare$

3 $50 \times 50 = \blacksquare$

$49 \times 51 = \blacksquare$

$48 \times 52 = \blacksquare$

$47 \times 53 = \blacksquare$

$46 \times 54 = \blacksquare$

REVIEW MODEL
Problem Solving Strategy
Solve a Simpler Problem

> Grant works 24 hours a week. How many hours does he work in 31 weeks?

Strategy: Solve a Simpler Problem

Read to Understand

What do you know from reading the problem?

Grant works 24 hours each week.

What do you need to find out?

the number of hours Grant works in 31 weeks

Plan

How can you solve this problem?

I can use the strategy *solve a simpler problem* to find 24 × 31.

Solve

How can you solve a simpler problem?

One Way: I can multiply 24 by 30 (which is simpler to compute mentally) and then make an adjustment by adding another 24.
24 × 30 = 720; 720 + 24 = 744

Another Way: I can split an area model and complete a puzzle.

	20	4
30	600	120
1	20	4

×	20	4	24
30	600	120	720
1	20	4	24
31	620	124	744

So, Grant works 744 hours in 31 weeks.

Check

Look back at the problem. Did you answer the questions that were asked? Does the answer make sense?

Problem Solving Practice

Solve a simpler problem to solve.

1 Pat's Pet Shop sells flea collars for $17. Last month they sold 23 collars. How much money did they take in on the sale of flea collars?

2 Chad earns $12 an hour. He worked 4 hours in January, 13 hours in February, and 23 hours in March. How much did he earn those three months?

Problem Solving Strategies

✔ Act It Out
✔ Draw a Picture
✔ Guess and Check
✔ Look for a Pattern
✔ Make a Graph
✔ Make a Model
✔ Make an Organized List
✔ Make a Table
✔ **Solve a Simpler Problem**
✔ Use Logical Reasoning
✔ Work Backward
✔ Write an Equation

Mixed Strategy Practice

Use any strategy to solve. Then explain what strategy you used and how you solved the problem on a separate piece of paper.

3 Anthony lives 4 blocks from school. How many blocks does he walk to school and back home in a week?

4 Michel's family is planning a trip. They can go to either Dallas or San Francisco. They can drive, fly, or take the train to their destination. How many choices do they have?

5 Katlin exercises for 2 minutes on Day 1, 4 minutes on Day 2, 8 minutes on Day 3, and 16 minutes on Day 4. If the pattern continues, how many minutes will she exercise on Day 7?

6 Students in kindergarten through fifth grade attend Garden Elementary School. There are 4 classes in each grade with about 25 students in each class. About how many students attend Garden Elementary School?

Emma made this table to show some popular dog breeds. Use the table for 7–9.

7 Which is the second most popular breed?

8 Which breeds are less popular than a Beagle?

9 List the breeds in order from most popular to least popular?

Most Popular United States Dog Breeds	
Dog Breed	**Number of Registered Dogs**
Beagle	45,033
Dachshund	39,473
German Shepherd	43,950
Golden Retriever	52,530
Labrador Retriever	144,934

Chapter 2 Vocabulary

Choose the best vocabulary term from Word List A for each sentence.

1 Multiples of 5 that end in 5 are __?__.

2 The numbers 4, 8, 12, and 16 are __?__ of 4.

3 The __?__ for 371 is $3 \times 100 + 7 \times 10 + 1 \times 1$.

4 You can estimate a product by __?__ factors and then multiplying them.

5 You can find the value of a number in expanded notation by __?__.

6 A(n) __?__ is a rectangle of rows and columns.

7 You can just round factors or use __?__ to estimate a product.

8 A(n) __?__ has a horizontal line of objects.

9 You can add __?__ to find the product of two numbers.

Word List A

adding products
array
compatible numbers
doubling products
estimating
expanded notation
factors
multiples
odd multiples
partial products
rounding
row
word

Complete the analogy using the best term from Word List B.

10 Ones is to thousands as billions is to __?__.

11 Horizontal is to vertical as rows are to __?__.

Word List B

arrays
billions
columns
trillions

Talk Math

Discuss with a partner what you have learned about multiplying large numbers. Use the vocabulary terms *product*, *square number*, *neighbor numbers*, and *steps away*.

12 How can you multiply 41×39?

13 How can you multiply an odd multiple of 5 by itself?

14 How can you multiply 56×64?

15 Create a concept map that shows different ways to multiply larger numbers.

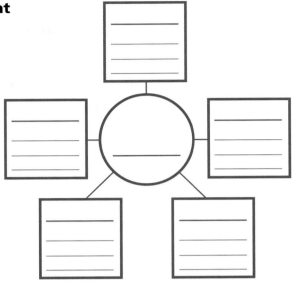

Analysis Chart

16 Create an analysis chart using the vocabulary terms *factors, rounding, compatible numbers,* and *neighbor numbers.* Use what you know and what you have learned about multiplying.

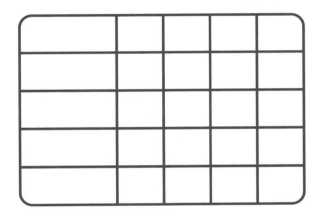

What's in a Word?

TRILLION Many familiar words begin with *tri-*. Some of them are *triangle, tricycle, trio,* and *triple.* Can you see what these words have in common? A triangle has three angles, a tricycle has three wheels, a trio is three people, and a triple is something that occurs three times. The prefix *tri-* means "three." The word *trillion* puts together the prefix *tri-* with *-illion* from the word *million* to get *trillion.* So, *million* is the first group of millions, billion is the second group of millions, and *trillion* is the third group of millions.

GO ONLINE Technology
Multimedia Math Glossary
www.harcourtschool.com/thinkmath

GAME

Product Grab

Game Purpose
To review basic multiplication facts through 12

Materials
• 48 index cards   • clock

Product Grab

| 5 | 2 | 9 | 4 |

How To Play The Game

1 Play this game with a partner. Use index cards to make 4 sets of number cards, each set numbered 1 to 12.

2 One player mixes up the cards, and deals them all face down.

3 Players turn over the top two cards from their piles at the same time and state the products.

• The player whose cards have the greater product grabs all 4 cards and sets them aside.

• If the products are equal, both players turn over two more cards. The player with the greater product takes all 8 cards.

Example: **Danielle's cards**   **Evan's cards**

6 2   5 7

The product of Evan's cards is 35, and the product of Danielle's cards is 12. Since 35 is greater than 12, Evan takes all 4 cards.

4 If you run out of cards from your original pile, mix up the cards you have grabbed, and use them to keep playing.

5 At the end of 10 minutes, the player with the greater number of cards wins the game. If a player runs out of cards before the 10 minutes are up, the other player wins the game.

GAME

Factor Search

> **Game Purpose**
> **To practice multiplication and division facts**
>
> **Materials**
> • Activity Master 9: *Factor Search Grid*
> • Activity Masters 10–13: *Factor Search Cards*
> • counters in two different colors • scissors

How To Play The Game

1 Play this game with a partner. Each player needs a set of counters and a *Factor Search* grid. Cut out all of the *Factor Search* cards.

2 Mix up the *Factor Search* cards, and place them face down in a pile. Each player takes a *Factor Search* card. The player who has the greater number goes first. Put those two cards at the bottom of the pile.

3 Take turns. Turn over the top card from the pile.
• Find a square on your *Factor Search* grid by naming two factors for the product shown on the *Factor Search* card.
• Put a counter on the grid at the product location.
• If there is no open square for a product, the player loses a turn.

Example: Emilee turns over this card.

| 27 |

Possible factors: The only possible factors are 9 and 3. The factors cannot be 1 and 27 because 27 is not a factor on the *Factor Search* grid.

Possible moves: There are two squares on the *Factor Search* grid on which Emilee could put a counter: 9 across and 3 down, and 3 across and 9 down.

4 The first player to put three counters in a line—horizontally, vertically, or diagonally—wins.

CHALLENGE

Hexagon Loop

Someone has left some mystery puzzles! Your skills will be tested as you try to solve them. Don't get dizzy!

- Figure out the relationship between the numbers in the rectangles and the hexagons in Puzzle A.
- Use that same relationship to solve Puzzles B and C.

A

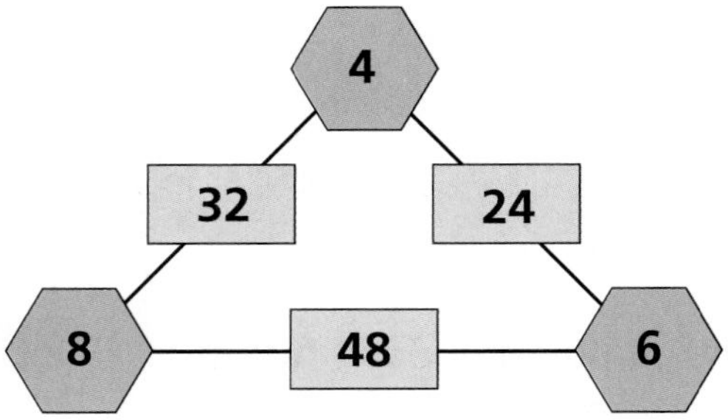

B

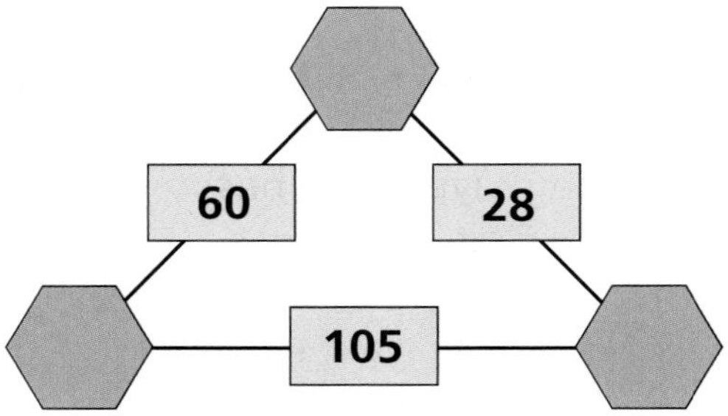

C

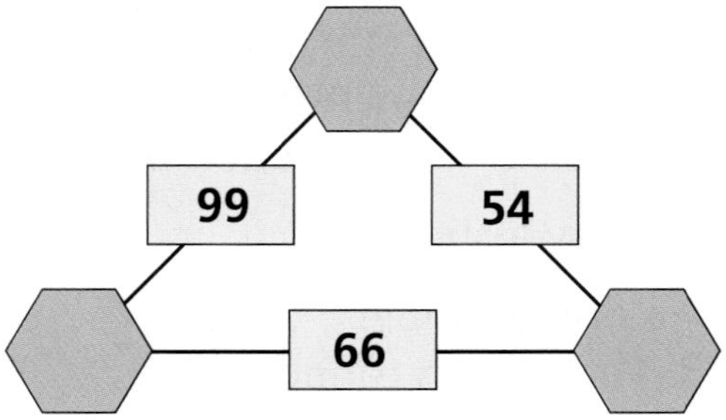

Now that you know what's going on, trace the outline of one puzzle, and make up your own. Challenge a classmate with it.

Chapter

3 Factoring and Prime Numbers

Dear Student,

Factories make various products. We use very similar words—factors and products—when we are talking about how some numbers can be multiplied together to make other numbers. The numbers we multiply are called factors, and the result of the multiplication is the product. In this chapter, you will learn more about putting numbers together and taking them apart using multiplication.

To begin exploring making and breaking numbers with multiplication, you will solve Mystery Number Puzzles with clues such as those at the right.

Puzzle

- ☑ I have 4 factors
- ☑ I am a 1-digit number
- ☑ I am not divisible by 4

Can you guess what the number is? Don't worry if you can't yet. By the end of the chapter you will know what each of these clues mean and be able to quickly solve the puzzle.

Mathematically yours,
The authors of *Think Math!*

Wild Rides

FACT·ACTIVITY 1

Modern roller coasters have train cars linked together, each carrying a number of people. Their hills can be hundreds of feet high.

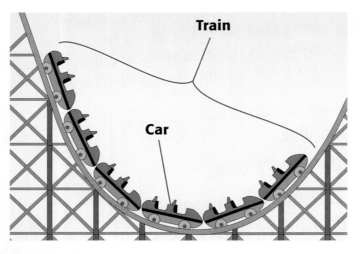

Train

Car

Number of Passengers in Some Roller Coasters	
Name of Roller Coaster	Number of Passengers
Kingda Ka	18
Superman Ride of Steel	36
Titan	30
Scream	32
Thunderbolt	24

① The *Scream* is a train of 8 cars. How many passengers does each car carry?

② Which ride in the table could use trains made of cars that carry 5 passengers each?

③ Suppose you were designing a new 18-passenger train for *Kingda Ka*. Think about how many different-sized cars could be used for 18 passengers if you want the same number of passengers to ride in each car. What are the different numbers of cars and passengers that could be used for the train?

④ Suppose you are designing a new 30-passenger train for *Titan*. Which of the cars you designed for *Kingda Ka* could be used for this train? (Hint: Think about factors of 30.)

This roller coaster design is supported by segments of vertical metal beams under the hills. To be cost effective, all hills must be built from segments of metal beams that are the same length.

1. What are the lengths of beam segments that could be used for the 81-ft support? What lengths could be used for the 36-ft support?

2. Which factors do these two numbers have in common? What is the largest segment of beam length that could be used for both supports?

3. The middle hill will use the same size beam segments used in Problem 2. Remember the middle hill is less than 81 ft but greater than 36 ft. List the possible number of beam segments for the middle hill and the possible heights of the hill.

CHAPTER PROJECT

With your group, build a model roller coaster train. Use 3 cardboard egg cartons. Each space for an egg represents a seat on your roller coaster. Cut and arrange the cartons to make trains. Each car in the train must have the same number of seats and the train must have a total of 36 seats.

- How many different car sizes will let 36 people ride the roller coaster train?

- Explain how these different car sizes are related.

- Write a description of another design with 60 seats. Explain the arrangement of cars and seats you choose. Write multiplication sentences to show your arrangement.

Materials

- string/yarn to connect the crates (cars)
- egg cartons
- needles
- scissors
- glue
- paint
- brushes

ALMANAC
Fact

Cedar Point, in Sandusky, Ohio, had 16 roller coasters in 2006. That was the most of any amusement park in the U.S.

EXPLORE
Mystery Number Puzzles

The boxes to the right of the clues show you the number of digits in the solution.

Make a list of numbers that match the first clue.

Use the other clues to help you eliminate numbers and cross them off your list.

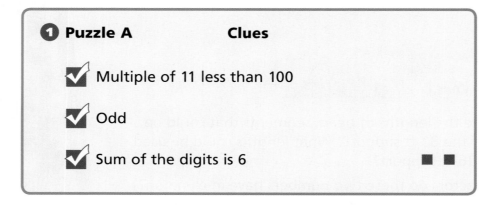

1 **Puzzle A**   **Clues**

☑ Multiple of 11 less than 100

☑ Odd

☑ Sum of the digits is 6   ■ ■

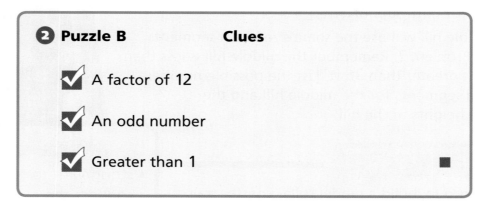

2 **Puzzle B**   **Clues**

☑ A factor of 12

☑ An odd number

☑ Greater than 1   ■

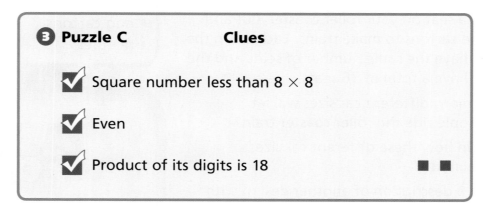

3 **Puzzle C**   **Clues**

☑ Square number less than 8 × 8

☑ Even

☑ Product of its digits is 18   ■ ■

EXPLORE
Finding Factors

Make a list of numbers from the first clue.
Use the other clues to eliminate some numbers.

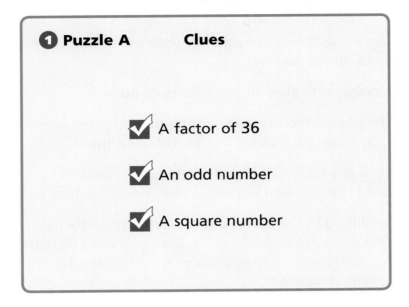

1 Puzzle A   Clues

☑ A factor of 36

☑ An odd number

☑ A square number

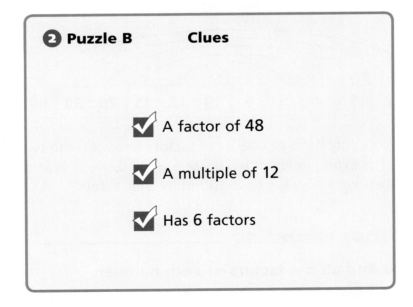

2 Puzzle B   Clues

☑ A factor of 48

☑ A multiple of 12

☑ Has 6 factors

REVIEW MODEL
Factors of a Number

One whole number is a factor of another whole number if, when you divide the second by the first, the quotient is also a whole number and the remainder is 0.

You can use a diagram as a way to organize your list to be sure that you have found all the factors.

Example Draw a diagram to find all the factors of 60.

Step ❶ Write the pair of factors that consists of 1 and the number itself. Leave space for other factors between them.

Step ❷ Decide if 2 is a factor. If 2 is a factor, name the other member of the pair and write this pair inside the first pair.

Step ❸ Continue filling in the factor pairs, listing the factors in increasing order from left to right. [As one factor increases, the other decreases, so they keep moving toward the center of the diagram.]

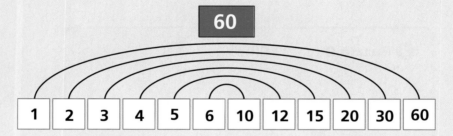

60

| 1 | 2 | 3 | 4 | 5 | 6 | 10 | 12 | 15 | 20 | 30 | 60 |

After each step, you only have to check for factors between the two closest numbers. For example, after we write 6 and 10, we check 7, 8, and 9 and then we know we have found all the factors.

✔ Check for Understanding

Draw a diagram to find all the factors of each number.

❶   18

❷   100

REVIEW MODEL
Common Factors

Factors of a number are the whole numbers that, multiplied by another whole number, make that particular product.

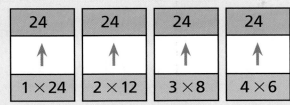

24	24	24	24
↑	↑	↑	↑
1 × 24	2 × 12	3 × 8	4 × 6

Factors → **1, 24**   **2, 12**   **3, 8**   **4, 6**

Common factors of two or more numbers are the factors that the numbers share.

Example Find the common factors of 80 and 100.

Step ❶ List the factors of both numbers.

80: 1, 2, 4, 5, 8, 10, 16, 20, 40, 80
100: 1, 2, 4, 5, 10, 20, 25, 50, 100

Step ❷ Find the numbers that are in both lists.

80: **1, 2, 4, 5,** 8, **10,** 16, **20,** 40, 80
100: **1, 2, 4, 5, 10, 20,** 25, 50, 100

So, 1, 2, 4, 5, 10 and are the common factors of 80 and 100.

✓Check for Understanding

Find common factors for each pair of numbers.

❶ 12 and 18

❷ 15 and 45

❸ 22 and 28

❹ 9 and 20

REVIEW MODEL
Prime and Composite Numbers

Numbers that have exactly two factors, 1 and the number itself, are prime numbers. Numbers that have more than two factors are composite numbers. 1 is neither prime nor composite. It has exactly one factor, 1.

Number	Prime or Composite?	Reason
2	Prime	1 and 2 are the only factors of 2.
6	Composite	1, 2, 3, and 6 are factors of 6.

A composite number can be expressed as a product of prime numbers. You can use a factor tree to help you find the prime factors of a number.

Example Write 24 as the product of prime factors.

Begin with any two pairs of factors for 24. Circle any prime factors, and continue to factor any composite numbers. The prime factors are always the same, no matter how you find them.

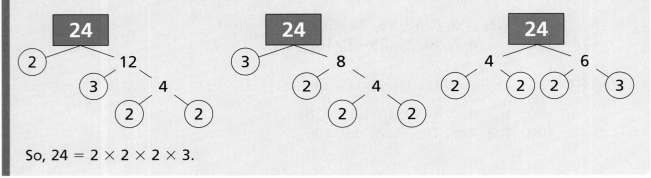

So, $24 = 2 \times 2 \times 2 \times 3$.

✔ Check for Understanding

Tell if each number is prime or composite.

1 3

2 15

3 11

4 18

5 24

Use a factor tree. Write each number as the product of prime numbers.

6 12

7 36

8 40

REVIEW MODEL
Divisibility Rules

A whole number is divisible by another whole number when the quotient is also a whole number and the remainder is zero.

Some numbers have a divisibility rule. Look at the rules in the table.

A number is divisible by	Divisible	Not Divisible
2 if the ones digit is an even number.	94	91
3 if the sum of the digits is divisible by 3.	51	52
5 if the ones digit is 0 or 5.	45	54
6 if the number is even and divisible by 3.	642	651
9 if the sum of the digits is divisible by 9.	729	971
10 if the ones digit is 0.	400	555

Example Determine if **18 is divisible by 2, 3, 5, 6, 9, or 10.**

18 is divisible by:
   2 because the last digit is an even number.
   3 because the sum of the digits is divisible by 3.
   6 because the number is even and divisible by 3.
   9 because the sum of the digits is divisible by 9.

✔Check for Understanding

Determine if each number is divisible by 2, 3, 5, 6, 9, or 10.

1 42   **2** 200   **3** 75   **4** 324

5 360   **6** 144   **7** 309   **8** 96

9 Write a number that is divisible by 3 and 5. Explain how you know the number is divisible by 3 and 5.

REVIEW MODEL
Problem Solving Strategy
Guess and Check

Katie wrote clues for a Mystery Number Puzzle. What is the solution to her puzzle?

> **Katie's Mystery Number Puzzle**
> ☑ I am a 2-digit multiple of 3.
> ☑ I am an odd number.
> ☑ My tens digit is greater than my ones digit.
> ☑ The sum of my digits is 15.

Strategy: Guess and Check

Read to Understand

What do you know from reading the problem?

I know that the number has to match all the clues that Katie gave.

What do you need to find out?

I need to find a number that is a 2-digit multiple of 3, is an odd number, has a tens digit greater than its ones digit, and has a digit sum that is 15.

Plan

How can you solve this problem?

I can use the first clue to make a systematic list of guesses for the number and then continue to check with each clue to see if the numbers still fit the clues.

Solve

How can you use guessing and checking to solve the problem?

12	21	30	42	51	60	72	81	90
15	24	33	45	54	63	75	84	93
18	27	36	48	57	66	78	87	96
	39			69				99

The choice of what clue to begin with can change the process. Here is one example: I can make a list of the numbers that match the first clue (2-digit multiple of 3). Then I look at each of the remaining clues and cross off any numbers that do not match until only one number remains.

Only 87 remains. So, the solution to the puzzle is 87.

Check

Look back at the problem. Did you answer the questions that were asked? Does the answer make sense?

Problem Solving Practice

Guess and check to solve.

1 An art teacher has 85 markers to distribute equally among students. No fewer than 2 markers and no more than 10 markers were given to any student. After the markers are distributed, there are no markers left over. How many students received markers? How many markers did each student receive?

2 Christopher bought two books about sharks at the aquarium gift shop. He spent $15.75 for the two books. One book cost $0.25 more than the other book. How much did Christopher pay for each book?

Problem Solving Strategies

✔ Act It Out
✔ Draw a Picture
✔ **Guess and Check**
✔ Look for a Pattern
✔ Make a Graph
✔ Make a Model
✔ Make an Organized List
✔ Make a Table
✔ Solve a Simpler Problem
✔ Use Logical Reasoning
✔ Work Backward
✔ Write an Equation

Mixed Strategy Practice

Use any strategy to solve. Explain.

3 Sarah cleans the hamster cage every fifth day. She cleans the bird cage every third day. If she cleans both cages today, in how many days will she clean both cages on the same day again?

4 Matt has a jar full of pennies. He puts the pennies in 29 stacks with 12 pennies in each stack. He has 3 pennies left over. How many pennies were in Matt's jar?

For 5–7, use the graph.

5 Soccer balls cost $15. How much did Sports and More take in on the sale of soccer balls in January and February?

6 In all, how many soccer balls did Sports and More sell during the first six months of the year?

7 How many more soccer balls were sold in the month when the most balls were sold than in the month when the fewest balls were sold?

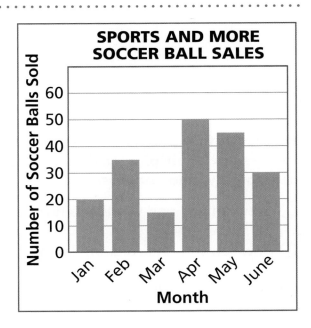

SPORTS AND MORE SOCCER BALL SALES

Chapter 3 Vocabulary

Choose the best vocabulary term from Word List A for each sentence.

❶ A number that is __?__ 10 ends in 0.

❷ A number is a(n) __?__ number if it has just two factors.

❸ A number is divisible by 6 if it is a(n) __?__ multiple of 3.

❹ A __?__ is a number that is multiplied by another number to find a product.

❺ A number is a(n) __?__ number if it has more than two factors.

❻ Some of the __?__ of 4 and 6 are 12, 24, 36, and 48.

❼ The __?__ of all prime factors of 30 is 30.

Word List A

common factors
common multiples
composite
divisibility
divisible by
even
factor
factoring
factors
multiple
multiples
odd
prime
product
square number

Complete the analogy using the best term from Word List B.

❽ Even is to odd as prime is to __?__ .

❾ Product is to __?__ as sum is to addend.

Word List B

composite
factor
multiple

Talk Math

Discuss with a partner what you have learned about factors and multiples. Use the vocabulary terms *factors*, *divisible by*, and *composite*.

❿ How can you find whether a number is prime or not?

⓫ How can you find common factors of two numbers?

⓬ How can you tell whether a number is a multiple of 3?

Analysis Chart

13 Create an analysis chart. Use what you know and what you have learned about *factors* and *multiples*.

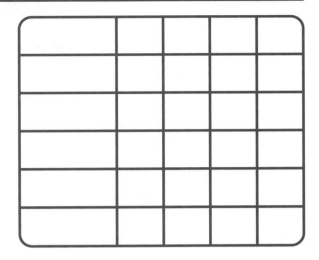

Tree Diagram

14 Create a tree diagram about numbers. Use what you know and what you have learned about *composite* numbers, *prime* numbers, *factors*, and *multiples*.

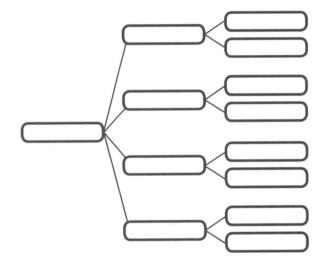

What's in a Word?

PRIME The word *prime* is a common word that is used in many ways. A person in his or her *prime* is one who is expected to accomplish more in the present than in the past or future. *Prime* can also mean a very good cut of meat, such as *prime* rib. It can mean first in importance, such as a *prime* example. It could mean having the greatest value, such as *prime* real estate. In mathematics, the word *prime* means that a number has exactly two factors, 1 and itself.

GO ONLINE Technology
Multimedia Math Glossary
www.harcourtschool.com/thinkmath

GAME

Factor Trees

Game Purpose
To practice finding prime factors of a number

Materials
- Activity Masters 10–13: *Factor Search* Cards
- 2 different colors of pencils or crayons
- several sheets of blank paper
- scissors

How To Play The Game

1 Play this game with a partner. Cut out all the *Factor Search* Cards. Remove all the prime number cards, and set them aside. They are not used in this game.

2 Mix up the cards. Place them face down in a pile. Decide who will play first.

3 Player 1 turns over the top card and writes that number at the top of a sheet of paper.

4 Player 2 begins a factor tree for the number and circles any prime factors using one color.

5 Player 1 continues the factor tree, if possible, by writing another factor pair and circles any prime factors using the other color.

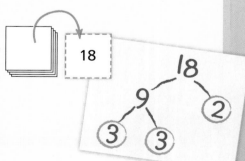

6 Take turns until all of the prime factors for the number have been found and circled. The player who has circled more prime factors is the winner.

7 Turn over a new card, and play the game again.

GAME

Click-Clack

Game Purpose
To practice naming numbers that are multiples of 2, 5, and 10

How To Play The Game

1 Four, five, or six players can play this counting game. Sit in a circle. Decide who will go first.

2 To start the round, Player 1 says "1." Continue counting around the circle in order. But if the number is
• a multiple of 2, say "click" instead.
• a multiple of 5, say "clack" instead.
• a multiple of 10, say "click-clack" instead.

Example: Starting at 1, the first 10 turns would be 1, click, 3, click, clack, click, 7, click, 9, click-clack.

3 If you make a mistake, you are out of the round.

4 When you reach 100, begin counting over at 1. Or you can count backward from 100, replacing multiples of 2, 5, and 10 with click, clack, and click-clack.

5 Play until there is only one player left. That player wins the round and 1 point. Play as many rounds as time allows. The player with the most points wins the game.

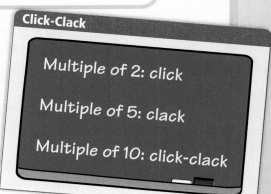

Click-Clack

Multiple of 2: click

Multiple of 5: clack

Multiple of 10: click-clack

Player 1
click-clack
clack
click
1
click
9
click
7
3
click
click

CHALLENGE

Greatest Common Factor Rectangles

What is the greatest common factor of 16 and 20? Follow these steps to find the answer. You will need 30 square tiles or small cubes.

Step ❶ Build all possible rectangles using 16 and 20 tiles.

Step ❷ Copy the rectangles onto grid paper and write their dimensions.

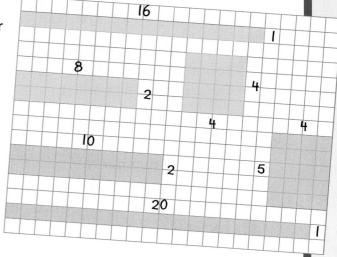

Step ❸ Use the same color to shade rectangles that have the same area.

Step ❹ What is the greatest length that is part of both the 16 square unit and the 20 square unit rectangles?

Step ❺ What is the greatest common factor of 16 and 20?

Follow the steps above to find the greatest common factor of these pairs of numbers.

❶ 9 and 12   **❷** 10 and 16   **❸** 14 and 10

❹ 14 and 27   **❺** 18 and 24   **❻** 20 and 24

❼ 11 and 15   **❽** 20 and 30   **❾** 16 and 28

❿ 21 and 18   **⓫** 28 and 14   **⓬** 24 and 15

4 Equivalence and Comparison of Fractions

Dear Student,

You already know a lot about fractions. In this chapter, "Equivalence and Comparison of Fractions," you may see fractions in a whole new way! You have certainly seen them represent a number of equal-sized pieces, like this:

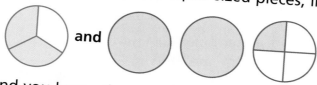 **and**

And you know that a fraction, like any other number, may be located on a number line.

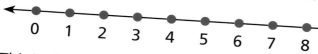

Think about where each of these numbers would be located: $\frac{1}{2}$, $1\frac{3}{4}$, $\frac{1}{3}$, and $7\frac{1}{4}$.

You probably haven't thought about fractions as instructions to multiply and divide numbers by certain amounts. Look at this new machine and its input and output.

Can you figure out how the machine works? You will know this and so much more about fractions by the end of this chapter!

Mathematically yours,
The authors of *Think Math!*

$9

2

3

$6

Growing Up, Measuring Up

Great White

All living things grow, but they grow at different rates. In the one year between your birth and first birthday, you probably grew about 10 inches. As incredible as that sounds, many animals grow even faster.

FACT·ACTIVITY 1

The whale shark is only about $\frac{1}{2}$ meter long at birth— about the length of a human baby. In time, the whale shark can grow to more than 18 meters in length, making it the world's largest fish.

Use the table and your answer for 1 to answer 2–4.

❶ Copy the three shapes below. Shade each shape to show three different ways to represent $\frac{1}{2}$.

❷ Is the annual growth of a sharpnose shark greater than or less than the annual growth of a thresher shark? Explain.

❸ Write equivalent fractions to help you compare the growth rates of all 3 sharks. Write the shark names in order from the one with the fastest growth rate to the one with the slowest growth rate.

❹ Based on the growth rate in the table above, how long does it take a great white shark to grow 1 meter? Explain.

Annual Growth Rate of Some Sharks	
Name of Shark	**Growth Rate (meters per year)**
Great White	$\frac{1}{3}$
Sharpnose	$\frac{1}{4}$
Thresher	$\frac{1}{2}$

Sharpnose

Thresher

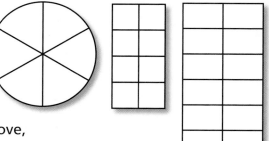

People grow at varying rates. From age 5 to age 10, Lanie grew the same amount, $2\frac{1}{2}$ inches, each year. The chart shows how much she grew in other years.

FACT·ACTIVITY 2

Use Lanie's growth chart for 1–4.

1. Write the number of inches Lanie grew between age 4 and age 5 as an improper fraction.

2. Lanie says that she grew more than $2\frac{1}{8}$ inches between age 10 and age 11. Is she right? Explain how you know.

3. Lanie's brother grew $2\frac{7}{8}$ inches between age 3 and age 4. Is that greater than or less than the number of inches Lanie grew at the same age? Explain how you know.

4. Write a mixed number in simplest form that is smaller than any number in the table.

Lanie Grows Up!	
Age from Birthday to Birthday	Inches Grown per Year
2–3	$3\frac{1}{4}$
3–4	$2\frac{3}{4}$
4–5	$2\frac{1}{2}$
10–11	$2\frac{1}{4}$
11–12	$3\frac{1}{3}$

CHAPTER PROJECT

Using library resources or the Internet, research domestic pets and choose one that is less than 6 feet tall. Write the breed or animal species on a card. Also write the typical height of the animal in feet, using fractions or mixed numbers. Then in groups of 4 or 5, combine your cards and order the animals' heights from least to greatest. You may have to convert from mixed numbers to improper fractions, use equivalent fractions, and simplify fractions.

ALMANAC

Fact

Baby blue whales are 25 feet long when born. Each day for the first seven to eight months, they grow up to one inch in length and gain 200 pounds.

EXPLORE
Two New Machines

Here is the first new machine.

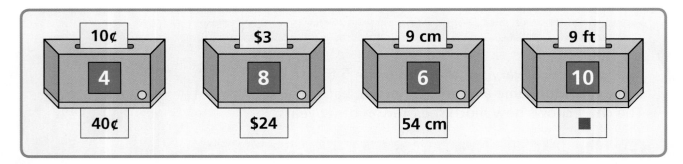

1 What does this machine do to the numbers on the cards that are put into its top?

Here is the second new machine.

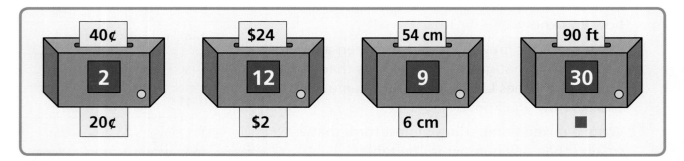

2 What does it do to the numbers on the cards that are put into its top?

Now the machines are put together.

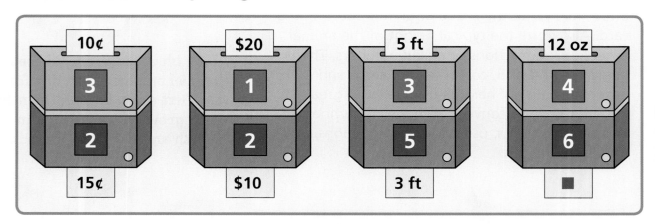

3 What does the combined machine do to the numbers on the cards?

EXPLORE
Order of Multiplying and Dividing

Dakota was experimenting with these fraction machines.

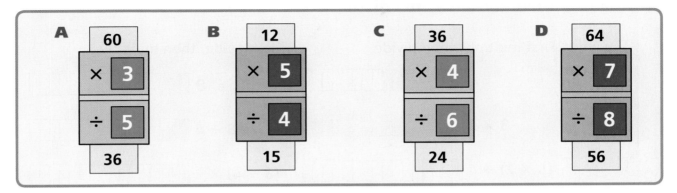

She wanted to divide first, because multiplying first gave large numbers.

1 Try Dakota's experiment. Was she correct that dividing first gives the same answers?

2 Will Dakota's method work for other fractions? Try some other fractions and input numbers. Show your experiments.

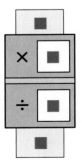

REVIEW MODEL
Using Fraction Machines to Multiply and Divide

You can use a model to help you investigate the order of operations for multiplication and division.

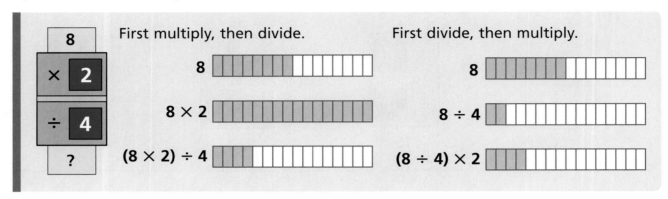

First multiply, then divide.

8

8 × 2

(8 × 2) ÷ 4

First divide, then multiply.

8

8 ÷ 4

(8 ÷ 4) × 2

You can multiply and then divide, or you can divide and then multiply. The outcomes are the same.

Example 1

The input, 48, is a large number, so you may want to divide first.

48 ÷ 8 = 6
6 × 3 = 18

The output is 18.

48
× 3
÷ 8
18

Example 2

The denominator is not a factor of the input, so you may want to multiply first.

15 × 8 = 120
120 ÷ 12 = 10

The output is 10.

15
× 8
÷ 12
10

✔ Check for Understanding

Multiply and then divide. Or, divide and then multiply.
Write the outputs.

❶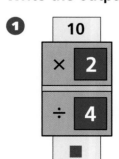

10
× 2
÷ 4
■

❷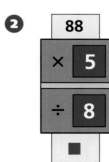

88
× 5
÷ 8
■

❸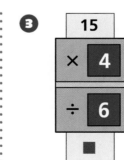

15
× 4
÷ 6
■

❹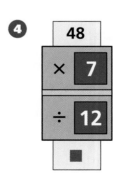

48
× 7
÷ 12
■

EXPLORE
Fraction Machine Experiment

Here are four fraction machines.

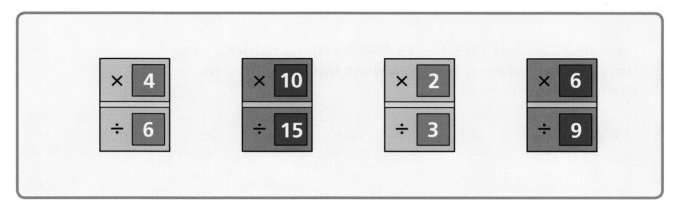

Try this experiment. Be prepared to discuss your results.

1 Choose three multiples of 3 as input numbers.

2 Find out what happens when you put your first number through all four machines.

3 Do the same with your other two numbers.

REVIEW MODEL
Writing Equivalent Fractions

You can use dot sketches to help you write equivalent fractions.

Example 1 Use dot sketches to find fractions equivalent to $\frac{5}{6}$. Note that all columns for equivalent fractions must be shaded the same way.

Draw a column of 6 open dots. Shade 5 of the dots to represent $\frac{5}{6}$.

Draw two columns of dots, each exactly like the first one to show $\frac{10}{12}$.

Draw three columns of dots, each exactly like the first one to show $\frac{15}{18}$.

$$\frac{5}{6} = \frac{10}{12} = \frac{15}{18}$$

The numerator shows the number of shaded dots.

The denominator shows the total number of dots.

You can also multiply or divide to write equivalent fractions.

Example 2 Multiply the numerator and the denominator by the same number to write fractions equivalent to $\frac{3}{5}$.

$$\frac{3}{5} = \frac{6}{10} = \frac{12}{20}$$

Multiply both the numerator and denominator of $\frac{3}{5}$ by 2.

Multiply both the numerator and denominator of $\frac{3}{5}$ by 4.

Example 3 Divide the numerator and the denominator by the same number to write fractions equivalent to $\frac{6}{12}$.

$$\frac{6}{12} = \frac{2}{4} = \frac{3}{6}$$

Divide both the numerator and denominator of $\frac{6}{12}$ by 3.

Divide both the numerator and the denominator of $\frac{6}{12}$ by 2.

✔Check for Understanding

Write two equivalent fractions for each fraction. Explain how you found the equivalent fractions.

1. $\frac{1}{6}$
2. $\frac{4}{16}$
3. $\frac{3}{10}$
4. $\frac{3}{8}$
5. $\frac{3}{4}$
6. $\frac{15}{20}$

REVIEW MODEL
Comparing Fractions

There are many different strategies you can use to compare fractions. For some pairs of fractions these strategies will work.

A If the denominators are the same, compare the numerators.

Bigger fraction has bigger numerator.

$$\frac{12}{16} > \frac{10}{16}$$

B If the numerators are the same, compare the denominators.

$$\frac{3}{8} > \frac{3}{12}$$

Smaller fraction has bigger denominator.

C Compare each fraction to $\frac{1}{2}$. If one is bigger than $\frac{1}{2}$ and other is smaller, it's easy to compare.

$$\frac{4}{6} > \frac{3}{8}$$

bigger than $\frac{1}{2}$

smaller than $\frac{1}{2}$

D Figure out which fraction is closer to 1. If both are less than 1, then the fraction closer to 1 is bigger.

$$\frac{15}{16} > \frac{3}{9}$$

$\frac{15}{16}$ is closer to 1.

If the strategies above do not help you, try this strategy.

E Write an equivalent pair of fractions with a common denominator. Then, compare the numerators.

15 is a common denominator.

$$\frac{3}{5} \enspace \blacksquare \enspace \frac{2}{3}$$

$$\frac{9}{15} \enspace < \enspace \frac{10}{15}$$

$\frac{10}{15}$ is equivalent to $\frac{2}{3}$.

$\frac{9}{15}$ is equivalent to $\frac{3}{5}$.

so $\frac{3}{5} < \frac{2}{3}$

12 is a common denominator.

$$\frac{5}{6} \enspace \blacksquare \enspace \frac{3}{4}$$

$$\frac{10}{12} \enspace > \enspace \frac{9}{12}$$

$\frac{9}{12}$ is equivalent to $\frac{3}{4}$.

$\frac{10}{12}$ is equivalent to $\frac{5}{6}$.

so $\frac{5}{6} > \frac{3}{4}$

✓ Check for Understanding

Copy and compare. Write <, >, or = between each pair of fractions.

1 $\frac{15}{16} \bullet \frac{12}{15}$

2 $\frac{3}{8} \bullet \frac{1}{2}$

3 $\frac{7}{8} \bullet \frac{9}{12}$

4 $\frac{3}{16} \bullet \frac{3}{18}$

5 $\frac{3}{4} \bullet \frac{6}{8}$

6 $\frac{5}{12} \bullet \frac{7}{12}$

7 $\frac{2}{3} \bullet \frac{4}{5}$

8 $\frac{6}{9} \bullet \frac{4}{6}$

EXPLORE
Fractions Greater Than 1

Solve the problems.

> Michaela made a number line showing her age and the ages of her two brothers. Michaela is $10\frac{1}{2}$, her younger brother is 8, and her older brother is $11\frac{1}{2}$.

1 Draw a number line to show Michaela and her brothers' ages.

> Justin's mother baked some cookies and then cut each in half. She told him that he could only eat three of the halves before supper.

2 How many cookies was Justin allowed to eat before supper?

3 If Justin ate the three cookie halves before supper and two more cookie halves for dessert, how many cookies did he eat?

REVIEW MODEL
Mixed Numbers and Improper Fractions

Mixed numbers and improper fractions are two different forms of numbers that are greater than 1 but are not whole numbers.

You can convert back and forth between the two forms.

You can use a number line to help you convert improper fractions to mixed numbers.

Example 1 Find a mixed number for $\frac{15}{4}$.

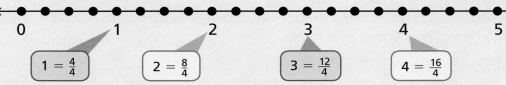

$1 = \frac{4}{4}$ $2 = \frac{8}{4}$ $3 = \frac{12}{4}$ $4 = \frac{16}{4}$

So, $\frac{15}{4}$ is between 3 and 4. You can write $\frac{15}{4}$ as $3\frac{3}{4}$.

You can use sketches to help you convert mixed numbers to improper fractions.

Example 2 Find an improper fraction for $2\frac{2}{3}$.

So, you can rewrite $2\frac{2}{3}$ as $\frac{8}{3}$.

There are $\frac{3}{3}$ in 1.

There are $\frac{6}{3}$ in 2.

There are $\frac{8}{3}$ in $2\frac{2}{3}$.

✔Check for Understanding

Write an improper number for each.

1 $2\frac{1}{6}$ **2** $1\frac{1}{5}$ **3** $2\frac{3}{4}$ **4** $3\frac{4}{7}$ **5** $1\frac{15}{16}$ **6** $3\frac{5}{6}$

Write a mixed number for each.

7 $\frac{7}{5}$ **8** $\frac{13}{10}$ **9** $\frac{11}{4}$ **10** $\frac{9}{2}$ **11** $\frac{11}{3}$ **12** $\frac{23}{16}$

REVIEW MODEL
Problem Solving Strategy
Draw a Picture

Last week Caleb and Isabelle each earned the same amount of money doing yard work. Caleb spent $\frac{3}{4}$ of his money and Isabelle spent $\frac{2}{3}$ of her money. Who spent more money?

Strategy: Draw a Picture

Read to Understand

What do you know from reading the problem?

Both people earned the same amount of money. Caleb spent $\frac{3}{4}$ of his money and Isabelle spent $\frac{2}{3}$ of hers.

What do you need to find out?

who spent more money

Plan

How can you solve this problem?

I can use the strategy *draw a picture* to help me find out who spent more money.

Solve

How can you *draw a picture* to solve the problem?

I can make two dot sketches and shade the dots for the fractions. Then I can compare the number of shaded dots to see who spent more.

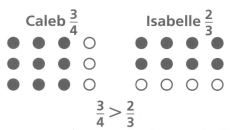

So, Caleb spent more money than Isabelle.

Check

Look back at the problem. Did you answer the questions that were asked? Does the answer make sense?

Problem Solving Practice

Draw a picture to solve.

❶ Ashley and Andy each order a small pizza. Ashley eats $\frac{2}{3}$ of hers. Andy eats $\frac{3}{5}$ of his. Who ate more pizza?

❷ Katie put 2 dozen flowers in a vase. $\frac{1}{2}$ of the flowers were daisies and $\frac{3}{8}$ of the flowers were roses. How many daisies and how many roses were in the vase?

Mixed Strategy Practice

Problem Solving Strategies

✔ Act It Out
✔ **Draw a Picture**
✔ Guess and Check
✔ Look for a Pattern
✔ Make a Graph
✔ Make a Model
✔ Make an Organized List
✔ Make a Table
✔ Solve a Simpler Problem
✔ Use Logical Reasoning
✔ Work Backward
✔ Write an Equation

Use any strategy to solve. Then explain what strategy you used and how you solved the problem on a separate piece of paper.

❸ Drew's goal is to practice the piano for 3 hours each week. He practiced for 40 minutes on Monday and 35 minutes on Tuesday. How much longer does he have to practice this week to meet his goal?

❹ Kyle paid $10.50 for one adult ticket and one student ticket to a play. The adult ticket cost $2.50 more than the student ticket. How much did each ticket cost?

❺ Ms. Blackwell deposited two checks in her checking account, one for $250 and one for $100. Later that day she withdrew $90 at an ATM. At the end of the day the balance in her account was $580. What was her balance at the beginning of the day?

❻ Raul can choose from these pizza crusts and toppings.
Crusts: thick, thin
Toppings: mushrooms, sausage, peppers, onions, pepperoni, ham.

How many different choices of crust and one topping does he have?

Use the spinner for 7–10. Suppose you spin the pointer on this spinner. Write *impossible, unlikely, likely,* **or** *certain* **to describe each event.**

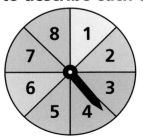

❼ Landing on a square number is ___?___.

❽ Landing on a multiple of 3 greater than 6 is ___?___.

❾ Landing on a number greater than 2×1, but less than 2×5 is ___?___.

❿ Landing on an even number or an odd number is ___?___.

Choose the best vocabulary term from Word List A for each sentence.

1 The ___?___ is the bottom number of a fraction.

2 A(n) ___?___ has both a fraction and a whole number.

3 The fractions $\frac{1}{4}$ and $\frac{3}{4}$ have a(n) ___?___.

4 A(n) ___?___ for $5\frac{1}{2}$ is $5\frac{6}{12}$.

5 When you put a number through a fraction machine, the machine gives you a(n) ___?___.

6 Equivalent fractions are ___?___ each other.

7 A(n) ___?___ has a numerator that is greater than the denominator.

8 A(n) ___?___ is an array that you can use to show equivalent fractions.

Word List A

common denominator
denominator
dot sketch
equal to
equivalent
equivalent mixed number
greater than
improper fraction
input
less than
mixed number
numerator
output
part of a whole
simplest form

Complete each analogy using the best term from Word List B.

9 Equal to is to = as ___?___ is to >.

10 Top is to bottom as ___?___ is to denominator.

11 Fraction is to equivalent fraction as ___?___ is to equivalent mixed number.

Word List B

greater than
improper fraction
less than
numerator
mixed number

Talk Math

Discuss with a partner what you have just learned about comparing fractions. Use the vocabulary terms *numerator* and *denominator*.

12 How can you tell when two unlike fractions are equivalent?

13 How can you tell when a fraction is in simplest form?

14 How can you tell when a fraction is an improper fraction?

Word Definition Map

15 **Create a word definition map for the term *equivalent*.**

A What is it?

B What is it like?

C What are some examples?

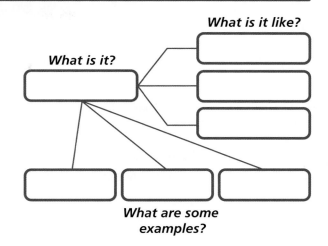

Concept Map

16 **Use what you know and what you have learned about fractions to create a concept map for terms related to *fraction*.**

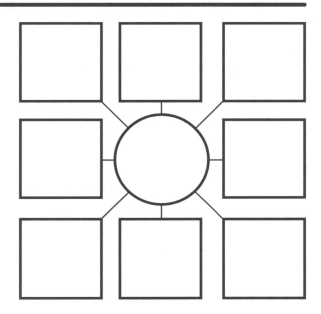

COMMON DENOMINATOR A *common denominator* is a trait or theme that different people or things have in common. A *common denominator* among the different members of a chess club is that they all like to play chess. A *common denominator* among tigers is that they have stripes. In math, a *common denominator* is the bottom number of a fraction that is the same for several different fractions.

GO ONLINE Technology
Multimedia Math Glossary
www.harcourtschool.com/thinkmath

GAME

Fraction Action

Game Purpose
To practice comparing fractions

Materials
- Activity Master 27: Fraction Cards 1
- scissors

How To Play The Game

1 Play the game with a partner. Cut out the fraction cards on Activity Master 27. Decide together whether you want the bigger or the smaller fraction to be the winner in each round.

2 One player mixes up the cards and gives 8 cards to each player. Put your cards face down in a pile.

3 Both players turn over their top card and compare the fractions. The player with the bigger (or smaller) fraction takes both cards and sets them aside.

Example: The bigger fraction wins. These are the first 2 cards.

Suzi   Adam

$$\frac{2}{5}$$ $$\frac{3}{10}$$

Suzi's fraction is bigger, so she takes both cards.

4 After both players have turned over their 8 cards, they mix up the cards they have won and keep playing.

5 There are two ways to win.
- You can win if you collect all 16 cards.
- You can win if you have more cards than your partner when time is called.

GAME

Fractiontration

Fractiontration

How To Play The Game

1 Play this game with a partner. Cut out all of the cards from Activity Masters 27–30.
   • Mix up all the cards, and place them face down in a pile.
   • Take the top 20 cards from the stack. Place them face down in 4 rows of 5 cards.

2 The goal is to find equivalent fraction pairs. Look for 2 cards that have:
   • equivalent written fractions.
   • equivalent shaded models.
   • a written fraction and a shaded model that are equivalent.

3 Take turns. One player turns over 2 cards.
   • If they show equivalent fractions, take them. Replace those cards with 2 cards from the pile, face down.
   • If they do not match, return the 2 cards to their places, face down.
   • Then it's the other player's turn.

Example:

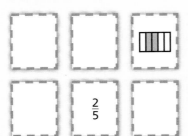

You turn over these two cards.

The written fraction and the shaded model show equivalent fractions.

So, you take those cards and replace them with 2 cards from the pile.

Now it's your partner's turn.

4 The winner is the player who has more cards at the end of the game.

CHALLENGE

Fraction Maze

Can you find a path through the maze? Begin at "Start" and end at "Finish". Here are the rules you must follow!

- You can only move from left to right.
- You can only move only from top to bottom.
- You can move horizontally, vertically, or diagonally.
- You can only move from a smaller fraction to a larger one.

The two orange fractions, $\frac{7}{28}$ and $\frac{1}{2}$, are hints for you.

Start

$\frac{1}{20}$	$\frac{1}{18}$	$\frac{5}{19}$	$\frac{3}{15}$	$\frac{3}{8}$	$\frac{7}{12}$	$\frac{3}{15}$	$\frac{1}{10}$	$\frac{6}{15}$	$\frac{1}{20}$
$\frac{6}{21}$	$\frac{1}{2}$	$\frac{3}{15}$	$\frac{1}{2}$	$\frac{9}{20}$	$\frac{1}{10}$	$\frac{1}{2}$	$\frac{7}{28}$	$\frac{1}{18}$	$\frac{9}{20}$
$\frac{1}{2}$	$\frac{9}{20}$	$\frac{7}{28}$	$\frac{1}{20}$	$\frac{2}{3}$	$\frac{6}{21}$	$\frac{1}{10}$	$\frac{2}{3}$	$\frac{2}{3}$	$\frac{7}{12}$
$\frac{6}{15}$	$\frac{7}{12}$	$\frac{2}{3}$	$\frac{5}{19}$	$\frac{6}{21}$	$\frac{3}{8}$	$\frac{1}{20}$	$\frac{7}{9}$	$\frac{1}{6}$	$\frac{5}{19}$
$\frac{9}{20}$	$\frac{3}{15}$	$\frac{1}{2}$	$\frac{7}{9}$	$\frac{7}{12}$	$\frac{2}{9}$	$\frac{6}{15}$	$\frac{5}{40}$	$\frac{3}{8}$	$\frac{1}{10}$
$\frac{7}{9}$	$\frac{1}{10}$	$\frac{6}{15}$	$\frac{1}{20}$	$\frac{2}{3}$	$\frac{5}{19}$	$\frac{7}{12}$	$\frac{9}{20}$	$\frac{1}{5}$	$\frac{4}{15}$
$\frac{6}{21}$	$\frac{5}{40}$	$\frac{3}{8}$	$\frac{1}{6}$	$\frac{1}{2}$	$\frac{6}{15}$	$\frac{1}{18}$	$\frac{1}{5}$	$\frac{1}{2}$	$\frac{9}{20}$
$\frac{1}{6}$	$\frac{1}{20}$	$\frac{9}{20}$	$\frac{1}{10}$	$\frac{3}{8}$	$\frac{2}{3}$	$\frac{1}{2}$	$\frac{1}{10}$	$\frac{7}{12}$	$\frac{4}{15}$
$\frac{7}{12}$	$\frac{9}{20}$	$\frac{2}{9}$	$\frac{1}{18}$	$\frac{7}{9}$	$\frac{1}{5}$	$\frac{4}{15}$	$\frac{7}{28}$	$\frac{2}{3}$	$\frac{1}{20}$
$\frac{5}{19}$	$\frac{1}{10}$	$\frac{3}{15}$	$\frac{2}{3}$	$\frac{6}{21}$	$\frac{1}{10}$	$\frac{3}{15}$	$\frac{1}{6}$	$\frac{3}{8}$	$\frac{7}{9}$

Finish

5 Recording Multi-Digit Multiplication

Dear Student,

In Chapter 2 you used area models and puzzles to make multiplication of 2-digit numbers easier. To multiply two large numbers, you broke each factor into two smaller numbers and multiplied the four smaller numbers like this.

	20	4
20	400	80
9	180	36

×	20	4	24
20	400	80	480
9	180	36	216
29	580	116	696

In this chapter, "Recording Multi-Digit Multiplication," you will multiply as you have before, but use a more compact way to record your work.

```
      2 4
 ×    2 9
 ─────────
    4 0 0
      8 0
    1 8 0
      3 6
 ─────────
    6 9 6
```

You will also investigate other ways to record the step-by-step process that you use to multipy large numbers. Whichever recording method you prefer, the process is always the same: to multiply large numbers, break the numbers into smaller ones!

Mathematically yours,
The authors of *Think Math!*

The Bear Facts

Admiralty Island is a thickly-forested and remote area in Alaska. Nine-tenths of the island is preserved as a national monument. All but two small sections of its 956,000 acres is designated as the *Kootznoowoo Wilderness. Kootznoowoo* means "Fortress of Bears" in the Native Alaskan language.

FACT·ACTIVITY 1:

People travel to Admiralty Island to observe the wildlife. The Pack Creek Air Taxi Service provides transportation to the island. Its costs are listed below.

Pack Creek Air Taxi Service
Round trip transportation only.
Departure times to be arranged.

Must have your *own* permits and gear.
2 passengers: $350 per person
3 passengers: $240 per person
4 passengers: $185 per person
5 passengers: $152 per person

❶ How much will the Air Taxi Service receive in fees if 2 people travel together? If 3 people travel together? If 4 people travel together?

❷ Describe the pattern in your answers to Problem 1.

❸ How much more will the Air Taxi Service receive if 5 passengers rather than 2 passengers travel together?

❹ The cost of a tour during peak season (June, July, and August) is $49 per person. Find the cost of the tour for 4 people.

❺ What is the total cost for air taxi service to Admiralty Island and the tour for 4 people?

Alaska is home to almost all of the brown bears in the United States. The table shows the estimated brown bear population on some of the Alaskan islands.

Approximate Brown Bear Population on Alaskan Islands			
Alaskan Islands	Area (km²)	Brown Bear Density (per 1,000 km²)	Estimated Total Number of Bears
Chicagof	5,000	300	1,500
Baranof	4,000	200	800
Admiralty	4,300	400	

1 Look at the numbers in each row. Explain a way to calculate the total number of bears from the area and the density.

2 Write an expression to calculate the total number of bears on Admiralty Island. Estimate the population of brown bears.

CHAPTER PROJECT

Admiralty Island is also home to many bald eagles, with about one eagle per 400 acres. Suppose a larger, nearby island has about one eagle per 400 acres. Copy the diagrams below; then make a 3-square by 3-square diagram and a 4-square by 4-square. Extend the table to record the data represented by the diagrams.

Eagle Population	
Area (square acres)	Number of Eagles
400	1
1,600	■

- Your diagrams and the numbers in the table should show the number of eagles in various numbers of acres.
- Describe the pattern of the numbers in the Number of Eagles column.
- Describe the pattern you see in the Area column.
- Extend the diagrams and the table further by adding two more rows.

ALMANAC Fact

About 1,700 brown bears, some more than 9 feet tall, live on Admiralty Island in Alaska. Bears outnumber the human population by 3 to 1.

EXPLORE
Exploring Records

1 As you solve this problem, think about the order in which you want to find the FOUR partial products. You may draw an area model if you wish.

```
        8 7
    ×   5 4
    _____
```

2 Mari did the problem by finding two partial products, like this.

A Where did the two partial products, 4,350 and 348 come from?

```
            8 7
        ×   5 4
        _____
    4 3 5 0
        3 4 8
    _____
    4, 6 9 8
```

B If Mari uses her "two partial products" method, how could she write a record for this multiplication?

```
        4 8
    ×   7 2
    _____
```

REVIEW MODEL
Strategies for Multiplying

You can use area models, puzzles, and vertical records to help you simplify a multiplication problem.

The example below shows these three strategies and how they can be used to find 35×24.

Example Find 35×24.

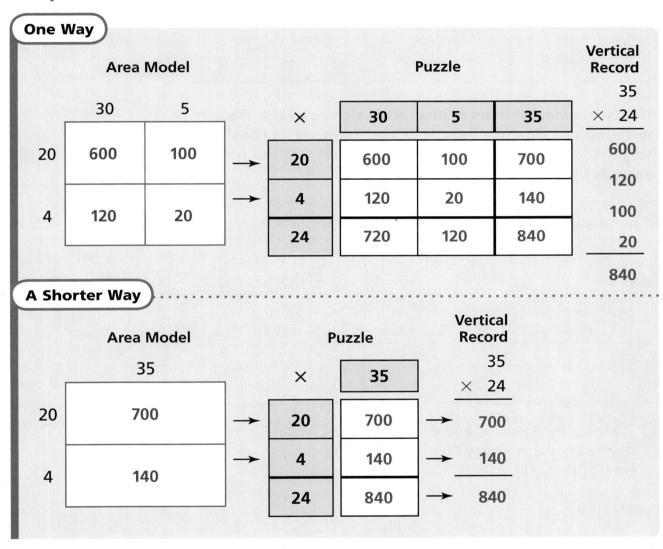

✓Check for Understanding

Find the product. Use area models, puzzles, or vertical records. Show your work.

① 24×17 **②** 28×16 **③** 33×21 **④** 45×25

EXPLORE
Floor Tiling

Marcus thought that the floor he wanted to cover with square tiles was a square.

He drew this sketch.

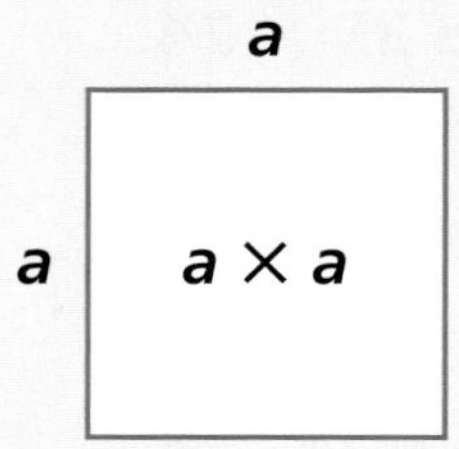

a

a | $a \times a$

However, when Marcus measured the sides of the floor, he found out that the length of the room was a foot longer than he first thought, and the width of the room was a foot shorter.

He drew a new sketch.

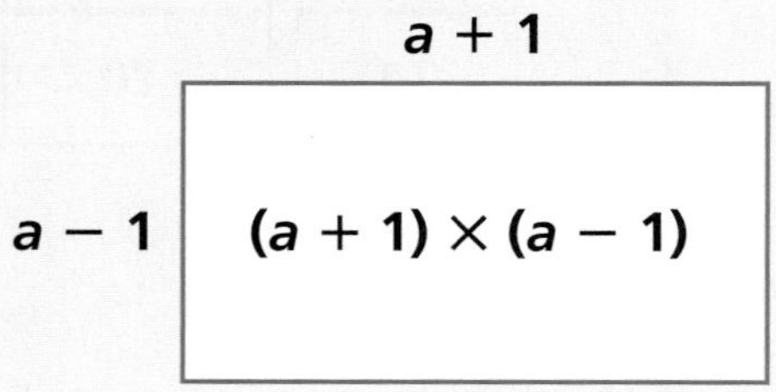

$a + 1$

$a - 1$ | $(a + 1) \times (a - 1)$

❶ Try some numbers for a to decide if Marcus would have ordered enough square tiles if he based his decision on his first sketch ($a \times a$).

❷ What numbers did you try?

REVIEW MODEL
Using Patterns in Square Number Differences

You can use patterns in square number difference to help you multiply large numbers.

Look at the products for the pairs of factors that are 1, 2, 3, and 4 steps away from 30. Then look at the table to see how the expressions with numbers and the expressions with letters are related.

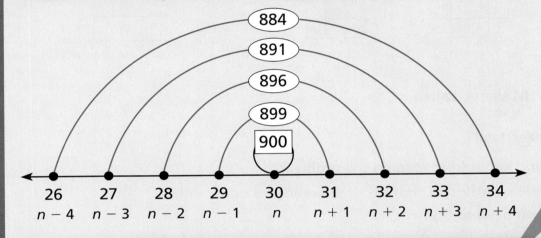

n^2 means "n squared" or $n \times n$.

	Expressions with Numbers	Expressions with Letters
Square Number	$30 \times 30 \rightarrow 900$	$n \times n \rightarrow n^2$
• 1 step away	$29 \times 31 \rightarrow 900 - 1$, or 899	$(n - 1) \times (n + 1) \rightarrow n^2 - 1$
• 2 steps away	$28 \times 32 \rightarrow 900 - 4$, or 896	$(n - 2) \times (n + 2) \rightarrow n^2 - 4$
• 3 steps away	$27 \times 33 \rightarrow 900 - 9$, or 891	$(n - 3) \times (n + 3) \rightarrow n^2 - 9$
• 4 steps away	$26 \times 34 \rightarrow 900 - 16$, or 884	$(n - 4) \times (n + 4) \rightarrow n^2 - 16$

✔Check for Understanding

Use a pattern to help you write the products

1 40×40
39×41

2 50×50
48×52

3 25×25
22×28

4 $\boxed{n = 10}$

$n \times n$
$(n - 1) \times (n + 1)$

5 $\boxed{a = 20}$

$a \times a$
$(a - 2) \times (a + 2)$

6 $\boxed{d = 12}$

$d \times d$
$(d - 3) \times (d + 3)$

REVIEW MODEL
Problem Solving Strategy
Make a Table

Kalista made these designs with green and orange square tiles.

 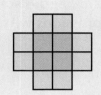 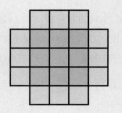

Which of these expressions give the number of orange tiles needed for a design with $n \times n$ green tiles?

| $2n + 2n$ | | $4n$ |

| $2n + 2$ |

Strategy: Make a Table

 Read to Understand

What do you know from reading the problem?

Kalista made a pattern of designs with green and orange tiles.

What do you need to find out?

which expressions show the number of orange tiles needed for a design with $n \times n$ green tiles

 Plan

How can you solve this problem?

I can use the strategy *make a table* to give me an organized way to test the expressions for various values for *n*.

 Solve

How can you *make a table* to solve the problem?

I can use the expressions as pattern indicators and see if they give numbers that match the number of orange tiles in the designs for various values for *n*.

So, *2n + 2n* and *4n* are correct expressions.

Expression	Values for *n*			Yes or No?
	1	**2**	**3**	
$2n + n$	4	8	12	Yes
$4n$	4	8	12	Yes
$2n + 2$	4	6	8	No

Check

Look back at the problem. Did you answer the questions that were asked? Does the answer make sense?

Problem Solving Practice

Make a table to solve.

① Lauren used dot paper to make a pattern with squares.

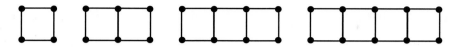

Which expessions give the number of dots needed to make *n* squares?

$$2 \times (n + 1) \qquad 2n + 1 \qquad 2n + 2$$

② Josh saved two pennies on Day 1, four pennies on Day 2, and eight pennies on Day 3. If he continues to double the number of pennies he saves each day, how many pennies will he save on the tenth day?

Problem Solving Strategies

✔ Act It Out
✔ Draw a Picture
✔ Guess and Check
✔ Look for a Pattern
✔ Make a Graph
✔ Make a Model
✔ Make an Organized List
✔ **Make a Table**
✔ Solve a Simpler Problem
✔ Use Logical Reasoning
✔ Work Backward
✔ Write an Equation

Mixed Strategy Practice

Use any strategy to solve. Explain.

③ Tanner's dad builds 3-legged stools and 4-legged tables. He used 40 legs to build 4 more stools than tables. How many stools and tables did he build?

④ Jason reads for a half-hour on Monday. Each day he reads for 10 minutes more than the previous day. How long does Jason read on Friday?

⑤ There are 40 rows with 36 seats each and 20 rows with 25 seats each in the auditorium. How many seats are in the auditorium?

⑥ A factory produces 56 machines each week. How many machines does it produce in a year?

For 7–10, use the menu.

⑦ Marliss bought a slice of pizza and two burritos. How much did she spend?

⑧ Glenn has $4.00. Can he buy a garden salad and lemonade?

⑨ Sheli bought 5 burritos. She gave the clerk a $20-dollar bill. How much change should she receive?

Today's Specials	
pizza slice	$2.50
garden salad	$3.75
burrito	$2.25
lemonade	$0.95

⑩ The snack bar owner has lots of extra pizza slices and decides to sell them for half price. How much will 10 half-price slices of pizza cost?

Choose the best vocabulary term from Word List A for each sentence.

Word List A

algebraic
 notation
area model
combined
 partial product
exponent
variable
vertical records

① A(n) __?__ is the part of the mathematical expression that can change.

② In a(n) __?__ for multiplication, the factors are outside the rectangle, and the partial products are inside it.

③ In __?__, the factors are in the top portion, and the total product is at the bottom.

④ When two partial products are added, the result is called a __?__.

⑤ In 4^3, the 3 is called the __?__.

⑥ __?__ is a kind of mathematical shorthand.

Complete each analogy using the best term from Word List B.

Word List B

area model
exponent
factor

⑦ A number-line model is to addition as a(n) __?__ is to multiplication.

⑧ Addend is to addition as __?__ is to multiplication.

⑨ Repeated addition is to multiplication symbol as repeated multiplication is to __?__.

Talk Math

Use the vocabulary term *area model* to discuss with a partner what you have learned about multiplying 2-digit numbers.

⑩ How can you multiply 2-digit numbers?

⑪ How do the numbers in area models relate to the numbers in vertical records?

⑫ How can you square a 2-digit number?

Concept Map

13 Create a concept map for words associated with multiplication. Use the terms *exponent, area model, vertical records,* and *combined partial product.*

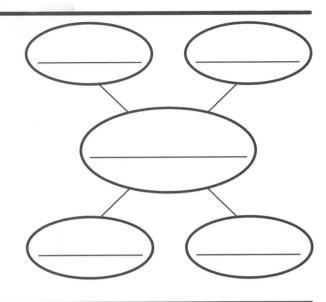

Word Definition Map

14 Create a word definition map using the term *algebraic notation.*

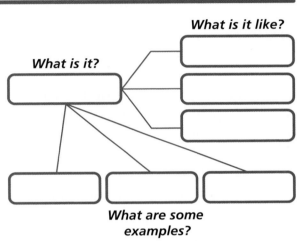

What is it?

What is it like?

What are some examples?

What's in a Word?

VARIABLE The word *variable* is a combination of the words *vary* and *able*. Vary means "to change." *Able* means "to have enough power, skill, or resources to do something." So, a *variable* is something that can change. *Variable* has the same meaning when it is used as an adjective in everyday language. The weather is *variable* because the temperature or amount of sunshine can change.

In mathematics, *variable* is a noun. A variable stands for a missing number. In arithmetic, it appears as an answer blank or a shape. In algebra, it appears as a letter. The value for the letter can change for every number sentence in which it is used. That's why it is called a *variable.*

GO ONLINE Technology
Multimedia Math Glossary
www.harcourtschool.com/thinkmath

GAME

Profitable Products

Profitable Products

29   53

20 × 50   20 × 3   9 × 50   9 × 3

How To Play The Game

1 Play this game with a partner. Cut out all the *Factor Search Cards* that show 2-digit numbers. Decide who will play first.

2 Player 1 mixes up the cards and puts them face down in a pile. Player 2 turns over the top two cards.
- Player 1 mentally computes one of the partial products and records it on paper. Since you earn more points for larger products, think before choosing.
- Player 2 mentally computes a different partial product and records it on paper.
- Take turns until all four partial products are listed.
- Player 1 adds the partial products. Player 2 checks the product with a calculator. If the product is not correct, decide together which partial products are incorrect.

3 To find your score, add your partial products. Then add **100** points for each correct partial product.

4 Player 2 starts the next round by turning over the next two cards and choosing the first partial product. Play as many rounds as you can so that both players start a round an equal number of times. Then add up each player's score to find the winner.

GAME

Favorable Factors

Game Purpose
To form factors that give the greatest product

Materials
• Number cards 1–9
• Paper and pencil for each player

Favorable Factors

How To Play The Game

1 Play this game with a partner. The goal is to make the greater product.

2 Mix up the cards. Place them face down in a pile. Turn four number cards face up. Both players record all four numbers on their papers.
• Secretly make two 2-digit factors from the four numbers.
• Find the product of your two factors without a calculator.
• Compare your products.
• The player with the greater product scores 1 point.

Example: These four cards are turned face up.

| 2 | 3 | 7 | 4 |

Player 1	Player 2
Makes factors 43 and 72.	Makes factors 37 and 24.
43 × 72 = 3,096	37 × 24 = 888
3,096 > 886	
Player 1 has the greater product. So, Player 1 scores 1 point.	

3 Mix up the cards again. Play until someone gets 10 points. If time is called, the player with more points wins.

You can change the game two ways:
• Turn over five cards. Make a 3-digit factor and a 2-digit factor.
• Change the goal to making the lesser product.

CHALLENGE

Choose Your Numbers

Test your estimation and mental math skills. Use numbers from the chart to solve Problems 1–7. Use a number only once for each problem. Solve each problem *without* using paper and pencil or a calculator.

9	3	19	4
6	15	30	2
20	7	12	5
8	50	10	40

1 Choose two numbers whose product is the greatest number less than 100.

2 Choose two numbers whose product is the least number greater than 100.

3 Choose three numbers whose product is exactly 1,000.

4 Choose three numbers whose product is between 5,000 and 6,000.

5 Choose three numbers whose product is an odd number greater than 1,000 but less than 2,000.

6 Choose three numbers whose product is an even number greater than 2,000 but less than 4,000.

7 Choose three numbers whose product is the greatest number less than 1,000.

After you have solved all the problems, follow these steps for each problem:

Step 1 Check your work with a calculator. Have you met the conditions of the problem? For example, if the problem asks for a product greater than 100, check to be sure that your product is greater than 100. If it is not, try again.

Step 2 If you think you have met all the conditions, check to see whether any other numbers would be a better solution. If not, you have solved the problem.

6 Grids and Graphs

Dear Student,

A computer screen is a rectangular array of hundreds of thousands of little dots (called "pixels"). By lighting certain ones and leaving others dark, the computer creates a picture. The pixels are so small that we do not see dots, but just see the pattern that they make.

When we type, a set of instructions (a program) that is already in the computer, tells the computer exactly which pixels to change to make each letter appear on the screen. The designer of that set of instructions refers to each pixel by giving the coordinates of its location. The coordinates are two numbers: one to say how far left or right that point is from a special point called the origin, and another to say how far up or down that point is.

Computer games use "moving" points. Well, the parts of the screen can't actually move around, so how does the computer show that movement? If a dark dot lights up and the light dot next to it becomes dark, then it looks like the light spot moved. To "move" an entire picture to the right, the programmer uses a rule that describes "slide to the right."

In this chapter, you will learn exactly how some of these rules work: rules for sliding, reflecting, or rotating points.

Mathematically yours,
The authors of *Think Math!*

Treasure Hunting

Treasure hunters search for buried or underwater artifacts to learn about past cultures, to find valuable treasures, and to enjoy the adventure of discovery.

People who love adventures play a game called *geocaching*. The goal is to find hidden "caches," which are containers with objects placed by other players.

FACT·ACTIVITY 1

Try geocaching! Begin at the first cache located at (3,2) where the trail and the creek intersect.

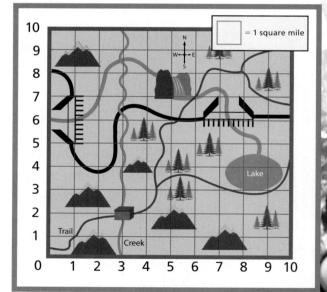

1. A clue in the first cache says: The coordinates of where you stand are *(x,y)*. Your next cache is at *(x + 3, y + 3)*. Go! What are the coordinates of the second cache?

2. A map in the second cache points you to the third cache, a big rock under the waterfall. The coordinates of the third cache are (5,7). Explain how you get there from the second cache.

3. The third cache clue says: Connect the points of the 3 caches and reflect the figure over the creek. Go 2 miles south of the point where the figures meet to find the buried treasure. Where is the buried treasure?

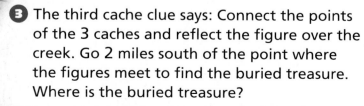

The *Senora de Atocha*, a Spanish ship, was lost at sea in 1622 near Key West, Florida. More than 350 years later, Mel Fisher, a treasure hunter, rediscovered the *Atocha's* cargo of gold and silver. Suppose Mel Fisher discovered these numbers of coins at different locations near Key West: 16, 31, 44, 25, 32, 15, 20, 17, 19, 22, 43, 29, 34, 17, and 11.

❶ What is the range of the number of coins found at the fifteen locations? the mean? the median?

❷ Explain how you might use these numbers to predict the number of coins at a sixteenth location.

CHAPTER PROJECT

Your class should be divided into 4 groups. On grid paper, each group draws a map of your classroom. Draw and label the *x*-axis and *y*-axis with positive and negative numbers so the origin is near the middle of the room.

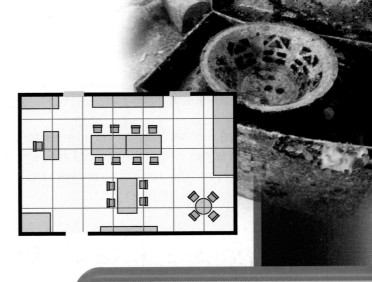

- Design a treasure hunt for another group. Select the starting point and 3 more points. The fourth point will be the location of your treasure. Each point must be a location on your map where you can hide the coordinates for the next location. Write the coordinates for the 4 locations on a slip of paper and place each one in a sealed envelope.

- Hide 3 of the envelopes. Place a small treasure such as a candy bar in the last location. Exchange maps and the first envelope with another group.

- Time each group's treasure hunt. Make a graph of the times. Describe and analyze your results.

ALMANAC
Fact

More than 40 tons of gold and silver worth about $400 million was recovered from the wreck of the *Senora de Atocha*.

EXPLORE
Introducing Translations

Katy is writing a computer game. This is the figure that will move across the screen.

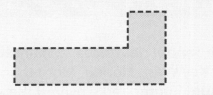

1 Cut out the ⌐---⌐ at the bottom of Activity Master 35: Blank Grid with an L and place it over the L on the activity master.

2 Record the coordinates of its vertices on a piece of scratch paper.

3 From here, move the L 3 spaces to the right (east). Record the new coordinates of its vertices on scratch paper. Describe how the coordinates have changed.

4 Move the L 2 spaces down (south). Record the new coordinates of its vertices on scratch paper. Describe how the coordinates have changed.

REVIEW MODEL
Translating a Figure

When you **translate** a figure you slide it in any direction without turning it or changing it in any other way.

- Increasing the *y*-coordinate of a point moves the point up.

- Increasing the *x*-coordinate of a point moves the point to the right.

- If you move all the vertices of a figure the same amount and in the same direction, and connect the new vertices the same way the originals were connected, you have translated the entire figure.

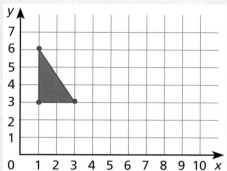

Example 1 Translate the blue triangle 4 spaces to the right and 1 space up. What are the coordinates of the new triangle?

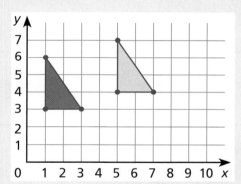

The coordinates of the new triangle are (5,4), (7,4), (5,7).

Example 2 Translate the blue triangle 1 space to the left and 2 spaces down. What are the coordinates of the new triangle?

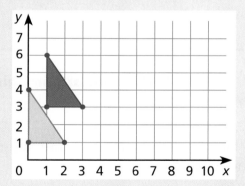

The coordinates of the new triangle are (0,1), (2,1), (0,4).

✔Check for Understanding

❶ Copy the triangle onto the grid on AM34. Translate the triangle 2 spaces to the right and 3 spaces down. Draw the new triangle.

❷ What are the coordinates of the vertices of the new triangle?

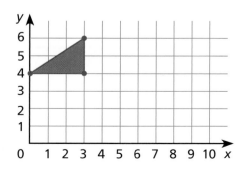

EXPLORE
Reflecting to Create Symmetrical Figures

Part A Create a symmetric design from an asymmetric one.

1 Choose one of the four figures on Activity Master 36: Asymmetrical Figures, color it or shade it, and then carefully cut it out.

2 On a piece of plain, unlined paper, carefully trace around your figure.

3 Trace the figure a second time so that you have made a symmetric design.

Part B Look at this figure and imagine it reflected across the dotted vertical line.

1 Think about where the reflection of Point A will be located.

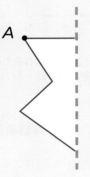

2 Be prepared to tell how you came up with that prediction.

REVIEW MODEL
Reflecting a Figure

When you **reflect** a figure across a line you make a mirror image of the figure as if the line were a mirror.

- Each vertex in the reflection is the same distance from the 'mirror' line as the corresponding vertex in the original figure.

This blue triangle has vertices at (1,4), (3,4), (1,7).

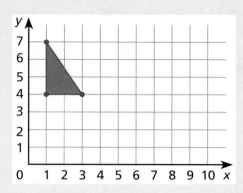

Example 1 Reflect the blue triangle over the dotted vertical line. How far are the two right-angle vertices from the mirror line?

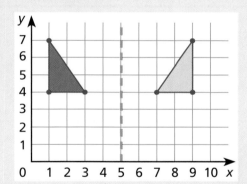

Both right-angle vertices are 4 units from the mirror line.

Example 2 Reflect the blue triangle over the dotted horizontal line. How far are the two right-angle vertices from the mirror line?

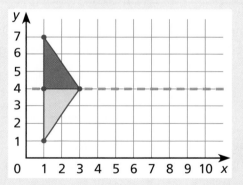

Both right-angle vertices are on the mirror line.

✔ Check for Understanding

1 Copy the triangle onto the grid on AM34. Reflect the triangle over the dotted line. Draw the new triangle.

2 How far are the two right-angle vertices from the mirror line?

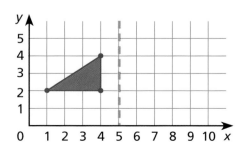

EXPLORE
Reflections of Reflections

Katy is making a background design for her computer game from copies of this figure. She knows how to reflect an image across an imaginary line on the computer screen. Help her experiment to find out what happens when she reflects a reflection.

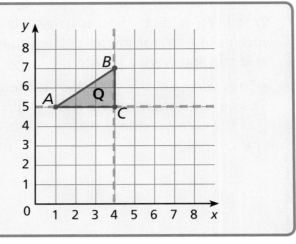

1 On Activity Master 39: Reflections, list the coordinates of the vertices of Figure Q in column Q.

2 Draw Figure R by reflecting Figure Q across the dotted vertical line. Fill in the column for Figure R.

3 Draw Figure S by reflecting Figure R across the dotted horizontal line. Fill the in column for Figure S.

4 Can you think of a way to transform Figure Q into Figure S in just one step?

REVIEW MODEL
Rotating a Figure

To rotate, or turn, a figure around a point, you must say which point to rotate around, and how much to turn.

The result will look different depending on what point the figure turns around and on how big the angle of the rotation is.

This blue triangle has vertices at (3,4), (5,4), (3,7).

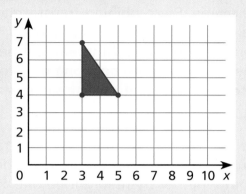

Example 1 Rotate the blue triangle 180° around the point (5,4).

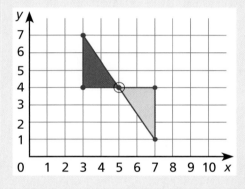

Example 2 Rotate the blue triangle 90° clockwise around the point (3,7).

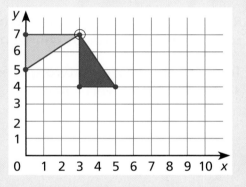

✔ Check for Understanding

❶ Copy the triangle onto the grid on AM34. Rotate the triangle 180° around the point (3,4). Draw the new triangle.

❷ How far is each vertex of the first triangle you drew from the point (3,4)? How far is each vertex of the rotated image from that point?

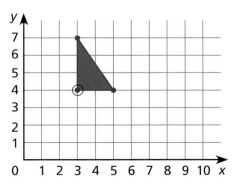

EXPLORE
Combining Transformations

Katy knows how to make the computer reflect, rotate, or translate a figure on the screen. By combining transformations, she can move figures in many ways. She wondered, though, if there might be times when she could use only one transformation instead of two, and get the same result.

Katy's figure

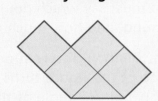

1 Use the following combinations of transformations of Katy's figure on Activity Master 40: Drawing Transformations. Think about whether there might be one transformation that will give the same result.

A Reflect the figure across the first dotted line and reflect the result over the second dotted line.

B Reflect the figure across the vertical dotted line and reflect the result over the horizontal dotted line.

C Translate the figure up two spaces and reflect the result across the dotted vertical line.

2 Is there a single translation, reflection, or rotation of any of the original figures that would give the same results as the transformations you just did? HINT: Cutting out the figure at the bottom of Activity Master 40 and moving it on the grids may help.

EXPLORE
Where Does Mr. Smith Live?

Marilyn drives a delivery truck for the Fancy Flower Shop. The directions that she was given were not very good!

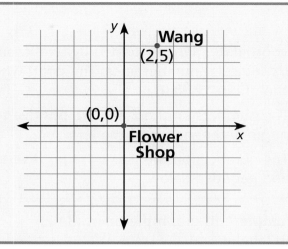

1 On Monday, Marilyn had to deliver some flowers to Mr. Smith. The directions just said, "Drive straight 5 blocks from the Flower Shop (0,0). Turn, then drive for 2 more blocks." Marilyn followed the directions, but ended up at Ms. Wang's house, instead. What went wrong?

2 Where might Mr. Smith's house be? On Activity Master 44: Marilyn's Map, mark all of the points that her directions could lead her.

3 Marilyn knew she needed better directions to Mr. Smith's. What could make the directions more useful?

REVIEW MODEL
Graphing on the Coordinate Plane

A coordinate plane is formed by two intersecting and perpendicular number lines. The point where they intersect is the origin, or (0,0).

- The numbers on the *x*-axis are positive to the right of the origin and negative to the left of it.

- The numbers on the *y*-axis are positive above the origin and negative below.

Example 1 To graph the point (3,⁻2) and label it

- Start at the origin.

- Move right 3 spaces.

- Move down 2 spaces.

- Plot the point and label it *A*.

Example 2 To name the coordinates for Point *B*

- Start at the origin.

- Move left 4 spaces.

- Move up 3 spaces.

- The coordinates for Point B are (⁻4,3)

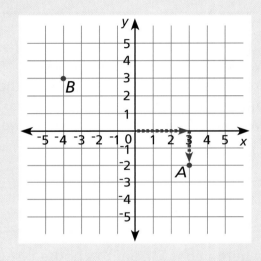

✓ Check for Understanding ———————

❶ Explain how you would graph the point (3,⁻2).

❷ Explain how you would graph the point (⁻3,0).

❸ What are the coordinates of Point *G*?

❹ What are the coordinates of Point *H*?

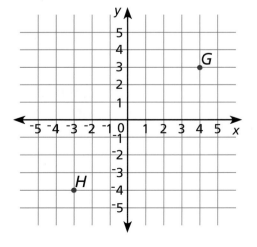

EXPLORE
Cafeteria Food

In an effort to provide the most popular and the most healthy food in the school cafeteria, your class is going to conduct a survey of students' food preferences.

> **These are the options being considered to replace the chips and cookies.**
>
> - Carrots and Dip
> - Pretzels
> - Fruit Cup
> - Red Apples
> - 1% Milk

1 Create a survey that will inform your recommendation to the cafeteria. You can use Activity Master 50: Survey Data as a guide.

2 Survey your classmates.

3 What will you recommend? Why?

REVIEW MODEL
Scatter Plots and Line Plots

Scatter plots and line plots are two types of frequency graphs. Frequency graphs give a visual picture of data and often reveal patterns and relationships in the data.

In a **scatter plot**, the values of two variables are used as coordinates of each point in the graph.

Example 1 The table shows the heights and number of points scored for 7 basketball players. Make a scatter plot of the data.

BASKETBALL PLAYERS							
Height (in inches)	54	57	57	56	60	60	58
Points Scored	8	9	7	10	4	9	10

- Find the minimum and maximum values for both variables (height and points scored). Use these values to help you label the horizontal and vertical axes of a grid.

- Plot the data. Title the graph.

BASKETBALL PLAYERS

In a **line plot**, the frequency of data is shown along a number line.

Example 2 The table shows the scores for the first 7 basketball games of the season. Make a line plot of the data.

- Draw a horizontal line.

- Find the minimum and maximum values for the data. Use these values to help you label the number line.

- Plot the data. Title the graph.

BASKETBALL SCORES							
Game	1	2	3	4	5	6	7
Score	78	76	78	76	80	77	70

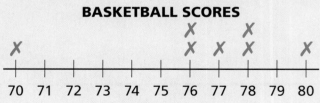

BASKETBALL SCORES

70 71 72 73 74 75 76 77 78 79 80

✔Check for Understanding

1 Make a scatter plot for this data.

STUDY TIME FOR MATH QUIZ							
Minutes Studying	15	20	17	5	20	12	18
Math Score	80	80	85	75	95	12	90

2 Make a line plot for this data.

PENCILS IN OUR DESKS							
Student	Al	Ed	Lou	Roe	Jay	Cal	Ana
Pencils in Desk	4	5	8	3	4	3	2

EXPLORE
Leveling Books

> **What is the difference between a 1st grade book and a 5th grade book?**

1 Choose a reading book from a 1st grade class and a book from your class.

2 Open each book to a random page and choose a sentence at random. Count the number of words in that sentence and record it in the table on Activity Master 51: Book Level Data.

3 Do the same for 12 more sentences from each book, making sure that you are always picking difference sentences. You should have a total of 13 numbers in the table for each book.

4 Use the tables to make a graph of the data for each book.

5 Find the **minimum, maximum, median, mode** and **range** of the number of words per sentence for the 1st grade book and then for the 5th grade book.

6 Which, if any, of these data seem useful in describing the differences between the reading levels for 1st grade and 5th grade books?

EXPLORE
Mean Towers

Part A Build 6 towers of cubes as indicated in the table.

Tower Number	1	2	3	4	5	6
Number of Cubes	2	3	6	5	3	5

❶ Record the moves you make as you now rearrange the cubes so that each tower is the same height. If you move more than one cube all at once from one tower to another, that is considered just "one move." Try to use as few moves as you can.

Examples of ways to record moves:
- 2 cubes from tower 3 to tower 1
- 2: 3 → 1

❷ When all the towers have been adjusted to the same height, that height is called the **mean height** of the towers. What is the **mean height** for these towers?

Part B Build 4 towers of cubes as indicated in this table.

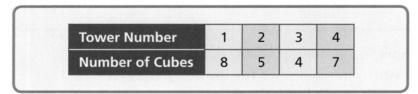

Tower Number	1	2	3	4
Number of Cubes	8	5	4	7

Without actually moving any cubes figure out what the mean height of these towers would be.

REVIEW MODEL
Describing Data

There are many ways to describe data. Mode, median, and mean are three ways you might choose a "typical" value for a set of data.

- The **mode** is the number or item that occurs most often in a set of data. There may be one mode, more than one mode, or no mode.

- The **median** is the middle value when the data are listed from minimum to maximum values. When there are two middle numbers, the median is the number halfway between the two middle values.

- The **mean** is the value you get from "evening out" all of the data values. You can find the mean by finding the sum of the values and then dividing the sum by the number of values.

Example

The table shows the number of pets some children have.

NUMBER OF PETS WE HAVE										
Child	Alex	Barb	Carl	Dean	Edie	Fran	Gail	Hal	Iris	Jake
Number of Pets	6	2	1	6	1	2	4	6	7	5

Find the mode, median, and mean for the data.

Ordering the data makes it easier to find the mode and the median for a set of data: 1, 1, 2, 2, 4, 5, 6, 6, 6, 7

- The number 6 occurs more than any other number, so 6 is the mode.

- The numbers 4 and 5 are the two middle numbers, so the median is 4.5.

- The sum of the numbers is 40 (1 + 1 + 2 + 2 + 4 + 5 + 6 + 6 + 6 + 7) and 40 ÷ 10 = 4, so 4 is the mean.

✔ Check for Understanding

1 Find the mode, median, and mean for the number of days of rain in a week.

DAYS OF RAIN										
Week	1	2	3	4	5	6	7	8	9	0
Number of Days	5	6	0	0	4	5	1	0	5	4

2 Find the median and mean for Jay's test scores.

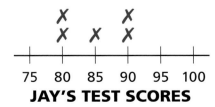

JAY'S TEST SCORES

REVIEW MODEL
Problem Solving Strategy
Act It Out

Jessie is making a design for a greeting card. She started with this triangle on a grid. She rotated the triangle 90° clockwise around the point (4,4) three times. Draw what the design looked like.

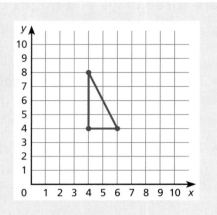

Strategy: Act it Out

Read to Understand

What do you know from reading the problem?

Jessie is rotating a triangle 90° clockwise around the point (4,4) three times to make a design.

What do you need to find out?

What the design looked like.

Plan

How can you solve this problem?

You use the strategy *act it out*.

Solve

How can you act it out?

You can cut out a shape to match the size and shape of the triangle on the grid. Then you can place the cut-out triangle on the triangle on the grid and see how the triangle looks as you rotate the cut-out triangle 90° clockwise around (4,4) three times.

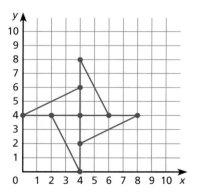

Check

Look back at the problem. Did you solve the problem that was given? Does your solution make sense?

Problem Solving Practice

Problem Solving Strategies

✔ **Act It Out**
✔ Draw a Picture
✔ Guess and Check
✔ Look for a Pattern
✔ Make a Graph
✔ Make a Model
✔ Make an Organized List
✔ Make a Table
✔ Solve a Simpler Problem
✔ Use Logical Reasoning
✔ Work Backward
✔ Write an Equation

Act it out to solve.

1 Bert started with this shape and translated it one space up and one space right. What are the vertices of the new shape?

2 Kristin reflected the shape over the dotted horizontal line. Draw what her design looked like.

Mixed Strategy Practice

Use any strategy to solve. Explain.

3 Ted read for 4 minute on Monday, 8 minutes on Tuesday, 16 minutes on Wednesday, and 32 minutes on Thursday. If the pattern continues, how many minutes will he read on Saturday?

4 At the snack bar, Marco bought a drink for $1.25, a sandwich for $3.45, and a bag of peanuts for $0.75 each. He was given $4.55 in change. How much money did he give the cashier at the snack bar?

5 The theater holds 542 people. If the theater was full for all 21 performances of a play. How many people attended the play?

6 The soccer team practices for 2 hours each Monday and for 1 hour and 30 minutes each Wednesday and Friday. For how many hours will the team practice in 8 weeks?

For 7–9, use the sign.

7 How much did it cost for the Blackwell family to buy two adult tickets and two tickets for their 12-year-old twins?

8 Mrs. Brewster paid $64 for a senior ticket for herself and for children's tickets for her grandchildren. How many tickets did she buy for her grandchildren?

9 Next year the amusement park will raise the price of all tickets by $2. How much will it cost a family to buy 2 adult tickets and 3 children's tickets next year?

RIDES GALORE AMUSEMENT PARK

Summer Admission Prices

Adults - $23

Children (Ages 4-15) - $15

Children (under 4) - Free

Seniors (ages 62 and over) - $19

Choose the best vocabulary term from Word List A for each sentence.

Word List A

average
axes
coordinates
endpoints
line of symmetry
mean
median
mode
ordered pair
outlier
quadrants
reflection
scatter plot
slide
transformation
translation
turn
x-axis
y-axis

1 The ___?___ is the value that occurs more often than any other in a set of data.

2 In the data set 2, 3, 9, 10, 72, the number 72 is a(n) ___?___.

3 A translation is another word for ___?___.

4 A line segment has two ___?___.

5 A diagonal of a square is a(n) ___?___ of the square.

6 A(n) ___?___ is a graph that can show whether two types of data are related.

7 The horizontal axis is called the ___?___.

8 The ___?___ of a set of data is the middle term when all the terms are listed in order.

9 The horizontal and vertical axes divide the coordinate plane into four ___?___.

10 A reflection is a type of ___?___.

Complete each analogy using the best term from Word List B.

Word List B

flip
line
maximum
range

11 Most is to ___?___ as least is to minimum.

12 Point is to rotation as ___?___ is to reflection.

Talk Math

Discuss with a partner what you have just learned about grids and graphs. Use the vocabulary terms *origin*, *vertical coordinate*, and *horizontal coordinate*.

13 How can you graph an ordered pair on a coordinate grid?

14 A square is graphed on a coordinate grid. How could you graph a translation of the square that is 3 spaces left and 2 spaces up?

15 A line segment is reflected across the horizontal axis. From there, it is reflected across the vertical axis. How can you describe the result as one transformation?

Venn Diagram

16 Create a Venn diagram for the words **vertical** and **horizontal**. Use vocabulary terms *horizontal axis*, *horizontal coordinate*, *ordered pair*, *origin*, *quadrants*, *vertical axis*, *vertical coordinate*, *x-axis*, and *y-axis*.

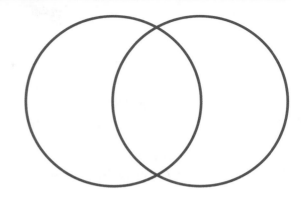

Word Web

17 Create a Word Web using the term *slide.* Use what you know and what you have learned about transformations.

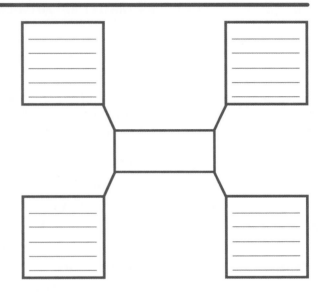

What's in a Word?

TRANSFORMATION, TRANSLATION Sometimes people confuse these words because they start and end the same way. The prefix *trans-* means "to change." So, the first part of each word means the same thing. And the last part *-tion* makes each word a noun.

The middle part of *transformation* is *-form-*. A form is a shape. In math, a transformation is what happens when a shape is changed somehow—moved to a new position, turned over, rotated. The middle part of translation comes from a Latin word that means "to carry." So, a math translation is changing by carrying, or moving, to a new position—but not changing in any other way. In math, a translation is a type of transformation.

GO ONLINE Technology
Multimedia Math Glossary
www.harcourtschool.com/thinkmath

GAME

Area Claim

Game Purpose
To practice identifying translations, reflections, and rotations

Materials
- Activity Master 41: *Area Claim* Grid
- Activity Master 42: *Area Claim* Figure Cards
- Activity Master 43: *Area Claim* Transformation Cards

How To Play The Game

1 This game is for 2 players. Cut out the Figure Cards and the Transformation Cards. Put each set in a separate pile, face down on the table. Decide who will be first.

2 Player 1 takes a Figure Card and a Transformation Card.
- Find the matching figure on the *Area Claim* Grid.
- Use the transformation named on the card to copy the figure to a new position. The new figure cannot overlap any figure already on the grid.
- Label the new figure with your initials. Put the used cards aside in discard piles.

3 Players take turns using a figure card and a transformation card to draw a figure on the grid.
- You must start from a figure that is printed on the grid or from one of your own figures. You must not use the other player's figures.
- Your turn ends after you have drawn a figure or if you cannot find space to draw a new figure.

4 When the cards run out, mix up the cards in the discard piles to start again. The game ends when you have gone through both piles twice. You can end the game early if you both agree that there is not enough space left to draw any of the figures.

5 When the game is over, both players find the total area of their figures. Whoever has the greater area wins.

Mean, Median, Mode

Game Purpose
To practice using and interpreting mean, median, and mode

Materials
- Activity Master 52: Data Measure Cards
- Index cards

How To Play The Game

1 This game is for 2 or 3 players.
- Make 4 sets of number cards, each set numbered 1–10.
- Cut out the cards from Activity Master 52. Make a group of word cards and a group of inequality cards. Mix up the cards in each group, and place them face down in 2 piles.
- Each player picks a word card and an inequality card. Don't show them to anyone—this is your secret goal. Any leftover cards are not used.

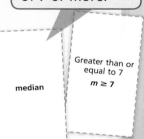

If you pick these two cards, your goal is a median of 7 or more.

median

Greater than or equal to 7
$m \geq 7$

2 Mix up the number cards. Choose one player to pass out 2 number cards to each player. The rest of the cards are put face down in a pile.

3 Players take turns creating a data set.
- Take the top number card. Now you will have 3 cards. Choose one of your cards and place it in the center.
- When there are 12 cards in the data set, the dealer turns over the top number card and adds it to the data set.

4 Work together to find the mean, median, and mode of the data set. If your goal is met, you win!
- There could be more than one mode. If any one of the modes matches a player's goal, that player wins.
- This game could have one winner, more than one winner, or no winners at all!

CHALLENGE

Reflections

How much do you know about a figure and its reflection?
To find out, follow the steps below and answer the questions.

You will need a sheet of grid paper.

Step 1 Draw a vertical line in the center of the grid paper. Then draw a triangle on the left side of the line. Label the vertices *A*, *B*, and *C*. Your drawing might look like this one.

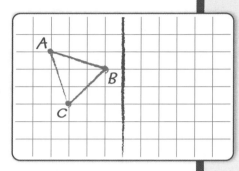

Step 2 Draw the reflection of the triangle across the line. Label the vertices of the reflected image *A'*, *B'*, and *C'*.

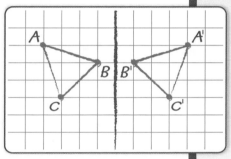

A How could you show that the triangle and its image are congruent?

Step 3 Draw a line segment from each vertex of the original figure to its image. That is, draw line segments *AA'*, *BB'*, and *CC'*.

B What type of angle does each segment make with the line of reflection?

C What else do you notice about the segments? Are any of the line segments parallel? How do their lengths on each side of the line of reflection compare?

Step 4 Mark any point on the original figure that is not a vertex. Label it point *M*. Draw a line segment from point M to its reflection image, point *M'*.

D Are your answers to questions **B** and **C** also true for line segment *MM'*?

Chapter

7 Decimals

Dear Student,

In this chapter, "Decimals," you will see how our base-ten place-value system extends in both directions from the decimal point. Directly to the left of the decimal point, there may be ones, and then tens, hundreds, thousands, ten-thousands, hundred-thousands, millions, and so on. To the right of the decimal point, there may be tenths, then hundredths, thousandths, and so on. This number system is based on ten, because the value of each place is ten times the value of the place directly to its right. As we go down the list, each number is 10 times the previous number. Just as 400 is 10×40, and 40 is 10×4, so the number 0.4 is 10×0.04. Another way of saying the exact same thing is that each number is one tenth of the next number.

You will begin the chapter by using decimal notation to name numbers within smaller and smaller spaces on the number line. Can you name several numbers between 16 and 17?

By the end of the chapter, you will know how to compare numbers with digits on both sides of the decimal point and also how to add, subtract, and multiply decimal numbers. You will also be more familiar with decimal names for some common fractions.

Mathematically yours,
The authors of *Think Math!*

0.04
0.4
4.0
40.0
400.0

Making Money

The U.S. Mint was founded in 1792. The Mint produced its first circulating coins in March 1793. Branches of the U.S. Mint in Denver, Colorado, and Philadelphia, Pennsylvania, currently make coins for circulation.

FACT·ACTIVITY 1

The tables below show the thickness of coins and the number of coins produced in a six month period.

Use the tables for 1–4.

1. Which coin is the thickest? Which is the thinnest?

2. Which has a thickness between that of the dime and the quarter? Explain using decimal values.

3. Margie says that the half dollar is 0.5 mm thicker than the quarter. Is she correct? Explain.

4. Which coin had more than 1 billion but less than 2 billion produced in the first 6 months of 2006?

Thickness of U.S. Coins						
	Penny	Nickel	Dime	Quarter	Half Dollar	Golden Dollar
Thickness (in millimeters)	1.55	1.95	1.35	1.75	2.15	2.00

Coin Production: January 2006 – June 2006 (in millions)						
	Penny	Nickel	Dime	Quarter	Half Dollar	Golden Dollar
Total Produced	6,171	1,122	2,126	2,025	4	8

You can take a tour to see how coins are made at the Philadelphia Mint.

The table shows the number of miles from the center of some cities to the Philadelphia Mint.

Distance by Car to Philadelphia Mint			
Starting City	**Number of Miles**	**Starting City**	**Number of Miles**
Albany, NY	231.76	Dallas, TX	1,465.87
Atlanta, GA	787.54	Hartford, CT	211.52
Baltimore, MD	105.15	Richmond, VA	254.23
Buffalo, NY	404.89	Tampa, FL	1,059.33

Use the table.

1 For which distances are the decimal part of the number about $\frac{1}{2}$? Explain.

2 Which number has a decimal part that is about $\frac{3}{4}$?

3 Tom's family drives from Buffalo, NY, to the Philadelphia Mint and then on to Richmond, VA. How many miles was the entire trip?

4 If Tom's family drives about the same number of miles each day for 4 days, about how many miles did they drive per day?

CHAPTER PROJECT

Some people collect commemorative coins, which honor people or events in history.

- Design a new coin with a new denomination. Draw a picture of your design on a poster and include its specifications such as its thickness and size, and the number that you would like produced per month. Explain why your coin is unique and what the design represents.

- Compare your coin with two of your classmates' coins. Use number sentences in your descriptions.

ALMANAC Fact

In June 2006, about $37 billion worth of coins were in circulation.

EXPLORE
The Same 3 Digits

1 Write all the whole numbers using the digits 3, 6, and 8, using each digit once (and only once) in each number.

2 Use the digits 3, 6, and 8 to make numbers with one or two digits after the decimal point. Use each digit once (and only once) in each number. Make as many different numbers as you can.

3 How can you be sure you found all the numbers?

REVIEW MODEL
Compare and Order Decimals

You can use a number line to compare and order decimals.

Example 1 Compare 1.13 and 1.8.

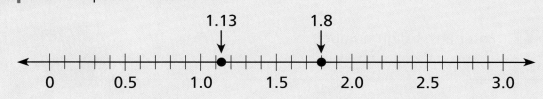

1.13   1.8

- 1.13 is to the left of 1.8, so 1.13 is less than 1.8.   1.13 < 1.8
- 1.8 is to the right of 1.13, so 1.8 is greater than 1.13.   1.8 > 1.13

You can also use place value to compare and order decimals.

Example 2 Order 5.035, 5.08, and 5.009 from least to greatest.
First, write the numbers with the decimal points aligned.
Then, compare the digits left to right until they are different.

Step ❶

Compare the ones
and tenths.
5.035
↓↓

5.08   same
↓↓

5.009

Step ❷

Compare the
hundredths.
5.035
↓

5.08   different
↓   0 < 3 < 8

5.009

Step ❸

Order the numbers.
5.009 < 5.035 < 5.08

✔Check for Understanding

Copy and complete. Write <, >, or = for each ●.

❶ 0.63 ● 0.625

❷ 8.35 ● 83.5

❸ 2.47 ● 2.470

❹ 8.34 ● 8.305

❺ Order from least to greatest.
2.14, 2.04, 2.41

❻ Order from greatest to least.
0.452, 0.367, 1.4, 0.60

EXPLORE
Shifting Place Value

Use a calculator.
Read all the directions before you begin.

Step 1   Enter any 1-digit number.

Step 2   Multiply the number by 10.   ■ × 10 =

Step 3   Read the number silently.

Step 4   Keep multiplying your number by 10 and silently reading each result.

Step 5   Stop when the calculator's window is filled with digits.

Step 6   Divide the number by 10.   ■ ÷ 10 =

Step 7   Keep dividing by 10 and reading the number silently each time.

Step 8   Stop when you see 0.00 ■.

↑———— Your starting number

Were there any numbers you could not name?
Describe how your number changed.

REVIEW MODEL
Connect Decimals to Fractions

You can use grids to help you connect decimals to fractions with denominators of 10 and 100.

Write a fraction or a mixed number and a decimal for each model.

1

6 out of **10** equal parts are shaded.

$\frac{6}{10}$ is shaded.

0.6 is shaded.

$\frac{6}{10} = 0.6$

2

75 out of **100** equal parts are shaded.

$\frac{75}{100}$ is shaded.

0.75 is shaded.

$\frac{75}{100} = 0.75$

3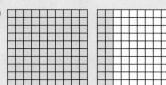

One whole plus **2** out of **10** parts are shaded.

$1\frac{2}{10}$ is shaded.

1.2 is shaded.

$1\frac{2}{10} = 1.2$

You can also use grids to help you connect decimals to familiar fractions with denominators that do not name tenths or hundredths.

3 out of **5** equal parts are shaded.

$\frac{6}{10} = \frac{3}{5} = 0.6$

3 out of **4** equal parts are shaded.

$\frac{75}{100} = \frac{3}{4} = 0.75$

One whole plus **1** out of **5** parts are shaded.

$1\frac{2}{10} = 1\frac{1}{5} = 1.2$

✔ Check for Understanding

Write a decimal for each fraction or mixed number.

1 $\frac{1}{4}$ **2** $4\frac{2}{5}$ **3** $7\frac{3}{100}$ **4** $\frac{1}{2}$

5 $2\frac{4}{10}$ **6** $20\frac{17}{100}$ **7** $3\frac{3}{4}$ **8** $10\frac{3}{5}$

EXPLORE
Decimal Notation for $\frac{1}{8}$

You previously used hundredths grids
to find decimals that are equivalent
to these fractions:

$$\frac{1}{4} \qquad \frac{3}{4} \qquad \frac{2}{5} \qquad \frac{3}{5} \qquad \frac{4}{5}$$

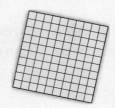

Use Activity Master 61: Shading $\frac{1}{8}$ with this activity.

1 Shade $\frac{1}{8}$ of the grid. You may shade parts of squares.

2 How would you write the decimal for $\frac{1}{8}$?

3 How would you complete this equation?

$$\frac{1}{8} = \frac{\blacksquare}{100} = \frac{\blacksquare}{1,000} = \blacksquare$$

REVIEW MODEL
Round Decimals

You can use a number line to help you round a decimal.

Example 1
Round 2.39 to the nearest whole number.

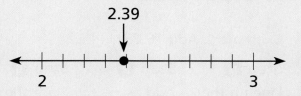

- Find the two whole numbers that 2.39 is between: 2 and 3.
- Determine which of these numbers is closer to 2.39. 2.39 is closer to 2. So, 2.39 rounded to the nearest whole number is 2.

Example 2
Round 0.763 to the nearest tenth.

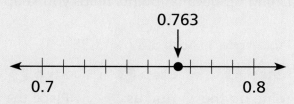

- Find the two tenths that 0.763 is between: 0.7 and 0.8.
- Determine which of these numbers is closer to 0.763. 0.763 is closer to 0.8. So, 0.763 rounded to the nearest tenth is 0.8.

When rounding to the nearest **whole number**, look at the **tenths** digit.   23.052 → 23

When rounding to the nearest **tenth**, look at the **hundredths** digit.   23.052 → 23.1

When rounding to the nearest **hundredth**, look at the **thousandths** digit.   23.052 → 23.05

Rounding Rules:
- Find the digit in the place to which you want to round.
- If the digit to the right is less than 5, round down.
- If the digit to the right is 5 or greater, round up.

✔Check for Understanding

Round to the nearest whole number.

1 45.8   **2** 102.35   **3** 3.5   **4** 78.28

Round to the nearest tenth.

5 3.45   **6** 45.08   **7** 117.88   **8** 20.582

Round to the nearest hundredth.

9 1.085   **10** 50.451   **11** 0.8091

REVIEW MODEL
Addition of Decimals

Use what you know about adding whole numbers to help you add decimals.

- Always add digits of like place value.
- Lining up decimal points helps you keep track of like place values.

Example 1 Add: 3.87 + 3.35

Step ①	**Step ②**	**Step ③**
Line up the decimal points.	Add as with whole numbers.	Place the decimal point.

Step ①:
$$3.87$$
$$+2.35$$

Step ②:
$$3.87$$
$$+2.35$$
$$\overline{6\ 22}$$

Step ③:
$$3.87$$
$$+2.35$$
$$\overline{6.22}$$

Check: Estimate the sum.

$3.87 \longrightarrow 4$ and $2.35 \longrightarrow 2$; $4 + 2 = 6$

6 is close to 6.22, so the answer is reasonable.

Example 2 Add 16.83 + 45.2

Step ①	**Step ②**	**Step ③**
Line up the decimal points.	Add as with whole numbers.	Place the decimal point.

Step ①:
$$16.83$$
$$+45.20 \leftarrow$$
Place a zero.

Step ②:
$$16.83$$
$$+45.20$$
$$\overline{62\ 03}$$

Step ③:
$$16.83$$
$$+45.20$$
$$\overline{62.03}$$

Check: Estimate the sum.

$16.83 \longrightarrow 17$ and $45.2 \longrightarrow 45$; $17 + 45 = 62$

62 is close to 62.03, so the answer is reasonable.

More Examples

A 9.52 + 14.08

$$9.52$$
$$+14.08$$
$$\overline{23.60}$$

B 56.1 + 14.52

$$56.10 \leftarrow \text{Place a zero.}$$
$$+14.52$$
$$\overline{70.62}$$

C 25.802 + 51.28

$$25.802$$
$$+51.280 \leftarrow \text{Place a zero.}$$
$$\overline{77.082}$$

✔Check for Understanding

Find the sum. Estimate to check.

❶ 3.95 + 0.56   ❷ 12.1 + 9.01   ❸ 57.81 + 12.65   ❹ 6.005 + 31.085

❺ 4.95 + 3.5   ❻ 7.32 + 12.9   ❼ 100 + 50.5   ❽ 3.2 + 6.4 + 10.5

EXPLORE
Decimal Subtraction

1 Solve. You may use the number sentence $64 - 57 = 7$ or base-ten blocks.

$$6 - 5 = \blacksquare$$

$$6.4 - 5 = \blacksquare$$

$$6 - 5.7 = \blacksquare$$

$$6.4 - 5.7 = \blacksquare$$

$$0.64 - 0.57 = \blacksquare$$

2 Solve. You may use the number sentence $55 - 28 = 27$ or base-ten blocks.

$$5 - 2 = \blacksquare$$

$$5.5 - 2 = \blacksquare$$

$$5 - 2.8 = \blacksquare$$

$$5.5 - 2.8 = \blacksquare$$

$$0.55 - 0.28 = \blacksquare$$

REVIEW MODEL
Subtraction of Decimals

Use what you know about subtracting whole numbers to help you subtract decimals.

- Always subtract digits of like place value.
- Lining up decimal points helps you keep track of like place values.

Example 1 Subtract: 5.14 − 0.86

Step ❶
Line up the decimal points.

```
  5.14
− 0.86
```

Step ❷
Subtract as with whole numbers.

```
  5.14
− 0.86
  4 28
```

Step ❸
Place the decimal point.

```
  5.14
− 0.86
  4.28
```

Check: Estimate the difference.

5.14 ⟶ 5 and 0.86 ⟶ 1; 5 − 1 = 4

4 is close to 4.28, so the answer is reasonable.

Example 2 Subtract: 62.4 − 9.15

Step ❶
Line up the decimal points.

```
  62.40
− 9.15
```
Place a zero.

Step ❷
Subtract as with whole numbers.

```
  62.40
− 9.15
  53 25
```

Step ❸
Place the decimal point.

```
  62.40
− 9.15
  53.25
```

Check: Estimate the difference.

62.4 ⟶ 62 and 9.15 ⟶ 9; 62 − 9 = 53

53 is close to 53.25, so the answer is reasonable.

More Examples

A 7.15 − 2.08
```
  7.15
− 2.08
  5.07
```

B 9 − 8.05
```
  9.00  ← Place zeroes
− 8.05
  0.95
```

C 8.52 − 5.1
```
  8.52
− 5.10  ← Place a zero
  3.42
```

✔Check for Understanding

Find the difference. Estimate to check.

❶ 1.5 − 0.7

❷ 11.4 − 6.6

❸ 7.095 − 5.64

❹ 4.578 − 1.123

❺ 14.1 − 8.65

❻ 17 − 8.7

❼ 21 − 15.06

❽ 6.85 − 1.486

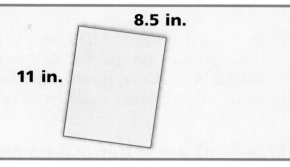

A standard piece of paper measures
$8\frac{1}{2}$ inches by 11 inches.

8.5 in.

11 in.

1 How would you find an estimate of the area
in square inches?

2 Try to find the exact area of an $8\frac{1}{2}$-inch by 11-inch piece of
paper without a calculator.

REVIEW MODEL
Problem Solving Strategy
Act it Out-Make a Model

Mr. Keys had five $10 bills, two $1 bills, five dimes, and three pennies. He spent $14.63 to buy a gift and put $26.50 in the bank. How much money does he have left? What bills and coins could he have?

Strategy: Act it Out-Make a Model

Read to Understand

What do you know from reading the problem?

Mr. Keys had some money: five $10 bills, two $1 bills, five dimes, and three pennies. He spent $14.63 and put $26.50 in the bank.

Plan

How can you solve this problem?

You can use bills and coins to *act out* the problem.

Solve

How can you *act it out?*

First, use bills and coins to show the amount of money Mr. Keys has. Record the amount ($52.53).

Then, take away the money he spent and the money he saved. To take away the $14.63 he spent, you have to first trade one $10 bill for ten $1 bills and trade one $1 bill for ten dimes. Take away the $14.63 he spent and the $26.50 he put in the bank.

The money that is left (one $10 bill, one $1 bill, and four dimes) represents the bills and coins Mr. Keys has left. He has $11.40 left.

Check

Look back at the problem. Did you answer the questions that were asked? Does the answer make sense? How could you check your answer?

You could use addition and subtraction to check your answer.

$14.63 $52.53
+ 26.50 − 41.13
$41.13 $11.40

Problem Solving Practice

Use the strategy *act it out–make a model* to solve.

1 Aaron, Brooke, Chris, Daniel, and Evan are waiting in line to buy ice cream. Brooke is in front of Daniel and after Chris. Aaron is between Chris and Brooke. Evan is after Daniel. Who is first in line?

2 Kristin and Theresa are playing a board game. In the first round, Kristin moves 6 spaces forward, 3 back, and 4 forward. Theresa moves 5 spaces forward, 2 back, and 5 forward. Who is ahead after the first round? How far ahead is she?

Problem Solving Strategies

✔ **Act It Out**
✔ Draw a Picture
✔ Guess and Check
✔ Look for a Pattern
✔ Make a Graph
✔ Make a Model
✔ Make an Organized List
✔ Make a Table
✔ Solve a Simpler Problem
✔ Use Logical Reasoning
✔ Work Backward
✔ Write an Equation

Mixed Strategy Practice

Use any strategy to solve. Explain.

3 Two numbers have a sum of 18 and a product of 56. What are the two numbers?

4 At the gymnastics vault competition, Robyn scored 9.925, Madison scored 9.950, and Belle scored 9.910. Which gymnast had the highest score?

5 Paul's checking account had a starting balance of $87.16. He wrote checks for $16.55 and $14.10. He made deposits of $20.50 and $19.50. What is his balance? Does Paul have enough money to write a check for $85.56?

6 Melissa can run a 100-meter dash in 10.49 seconds. Will her team beat the 400-meter record of 41.37 seconds if her three teammates also run 100 meters in 10.49 seconds?

For 7–9, use the table.

7 On which day did the temperature drop from morning to afternoon?

8 On which days was the afternoon temperature more than 10 degrees warmer than the morning temperature?

9 On which day was there the greatest difference between the morning and the afternoon temperatures? What was the difference?

Temperatures (in degrees F)		
Day	Morning	Afternoon
Monday	67.2°	76.9°
Tuesday	59.3°	70.4°
Wednesday	60.4°	70.7°
Thursday	68.4°	56.8°
Friday	53.1°	65.4°

Choose the best vocabulary term from Word List A for each sentence.

1 Numbers with one or more digits to the right of the decimal point are called ___?___.

2 The digit 9 in the number 9,876,543,210 is in the ___?___ place.

3 When you multiply a whole number by ___?___, you write zeros at the end of the whole number.

4 The ___?___ of 8 in 4.89 is 8 tenths.

5 Sometimes ___?___ are used to estimate the value of a decimal number.

6 The ___?___ place is two places to the right of the decimal point.

7 You can ___?___ the number 429 to the nearest ten or hundred.

8 The mixed numbers $4\frac{3}{1,000}$ and $7\frac{3}{100}$ are examples of ___?___.

Word List A

area
benchmark fractions
billions
comparing
decimals
fractions that name tenths and hundredths
hundredths
like place values
millions
ordering
place value
powers of 10
product
round
sum
tenths

Complete each analogy using the best term from Word List B.

9 Ones is to hundreds as ___?___ is to tenths.

10 Mixed number is to fraction as decimal number is to a ___?___.

Word List B

decimal part of a number
hundredths
tenths
thousandths

Talk Math

Discuss with a partner what you have just learned about large and small numbers. Use the vocabulary term *place-value position*.

11 How can you compare two decimal numbers?

12 How can you use rounding to estimate the value of a decimal number?

13 How can you add two decimal numbers?

Word Line

14 Create a word line for the terms *billions, hundredths, millions,* and *thousandths.*

Words:
Sequence:
_____

Word Definition Map

15 Create a word definition map using the word *decimal.* Use what you know and what you have learned about large and small numbers.

A What is it?

B What is it like?

C What are some examples?

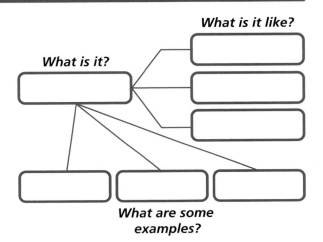

What is it?

What is it like?

What are some examples?

What's in a Word?

HUNDREDS, HUNDREDTHS These two words are similar. But two letters—*th*—make a big difference between them. *Hundreds* means the numbers 100 to 999. *Hundredths* are 100 equal parts of one whole. When you write a decimal as a fraction, you can see how *hundreds* and *hundredths* are related. The number of zeros in 100 (one *hundred*) is the same as the number of zeros used in $\frac{1}{100}$ (one *hundredth*).

The place-value positions of *hundreds* and *hundredths* are not the same on opposite sides of the decimal point. Each place-value position is one-tenth the value of the position to its left. So, the *hundreds* position is the third place to the left of the decimal point. And the *hundredths* position is the second place to the right of the decimal point.

GO ONLINE
Technology
Multimedia Math Glossary
www.harcourtschool.com/thinkmath

GAME

I Have . . ./Who Has . . .

Game Purpose
To practice estimation and comparison of decimals

Materials
- Activity Masters 62–63: *I Have . . ./Who Has . . .* cards
- Scissors
- Glue or tape

How To Play The Game

1 Play this game in a small group. Cut out all the *I Have . . .* cards and *Who Has . . .* cards. Make one set of **30 cards** by gluing or taping two cards together so that one side shows an *I Have . . .* number and the other shows a *Who Has . . .* question.

2 Mix up the cards, and give an equal number to each player. Some players might have more cards than other players. Decide who will be first.

3 Player 1 reads the *Who Has . . .* question on one of his or her cards. Everyone else checks the *I Have . . .* side of their cards.
- Raise your hand if you think your number is close.
- If more than one player raises a hand, compare all the numbers to see which is the closest.

Example:

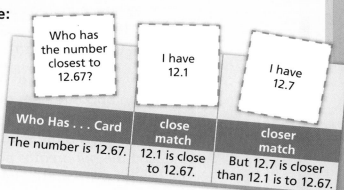

Who Has . . . Card	close match	closer match
The number is 12.67.	12.1 is close to 12.67.	But 12.7 is closer than 12.1 is to 12.67.

4 Whoever has the closest number turns over that card and reads the *Who Has . . .* question on the back.

5 Keep playing until all questions and answers have been matched.

GAME

Hit the Target

Hit the Target!

How To Play The Game

1 Play this game with a partner. Both players start with a score of 0. The goal is to reach a target number before your partner does.

2 Let one player toss both number cubes to make a target number.

Example: You toss

Decide whether the target number will be 34 or 43.

3 Take turns.
• Toss the number cubes, and make a decimal number between 1 and 10.

Example: You toss

Decide whether your number will be 2.5 or 5.2.

• Add the decimal number to your score. If your score is close to the target number, you can subtract the decimal number so that you do not go over the target number.

4 The game is over if:
• you hit the target number exactly. You win!
• your partner goes over the target number. You win!
• no one has hit the target or gone over after 10 tosses. If that happens and your score is closer to the target number, you win!

CHALLENGE

Rounded Numbers

This is a game for 2 players. A third student can act as a referee if needed.

GET READY
- Each player writes the digits 2, 3, 7, 9, and 0 on index cards. Write a decimal point on a sixth card.

RULES
- Use all 6 cards to make a number that matches each statement below. There might be more than one correct number for a statement.
- After you have made all 10 numbers, check each other's numbers. Ask a referee if you cannot agree that a number is correct. You get 1 point for each correct number. The player with more points wins!

Make a number that rounds to . . .

1 327.1 when rounded to the nearest tenth.

2 79.30 when rounded to the nearest hundredth.

3 29 when rounded to the nearest whole number.

4 790.3 when rounded to the nearest tenth.

5 30.28 when rounded to the nearest hundredth.

6 907 when rounded to the nearest whole number.

7 73.2 when rounded to the nearest tenth.

8 73.3 when rounded to the nearest tenth.

9 9,702 when rounded to the nearest whole number.

10 371 when rounded to the nearest whole number.

8 Developing a Division Algorithm

Dear Student,

You already know a lot about multiplication, like what is 3×7, and how to find products with larger factors, like 35×74. And you know how to use one multiplication problem to solve a related one. For example, you can use:

$$35 \times 74 = 2{,}590$$

to solve: $70 \times 74 = \blacksquare$

You also know connections between multiplication and division. Can you complete these related sentences?

$$35 \times 74 = 2{,}590$$
$$2{,}590 \div 35 = \blacksquare$$
$$\blacksquare \times \blacksquare = \blacksquare$$
$$\blacksquare \div \blacksquare = \blacksquare$$

There are other ways to connect multiplication and division. For example, you can use:

$$35 \times 74 = 2{,}590$$

to solve: $70 \times \blacksquare = 2{,}590$

In this chapter, you will learn how to use what you already know—especially the connection between multiplication and division—to solve more difficult division problems, for example, $3{,}818 \div 46$. You will also learn more about remainders.

Mathematically yours,
The authors of *Think Math!*

Marching Bands

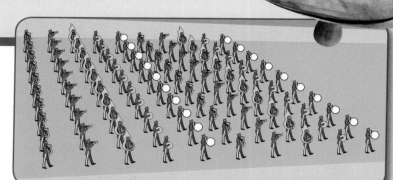

Have you ever seen a marching band in a parade or at a sporting event? Some elementary schools have marching bands, but you can see larger marching bands in high schools and colleges.

FACT·ACTIVITY 1

1. Suppose the University of Texas Longhorn Marching Band has 350 members. At the beginning of a performance, band members march in rows of 10. Describe what the missing factor in the equation tells you. $10 \times \blacksquare = 350$

2. Find the missing factor in Problem 1. Then, write a related division sentence.

3. If the marchers were arranged in rows of 5 instead of rows of 10, how many rows of marchers will there be? Explain how your answer is related to the answer to Problem 1.

4. Use an area model to show how the 350 Texas Longhorn marchers can be arranged in 25 rows. How many marchers will be in each row?

The Texas Longhorn Marching Band has played Presidential Inaugural events including the inauguration of Presidents George H. W. Bush and George W. Bush.

FACT·ACTIVITY 2

If you study a band instrument, it is likely to be one of three types: woodwind, brass, or percussion.

Use area models for 1–3.

1 Suppose the OMTAAMB band has 320 brass players, 128 woodwind players, and 112 percussion players. Group each section of the band so that there are 16 members in each row. How many rows will each section of the marching band have?

Brass: $320 \div 16 = \blacksquare$

Woodwind: $128 \div 16 = \blacksquare$

Percussion: $112 \div 16 = \blacksquare$

2 If two of the drummers cannot march, what happens to the arrangement of percussion marchers?

3 Write a division sentence which shows the number of complete rows and the number of marchers left over if there are only 110 percussion marchers. Then check your answer using multiplication.

CHAPTER PROJECT

Pretend you are the band director for a marching band. Decide on the number of people in your band and how many are in each section (brass, percussion, and woodwind). Some bands also have flag twirlers, called color guards. Decide if they will be a part of your band.

Then, develop 3 different marching arrangements (formations) for the different sections of your band. Your first formation should be an attempt to have the band march into the stadium in equal rows. Use area models on grid paper, multiplication, and related division sentences for help if you wish. (Hint: The sections can be "rectangles" of different sizes.) Decide what you will do if there are "remainders."

Present your formations to the class. Use equations to explain the number of rows and the number of people in each row for each section.

ALMANAC Fact

The One More Time Around Again Marching Band (OMTAAMB) is the world's largest marching band. There are about 560 members in the band from far away places including Japan and New Zealand. The band played at the 2000 Olympic Games in Sydney, Australia.

EXPLORE
Shipping Stamps

Sheila's Shipping Company ships packages. The company uses special shipping stamps that look like this.

| 10¢ | 20¢ | 30¢ | 40¢ | 50¢ | 60¢ | 70¢ | 80¢ | 90¢ |

| 1¢ | 2¢ | 3¢ | 4¢ | 5¢ | 6¢ | 7¢ | 8¢ | 9¢ |

The clerks quickly discovered that any amount of postage under $1.00 could be made with no more than one stamp of each color.

Sheila's Shipping Company shipped 4 packages, each with the same amount of postage. If the total postage was $1.52, how much postage was on each package?

Remember that each package has only one stamp of each color.

Here is a diagram to help you think about the problem.

Number of packages:	1	▣	▣	■	Postage on each package
Number of packages:	4	■	■	$1.52	Total Postage

EXPLORE
Multiplying and Un-Multiplying

You already know that you can figure out a large product by multiplying one part at a time and then adding the results.

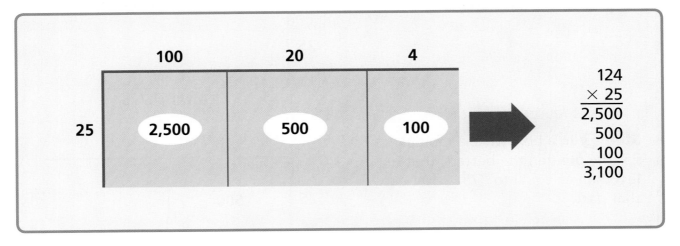

Use what you know to solve this problem.

A tile layer set 925 square tiles in 25 equal rows. How many tiles were in each row?

Draw the area model on a separate piece of paper. Use it to help you solve this problem any way you like.

REVIEW MODEL
Dividing Using an Area Model

You can use an area model to divide a large number. The model below shows how to divide 775 ÷ 25.

Step ❶ Draw the area model.

25 [ ]

Total = 775

Step ❷ In a box, write a multiple of 25 (the greater, the better!) that is less than or equal to 775. Carve out that part.

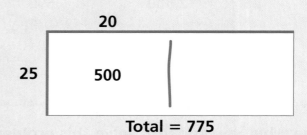

Total = 775

Step ❸ Subtract to find out how much of the 775 is left; 775 − 500 = 275. Now, find a multiple of 25 that is less than or equal to 275. Carve out that part. Above the model, write how wide that part must be.

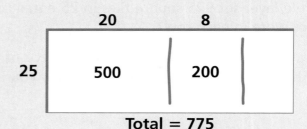

Total = 775

Step ❹ Subtract to find out how much of the 275 is left; 275 − 200 = 75. Find a multiple of 25 that is less than or equal to 75. Above the model, write how wide that part must be.
20 + 8 + 3 = 31
So, 775 ÷ 25 = 31

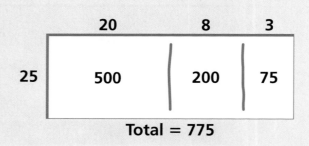

Total = 775

✔Check for Understanding

Use an area model to divide.

❶ 375 ÷ 25   ❷ 625 ÷ 25   ❸ 950 ÷ 25   ❹ 800 ÷ 25

REVIEW MODEL
Finding Multiples

You can use mental math strategies to make a table of multiples. Here is one way to find multiples of 12.

First, find 12 times 1, 2, 4, and 8.

×	1	2	3	4	5	6	7	8	9	10
12	12	24		48				96		

$12 \times 1 = 12$ Double what you wrote in the "× 1" box.   Double what you wrote in the "× 2" box.   Double what you wrote in the "× 4" box.

- -

Now, find 12×10. Use the product to find 12×5.

×	1	2	3	4	5	6	7	8	9	10
12	12	24		48	60					120

Halve 12×10.   Write a "0" after 12.

- -

Finally, use addition to find the remaining products.

×	1	2	3	4	5	6	7	8	9	10
12	12	24	36	48	60	72	84	96	108	120

$3 = 1 + 2.$ So, add $12 + 24.$ $6 = 5 + 1.$ So, add $60 + 12.$ $7 = 5 + 2.$ So, add $60 + 24.$ $9 = 5 + 4.$ So, add $60 + 48.$

✔ Check for Understanding

Copy and complete the table of multiples of 16.

×	1	2	3	4	5	6	7	8	9	10
16	■	■	■	■	■	■	■	■	■	■

EXPLORE
What Remainders Are Possible?

When you divide 84 by 3 the way you did in class, the record ends with "0 left over."

```
          8
        2 0
    3)8 4  Total
     - 6 0
        2 4  Left
      - 2 4
          0  Left
```

When you divide 97 by 3 the way you did in class, the record ends with "1 left over."

```
          2
        3 0
    3)9 7  Total
     - 9 0
          7  Left
        -   6
          1  Left
```

1 What other leftovers can a division by 3 record end with?

Experiment with some numbers, or find another way to support your answer.

---

2 What leftovers can a division by 12 record can end with?

Be ready to give a reason that supports your answer.

REVIEW MODEL
Dividing Using a Grid

You can use a grid to find both the whole-number quotient and the remainder in a division problem. The following steps show how to use a grid to find 42 ÷ 5.

Step ❶

Estimate the quotient. On grid paper, sketch a rectangle with a width greater than your estimate, and a height equal to the divisor.

Divisor and height are 5.

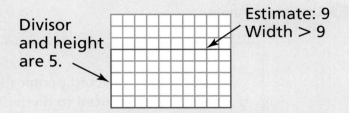

Estimate: 9
Width > 9

Step ❷

Begin filling in columns, moving left to right. Count squares as you go. Stop when the number of squares you have filled equals the dividend.

42 squares filled

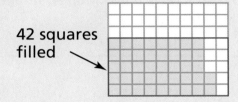

Step ❸

The whole-number part of the quotient is the number of columns you have filled. The remainder is the number of boxes you have filled in the last unfilled column.

So, 42 ÷ 5 = 8 r2 or $8\frac{2}{5}$.

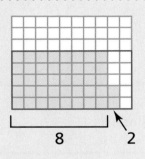

8   2

✔ Check for Understanding

Find the whole-number quotient and, if present, the remainder. You can use a grid to help you.

❶   28 ÷ 5   ❷   58 ÷ 9   ❸   55 ÷ 7

❹   78 ÷ 6   ❺   93 ÷ 4   ❻   79 ÷ 8

EXPLORE
What Do I Do About the Remainder?

For each problem, divide and then decide what to do about the remainder.

1 Sharing pennies.

> First graders collected pennies in a jar all year to give to charity. They wanted to divide the money evenly among a dozen favorite charities. When they had collected $9.17, how much money, in pennies, would each charity have received?

2 Sharing dollars.

> The first graders realized that a dozen charities was too many. They narrowed the number to only eight, and asked parents to help them raise more money. When the students had collected exactly $100, they divided it evenly among the eight charities. How much did each charity get?

REVIEW MODEL
Interpreting Remainders

When you divide with whole numbers, there is sometimes a remainder. What you do about the remainder depends on the situation in the problem.

Ignore the Remainder

Emma made punch with 12 ounces of cranberry juice, 64 ounces of orange juice, and 32 ounces of pineapple juice. How many 8-ounce servings did she make?

$$
\begin{array}{r}
1\,2 \\
6\,4 \\
+\,3\,2 \\
\hline
1\,0\,8
\end{array}
\qquad
\begin{array}{r}
1\,3 \\
8\,)\overline{1\,0\,8} \\
-\,8 \\
\hline
2\,8 \\
-\,2\,4 \\
\hline
4
\end{array}
$$

She made 13 eight-ounce servings.

Ignore the remainder because the 4 ounces that are left over are not enough to make a serving.

Include the Remainder as a Fraction or Decimal

James has a 270-foot piece of rope that he will cut into 12 equal lengths to make jump ropes. How long will each jump rope be?

$$
\begin{array}{r}
2\,2\,\tfrac{1}{2}\text{, or } 2\,2.5 \\
1\,2\,)\overline{2\,7\,0} \\
-\,2\,4 \\
\hline
3\,0 \\
-\,2\,4 \\
\hline
6
\end{array}
$$

Each jump rope will be $22\tfrac{1}{2}$, or 22.5, feet long.

Write the remainder as a fraction or a decimal because it makes sense to have a part of a foot.
$\frac{6}{12} = \frac{1}{2} = 0.5$

Round the Quotient Up

There are 1,245 students and parents who signed up for the annual school picnic. Each table will seat 8 people. How many tables will they need?

$$
\begin{array}{r}
3\,1 \\
8\,)\overline{2\,5\,0} \\
-\,2\,4 \\
\hline
1\,0 \\
-\,8 \\
\hline
2
\end{array}
$$

They will need 32 tables.

Round up the quotient to the next whole number because 31 tables will not be enough to seat everyone.

✔ Check for Understanding

Solve each problem. Explain how you decided what to do about the remainder.

1 A total of 124 players are riding a bus to the soccer game. If 25 players can ride in each bus, how many buses are needed?

2 The bakery sells boxes of a dozen muffins. They have 256 muffins ready to put into boxes. How many boxes can they fill?

3 Todd saved the same amount of money each week for 52 weeks. At the end of 52 weeks he had saved $754. How much did he save each week?

REVIEW MODEL
Problem Solving Strategy
Draw a Picture

Ashley rode her bike 13 miles due east from her house to the art museum. From there she rode 4 miles south to the mall, 2 miles west to the swimming pool, 4 miles north to the library, and then home. If she rode 6 miles per hour, how long did it take her to ride home from the library?

Strategy: Draw a Picture

Read to Understand

What do you know from reading the problem?

the speed, distances, directions, and destinations to which Ashley rode on her bike

What do you need to find out?

how long it took Ashley to ride from the library to her home

Plan

How can you solve this problem?

It's hard to tell where the library is in relation to Ashley's home, so draw a picture of her ride.

Solve

How can you draw a picture of the problem?

The drawing shows Ashley's ride. The library is 13 miles − 2 miles, or 11 miles from her house. Since she rode 6 miles per hour, you can divide 11 by 6 to find how long it took her to ride home from the library. $11 \div 6 = 1$ r5 hr, or $1\frac{5}{6}$ hr or 1 hr 50 min.

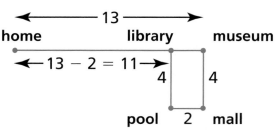

Check

Look back at the original problem. Did you answer the question that was asked? Does your answer make sense?

Problem Solving Practice

Use the strategy *draw a picture* to solve.

1 Sixteen teams are entered in a soccer tournament. A team is eliminated if it loses a game. The Jaguars won the tournament. How many games did they win?

2 A game board is in the shape of a hexagon. A line is drawn from each corner of the board to every other corner. How many lines are there on the game board?

Problem Solving Strategies

✔ Act It Out
✔ **Draw a Picture**
✔ Guess and Check
✔ Look for a Pattern
✔ Make a Graph
✔ Make a Model
✔ Make an Organized List
✔ Make a Table
✔ Solve a Simpler Problem
✔ Use Logical Reasoning
✔ Work Backward
✔ Write an Equation

Mixed Strategy Practice

Use any strategy to solve. Explain.

3 Martina has a nickel, a dime, a quarter, and a half dollar. How many different values can she make using combinations of one or more coins?

4 The sum of Andy's and Mandy's ages is 22. The product of their ages is 96. If Andy is older than Mandy, how old is Andy?

5 Brett wants to save $750 for his vacation. When he has saved 3 times as much as he has saved already, he will need only $27 more. How much has he already saved?

6 Amy started on the 8th floor of a skyscraper. She went up 13 floors, down 19 floors, up 7 floors, and down 5 floors. When she finished, how many floors from her starting point was she? Was she above or below?

7 A drawer contains 8 red socks and 8 white socks. How many socks must you remove to be sure you have two of the same color?

8 Jeff plans to build a 95-yard-long fence. He will put a post every 5 yards. Each post costs $8. How much will it cost him to buy the posts?

9 The first digit of Mr. Valvano's age is an even number. The second digit is one-third the first. How old is he?

10 There are 88 keys on a piano. Fifty-two of the keys are white. The rest are black. How many more white keys are there than black keys?

Vocabulary

Choose the best vocabulary term from Word List A for each sentence.

1 To __?__ a number is to break it into smaller parts that total the given number.

2 When deciding how to report a remainder, you need to make the most sensible or __?__ choice.

3 In division, the __?__ is the number that is left over when one number does not divide into another evenly.

4 In a division problem, the number you divide into is called the __?__.

5 The result of multiplying two or more numbers together is a(n) __?__.

6 Multiplication and division are __?__ operations because each undoes the other.

7 In a division problem, the number you divide by is called the __?__.

8 An approximation and a(n) __?__ are both guesses that are near an exact answer.

9 In division, adding 1 to the quotient and dropping the remainder is called __?__.

10 __?__ are numbers used to estimate the quotient of a division problem.

Word List A

approximation
compatible
  numbers
dividend
division
divisor
estimation
factor
inverse
output
partition
product
quotient
reasonable
remainder
rounding up
  the quotient

Complete each analogy using the best term from Word List B.

11 Addend is to sum as __?__ is to product.

12 Subtraction is to difference as division is to __?__.

Word List B

dividend
divisor
factor
quotient

Talk Math

Discuss with a partner what you have just learned about division. Use the vocabulary terms *dividend*, *divisor*, and *quotient*.

13 How can you use compatible numbers to find a partial quotient?

14 How do you know whether a division problem has a remainder?

15 How can you use multiplication to check a division problem?

Word Web

16 Create a word web for the word *divide.* Use what you know and what you have learned about division.

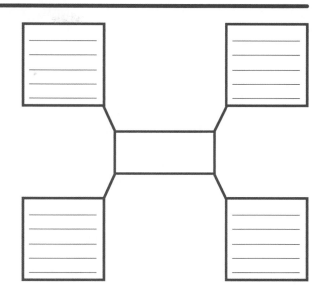

Tree Diagram

17 Create a tree diagram using the word *operation.* Use what you know and what you have learned about *addition, subtraction, multiplication,* and *division.*

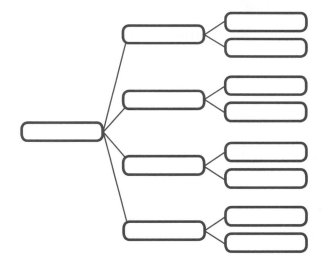

What's in a Word?

PRODUCT The word *product* has two different meanings. In everyday conversation, a *product* is the result of work. The *product* of an athletic equipment company could be a soccer ball or a tennis racket. In mathematics, a *product* is the result of multiplying two or more numbers together. In both cases, a *product* is the result of some action, but the actions are different.

GO ONLINE Technology
Multimedia Math Glossary
www.harcourtschool.com/thinkmath

GAME

200 Zoom

Game Purpose
To practice multiplication and addition

Materials
• 4 sets of number cards (1 to 12)

200 Zoom

How To Play The Game

1 Play this game with up to 3 other students. The goal is to score as many points as possible without going over 200. Decide who will go first.

2 The first player mixes up all the cards, and places them face down in a pile. The same player turns over the top card and says the "Zoom" number for that round. A "Zoom" number is the number on a card plus 10.

Example: The *top* card is a 4.
Zoom number = 10 + 4, or 14.

3 Take turns, moving clockwise from the first player. Take one card from the pile, and keep the number secret.

• Secretly multiply your number by the *Zoom* number. That is your score.

• You can increase your score by taking more cards from the pile. Put each of those cards face up in front of you. If you have more than one card, your score is the sum of the numbers on the cards times the "Zoom" number.

Example: Zoom number: 14   Cards drawn: 3, 7, 1
Score: 3 + 7 + 1 = 11, 11 × 14 = 154

• If your score is more than 200, you are out and must show all your cards.

4 Once everyone who is not out has all the cards they want, calculate and say your scores. Whoever is the closest to 200 without going over wins the round.

5 Play more rounds until all the cards have been taken. Whoever is the closest to 200 without going over wins the final round.

GAME

Don't Overestimate

Game Purpose
To practice estimating partial quotients

Materials
• 4 sets of number cards (1 to 9)

How To Play The Game

1 Play this game with a partner.
• Make a game mat. Draw a division box that is almost as large as a sheet of paper.
• Mix up the number cards. Place them face down in a pile.

2 The first player takes four cards. Place them on the mat side-by-side to make your dividend. Then take two more cards and place them side-by-side to make your divisor. Place the cards in the order in which they are picked.

Example: Max picked: 2, 4, 8, 5, 4, 6.

3 The same player tries to estimate the quotient *without* going over the actual quotient.
• The estimate can only have one non-zero digit.
• Numbers such as 30, 70, 100, 400, 900 are allowed. Numbers such as 12, 150, and 410 are not.

4 After the first player names a number, the second player may challenge it by offering a different estimate if he or she thinks that:
• a better estimate is possible; or
• the first estimate is already too high.
Otherwise, the second player passes.

5 Multiply each estimate by the divisor. If your product is less than the dividend, your product is your score. If your product is greater than the dividend, your score is 0.

6 Switch roles to complete the round. At the end of each round, calculate your scores. Whoever gets to 10,000 first wins!

CHALLENGE

Quotient Families

Sixteen division problems are grouped into four quotient families.

Blue Family

818 ÷ 24

618 ÷ 18

1,404 ÷ 41

1,193 ÷ 35

Yellow Family

1,013 ÷ 36

2,671 ÷ 62

1,088 ÷ 19

413 ÷ 24

Red Family

529 ÷ 23

1,225 ÷ 35

361 ÷ 19

1,681 ÷ 41

Green Family

1,532 ÷ 14

2,298 ÷ 21

3,498 ÷ 32

4,907 ÷ 45

1 Be a quotient detective. Look at each quotient family. How are the problems in each family alike?

2 Now use what you know about each quotient family to match each of these division problems with its quotient family.

A 5,017 ÷ 46

B 1,201 ÷ 46

C 1,573 ÷ 46

D 2,116 ÷ 46

Chapter

9 Attributes of Two-Dimensional Figures

Dear Student,

You already know quite a bit about two-dimensional figures, such as quadrilaterals and triangles and their parts, such as sides and angles. In this chapter, you will extend this knowledge. You will concentrate on studying angles and on developing different methods of comparing and finding angle sizes. For example, what do you notice about these two angles?

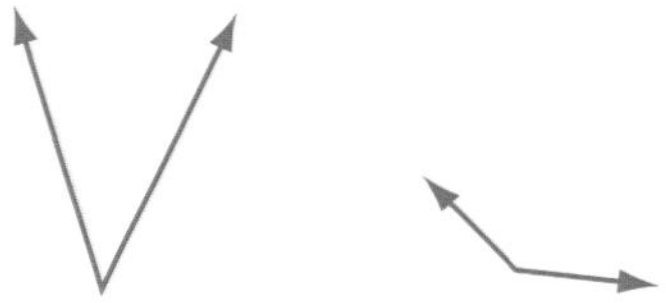

Not only will you learn to measure angles, but you will also learn other strategies for finding the size of certain angles without measuring.

Here are two angles:

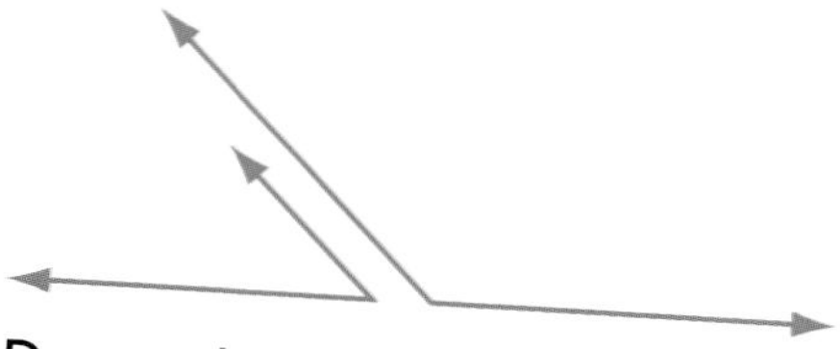

Do you know the sum of the measures of these two angles? You will know this answer (without measuring) and many more facts about angles and two-dimensional figures by the end of this chapter.

Mathematically yours,
The authors of *Think Math!*

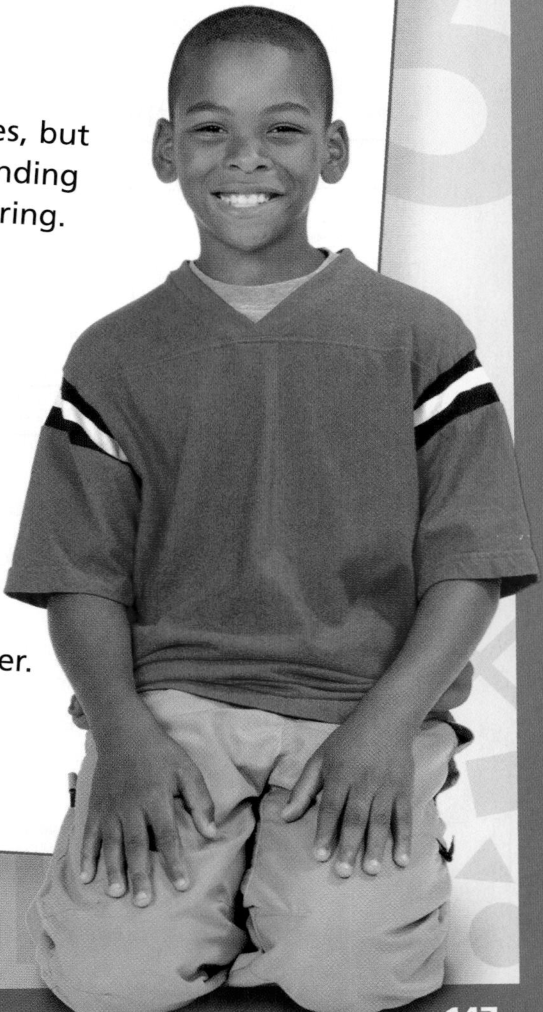

Patterns in Play

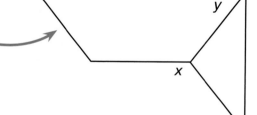

What could a soccer ball have in common with a brick wall? What about a quilt and a checker board? All of these objects are put together with a similar pattern called a tessellation. A tessellation is the tiling of a surface using a pattern of figures or polygons. Can you think of any other objects that have tessellations?

FACT·ACTIVITY 1

Look at the design below.

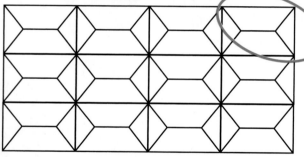

1. Use a protractor to measure angles *x* and *y*.

2. Is the triangle shown an acute, right, or obtuse triangle? Use a protractor to measure its angles.

3. Draw the triangle on a piece of paper so that the longest side measures 6 cm. About how long are the other 2 sides?

M.C. Escher is the father of modern tessellation art. The design below is an example of tessellation art. The white and green triangles are congruent.

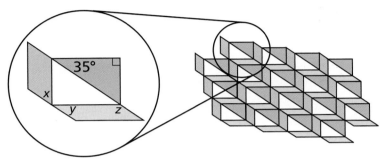

Trace the enlargement of the single set of figures. Shade the sections blue, yellow, and green as shown. Use your drawing to answer the questions below.

1 Look at the blue quadrilateral. Which angle is congruent to *x*? Label the congruent angle *x*.

2 Find other angles that are congruent to *x*. Label them *x*, also.

3 Look at the yellow quadrilateral. Which angle is congruent to *y*? Label it *y*. Which angle is congruent to *z*? Label it *z*.

CHAPTER PROJECT

Make your own tessellating pattern. Draw a triangle or quadrilateral on an index card. Within the figure, draw 2 segments to divide your figure into 3 smaller figures (triangles or quadrilaterals).

Cut out the 3 figures and trace multiple copies of each one on a different color of construction paper. Cut out at least 10 pieces of each figure. Arrange and glue the pieces to a larger sheet of cardboard or poster board to form a tessellating pattern. Remember, there should be no gaps or open spaces between figures. Display your tessellation in your classroom.

ALMANAC
Fact

M.C. Escher created over 2,000 drawings and sketches and about 450 lithographs, woodcuts, and engravings.

EXPLORE
An Experiment with a Triangle

Try this experiment and compare your results to your classmates' results.

Step 1 Use a ruler to draw a large triangle on a blank sheet of paper. Try to make all the sides different lengths. Label the angles on the inside of the triangle *A, B,* and *C,* or use a different-color dot in each corner of the triangle.

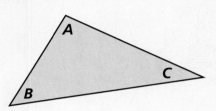 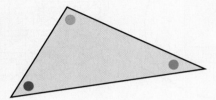

Step 2 Cut out your triangle and tear off the three corners.

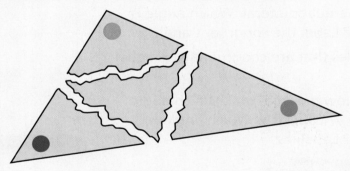

Step 3 Fit the three marked pieces together so that the dotted corners all meet at a single vertex. Tape them together as closely as possible without overlapping, like these two.

Sketch what you see and describe the result in words.

EXPLORE
How to Use a Protractor

Follow these steps to use a protractor to measure angles.

1 Match the circle in the center of the straight side of the protractor to the vertex of the angle you want to measure.

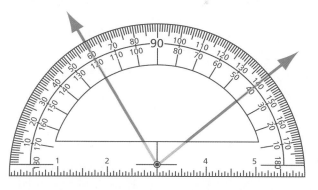

2 Match the zero mark on the protractor to one of the lines, or parts of lines, that form the angle.

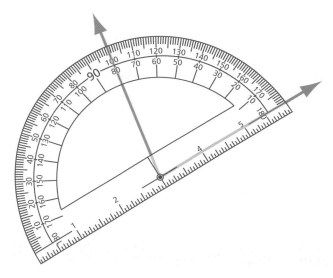

3 The other line, or part of a line, must cross the curved side of the protractor. Read the measurement from the curved side. For **acute angles**, use the smaller number. For **obtuse angles**, use the larger number.

REVIEW MODEL
Classifying Triangles

You can classify triangles by the measure of their angles or by the lengths of their sides.

Classifying by Angles	Classifying by Sides
A triangle is **right** if it has an angle that measures 90°. 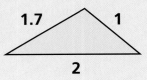	A triangle is **scalene** if all of its sides have different lengths. 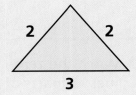
A triangle is **acute** if all the angles measure less than 90°. 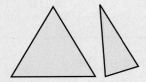	A triangle is **isosceles** if at least two of its sides have the same length. The two sides are congruent. 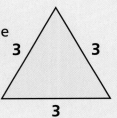
A triangle is **obtuse** if one angle measures more than 90° and less than 180°. 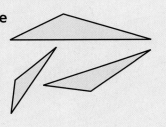	A triangle is **equilateral** if all of its sides have the same length. All three sides are congruent. 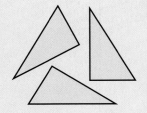

✔ Check for Understanding

Classify each triangle. Write *right*, *acute*, or *obtuse*.

1 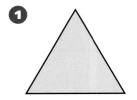   **2** 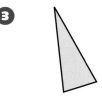   **3** 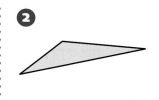   **4**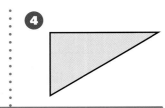

Classify each triangle. Write *scalene*, *isosceles*, or *equilateral*.

5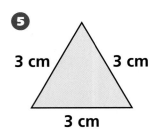
3 cm / 3 cm
3 cm

6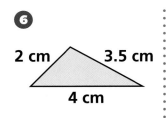
2 cm / 3.5 cm
4 cm

7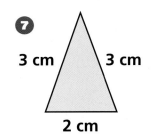
3 cm / 3 cm
2 cm

8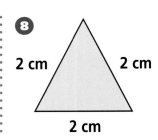
2 cm / 2 cm
2 cm

REVIEW MODEL
Constructing Triangles

Side-Angle-Side

If you know the measurements of two sides of a triangle and the angle between them, you can construct the triangle.

For example, if △*ABC* has:

Length of $\overline{AB}$	5 cm
Length of $\overline{AC}$	4 cm
Measure of ∠*A*	45°

1 Use a ruler to draw either segment, using the correct length. Label the endpoints.

5 cm

A   B

2 Use a protractor to draw the angle you know.

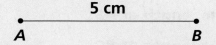

45°

A   B

3 Extend or shorten the segment you drew until it is the correct length for the second side you know. Label the new endpoint and draw the third side.

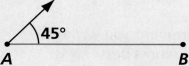

Angle-Side-Angle

If you know the measurements of two angles of a triangle and the side between them, you can construct the triangle.

For example, if △*ABC* has:

Length of $\overline{AB}$	7 cm
Measure of ∠*A*	30°
Measure of ∠*B*	45°

1 Use a ruler to draw a segment with the correct length. Label the endpoints.

7 cm

A   B

2 Use a protractor to draw the two known angles at the endpoints.

30°   45°

A   B

3 Extend the two new sides until they intersect. Label the intersection as the third vertex.

✔Check for Understanding

Use a ruler and a protractor to construct a triangle for each group of measures.

1 △*ABC* has
length $\overline{AB}$: 6 cm
length $\overline{AC}$: 5 cm
measure of ∠*A*: 60°

2 △*DEF* has
length $\overline{DE}$: 7 cm
length $\overline{DF}$: 4 cm
measure of ∠*D*: 90°

3 △*GHJ* has
length $\overline{GH}$: 8 cm
measure of ∠*G*: 45°
measure of ∠*H*: 90°

4 △*KLM* has
length $\overline{KL}$: 10 cm
measure of ∠*K*: 30°
measure of ∠*L*: 60°

EXPLORE
Shrinking a Triangle

For this exploration, you need one of the Measure Me Activity Masters (AM70–AM73). Your goal is to make a triangle, △ABC, whose sides are half the size of the sides of △ABC on your Measure Me page, but which has the same angle measures.

DIRECTIONS:

A Measure the sides and angles of the triangle on your **Measure Me** page and record them. You will have 6 measurements (3 angles and 3 sides).

B Use your measurements to calculate the lengths of the half-sized triangle's sides:

The length of $\overline{XY}$ is half the length of $\overline{AB}$.

The length of $\overline{YZ}$ is half the length of $\overline{BC}$.

The length of $\overline{XZ}$ is half the length of $\overline{AC}$.

C On blank paper, draw $\overline{XY}$, using the measurement you wrote in Step B. Label its endpoints **X** and **Y**. (This works best if **X** is near the bottom left of your paper).

D You know how long $\overline{XZ}$ should be, but where does it go? At point **X**, measure the angle you need, and sketch the line that $\overline{XZ}$ is part of. Don't worry about that line's length.

E Now measure the correct distance from point **X** along your new line and label that point **Z**.

F Use your ruler to connect points **Y** and **Z**.

G Measure $\overline{YZ}$. Is it within one cm of the length you expected?

EXPLORE
Angles Formed by Intersecting Lines

In this activity, m∠E, m∠F, m∠G, and m∠H represent the measures of the angles formed by the intersecting lines.

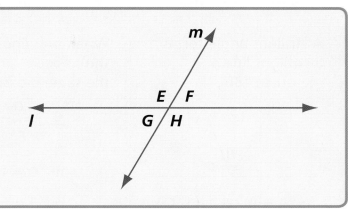

1 Without using a protractor, what can you say about the following sums of angle measures?

A m∠E + m∠F = ■   **B** m∠H + m∠F = ■

2 Find **m∠F** with a protractor. **m∠F** is about ■

3 Without using a protractor, find **m∠E** and **m∠H.** Look back at your answer to Problem 1 if you are not sure.

m∠E is about ■   **m∠H** is about ■

4 What can you say about **m∠E** and **m∠H?**

5 Without using a protractor, what can you say about the following?

A m∠G + m∠E = ■   **B** m∠G + m∠H = ■

6 Which of the following is true? Explain your answer.

m∠G < m∠F
m∠G > m∠F
m∠G = m∠F

REVIEW MODEL
Angle Measures

You can use what you know about straight angles, opposite angles, and Zs to figure out missing angle measures.

A straight angle forms a straight line and measures 180°.

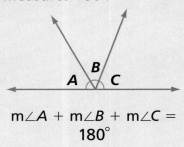

$$m\angle A + m\angle B + m\angle C = 180°$$

When two lines cross, the opposite angles have the same measure.

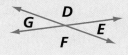

$$m\angle D = m\angle F$$

$$m\angle E = m\angle G$$

When two parallel lines have another line crossing them, the angles in the elbows of the Zs have the same measure.

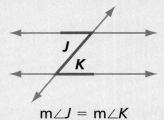

$$m\angle J = m\angle K$$

Example 1

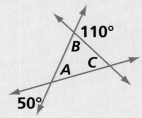

- ∠A measures 50°. It is opposite an angle that is 50°.

- ∠B measures 70°. It forms a straight angle with an angle that is 110° and 180° − 110° = 70°.

- ∠C measures 60°. The sum of the measures of the angles in a triangle is 180° and 180° − (50° + 70°) = 60°.

Example 2

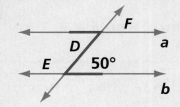

- ∠D measures 50°. It has the same measure as the 50° angle that is in the other elbow of the Z.

- ∠E measures 130°. It forms a straight angle with an angle that is 50° and 180° − 130° = 50°.

- ∠F is 50°. It is opposite an angle that is 50°.

✓ Check for Understanding

Without using a protractor, find the missing angle measures.

1

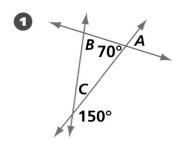

2 a∥b

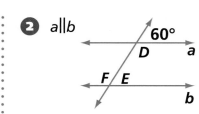

EXPLORE
Sorting Figures

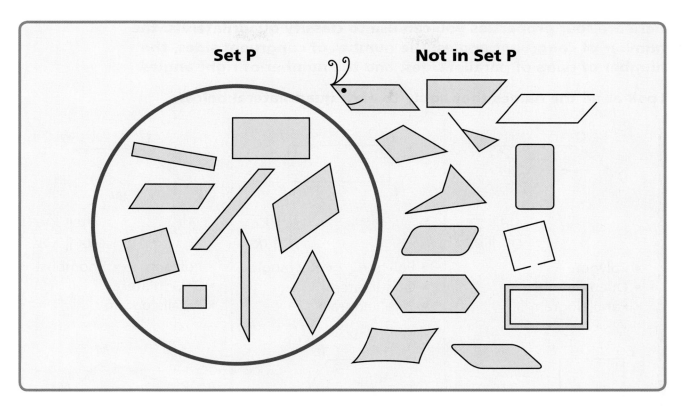

Set P   **Not in Set P**

1 Which of these figures belong in Set P?

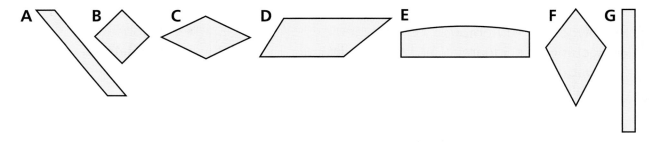

A   B   C   D   E   F   G

---

2 Without using the names of any polygons, write a set of rules to sort any figure properly.

The rules will include, "To be set in P, a figure has to have four sides," but you will need other rules as well.

REVIEW MODEL
Classifying Quadrilaterals

Here are four properties you can use to classify quadrilaterals: the number of congruent angles, the number of congruent sides, the number of pairs of parallel sides, and the number of right angles.

Look at all the names that apply to each quadrilateral below.

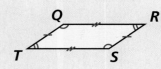

$$\overline{QR} \parallel \overline{ST}$$
$$\overline{QT} \parallel \overline{RS}$$

- Polygon
- Quadrilateral
- Parallelogram

$$\overline{IJ} \parallel \overline{KL}$$
$$\overline{IL} \parallel \overline{JK}$$

- Polygon   • Rectangle
- Quadrilateral
- Parallelogram

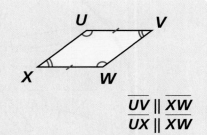

$$\overline{UV} \parallel \overline{XW}$$
$$\overline{UX} \parallel \overline{XW}$$

- Polygon   • Rhombus
- Quadrilateral
- Parallelogram

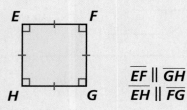

$$\overline{EF} \parallel \overline{GH}$$
$$\overline{EH} \parallel \overline{FG}$$

- Polygon   • Rhombus
- Rectangle • Square
- Quadrilateral
- Parallelogram

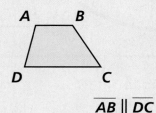

$$\overline{AB} \parallel \overline{DC}$$

- Polygon
- Quadrilateral
- Trapezoid

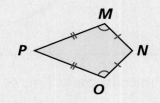

- Polygon
- Quadrilateral
- Kite

✔ Check for Understanding

Choose all the names from the box that apply to each figure.

| polygon   quadrilateral   parallelogram   rectangle   rhombus   square   kite   trapezoid |

1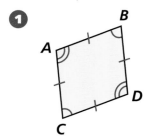

2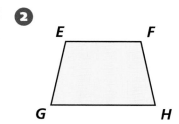

3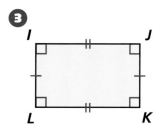

EXPLORE
An Experiment with a Quadrilateral

Remember the triangle experiment you did at the beginning of this chapter? Try this experiment with a quadrilateral and compare your results to your classmates' results.

> **You will need a copy of one of the Activity Masters 80–84: Quadrilateral Experiment 1–10. Each activity master has two copies of the same quadrilateral on it. The angles of the quadrilateral are labeled *q*, *r*, *s*, and *t*. The midpoints of the sides are marked and labeled *M*, *N*, *O*, *P*.** Here's an example, although your quadrilateral may look different from this one:
>
>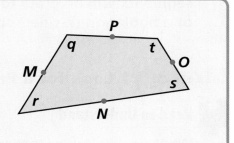

Step ❶ Using a straightedge, neatly connect points *M*, *N*, *O*, and *P* this way:

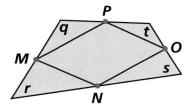

Step ❷ Cut out your quadrilateral. Then carefully cut along the lines you just made.

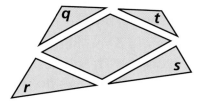

Step ❸ Fit the corner pieces together so that the labeled angles all meet at a single vertex. Fit them together as closely as possible without overlapping, like these two.

Sketch what you see and describe the result in words.

REVIEW MODEL
Problem Solving Strategy
Look for a Pattern

Andrew drew 2 line segments to connect the vertices of a square and 5 line segments to connect the vertices of a pentagon. How many segments will he draw to connect the vertices of a heptagon (7-sided polygon)?

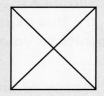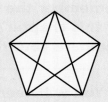

Strategy: Look for a Pattern

Read to Understand

What do you know from reading the problem?

Andrew drew 2 segments to connect the vertices of a square and 5 segments to connect the vertices of a pentagon.

What do you need to find out?

the number of segments needed to connect the vertices of a heptagon

Plan

How can you solve this problem?

You can look for a pattern in the number of segments needed to connect the vertices of polygons that have fewer than 7 sides.

Solve

How can you look for a pattern to solve this problem?

Draw polygons with fewer than 7 sides and draw the segments connecting the vertices.

Look at the 6-sided figure. There are 3 segments (3 less than the number of sides) from each of the 6 vertices. BUT, this counts each segment twice, once from each vertex that it connects. So, we do not really have 18 segments but half that amount, or 9 segments.

Check this pattern for the other polygons above. For a polygon with n sides, the number of segments is always half the number of sides multiplied by the number of sides minus 3, or half of $n \times (n - 3)$. So, for a heptagon, the number of segments is half of 7×4, or 28. Half of 28 is 14. So, there are 14 segments connecting the vertices in a heptagon.

Check

Look back at the problem. Did you answer the question that was asked? Does the answer make sense?

Problem Solving Practice

Problem Solving Strategies
✔ Act it Out
✔ Draw a Picture
✔ Guess and Check
✔ **Look for a Pattern**
✔ Make a Graph
✔ Make a Model
✔ Make an Organized List
✔ Make a Table
✔ Solve a Simpler Problem
✔ Use Logical Reasoning
✔ Work Backward
✔ Write an Equation

Use the strategy *look for a pattern* to solve.

1 Jacob is making a design using blue and white square tiles. How many tiles will he need to make the sixth figure in the pattern?

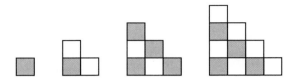

2 Rachel is making a quilt. She puts the squares in a repeating pattern of red, green, blue, yellow, white. What color will the 29th square be?

Mixed Strategy Practice

Use any strategy to solve. Explain.

3 One row of carrots produces 6.5 pounds of carrots. One row of beets produces 5.1 pounds of beets. How many more pounds of carrots than beets would come from 3 rows of carrots and 3 rows of beets?

4 The drama club will present a play to 912 students in 4 different performances. If each performance has the same number of students, how many students will be at each performance?

5 Sophia read 45 pages on Sunday, 90 pages on Monday and 135 pages on Tuesday. If she continues this pattern, how many pages will she read on Friday?

6 Jason spent half of his money on a CD. After he spent half of what was left on lunch, he had $5.75 left. How much did he have to start?

For 7–10, use the diagram. The sum along each side of this triangle is the same.

7 What is the value of *x*?

8 What is the value of *y*?

9 If you multiply each number in a blue circle by 2, how will *x* and *y* change?

10 How can you check that your answer to 9 is correct?

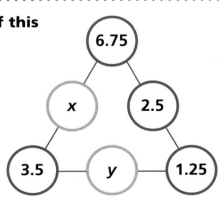

Chapter 9 Vocabulary

Choose the best vocabulary term from Word List A for each sentence.

Word List A

acute angle
concave
congruent figures
convex
equilateral triangle
isosceles triangle
kite
obtuse angle
opposite angles
parallel (||)
parallelogram
perpendicular
quadrilateral
rectangle
rhombus
right angle
scalene triangle
similar
straight angle
trapezoid
vertex

1 An angle that forms a square corner is called a(n) __?__.

2 A polygon with four sides is called a(n) __?__.

3 Two figures are __?__ if they have the same shape and the same or a different size.

4 A quadrilateral with two pairs of parallel sides, two pairs of congruent sides, and four right angles is a(n) __?__.

5 Figures with the same size and shape are __?__.

6 An angle with a measure less than a right angle is a(n) __?__.

7 A triangle that has three congruent sides is a(n) __?__.

8 A quadrilateral with four congruent sides and two pairs of parallel sides is a(n) __?__.

9 A quadrilateral with two pairs of parallel sides and two pairs of congruent sides is a(n) __?__.

10 Two lines that intersect at right angles are __?__.

Complete each analogy using the best term from Word List B.

Word List B

right angle
congruent figures
quadrilateral
square

11 Rectangle is to __?__ as equilateral triangle is to triangle.

12 Acute angle is to equilateral triangle as __?__ is to rectangle.

Talk Math

Discuss with a partner what you have just learned about attributes of two-dimensional figures. Use the vocabulary terms *acute angle*, *obtuse angle*, *right angle*, and *congruent*.

13 How can you tell whether a triangle is a scalene triangle?

14 How can you describe the angles formed by two intersecting lines?

15 How can you describe a parallelogram?

Degrees of Meaning Grid

16 Create a degrees of meaning grid. Start at least two rows with the word *triangle* and at least two rows with the word *quadrilateral*. Use what you know and what you have learned about quadrilaterals and triangles.

General	Less General	Specific

Analysis Chart

17 Create an analysis chart. List various polygons. Show the greatest number of right angles, acute angles, obtuse angles, and pairs of parallel sides the polygons can have.

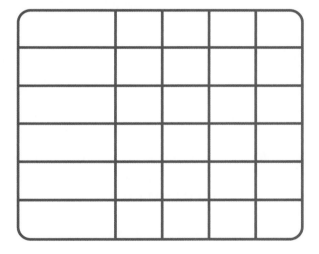

What's in a Word?

KITE There is a small hawk called a *kite* because the word *kite* sounds a bit like the bird's cry. Toy *kites* are made of paper, lightweight wood, and string. Because toy *kites* hover and glide like the bird, they were named after it. The quadrilateral *kite* gets its name from the toy because its shape is like the shape of some toy *kites*.

GO ONLINE Technology
Multimedia Math Glossary
www.harcourtschool.com/thinkmath

Triangle Maze

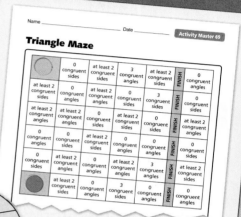

How To Play The Game

1 Play this game with a partner. Use the pencil and paper clip to make a spinner on Activity Master 69.

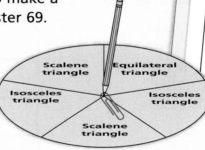

2 Each player should use a different color counter. Put your counter on one of the START corners of the Triangle Maze. Players should start in different corners.

3 Take turns spinning the pointer.
- After your spin, move your counter to a square that shares a side (not just a corner) with the square you are in AND describes the type of triangle shown by your spin.

  Hint: You can look at the examples of different types of triangles shown beside the spinner on Activity Master 69.

- You *must* move your counter if you can, even if you have to move backward.

4 The first player to cross the finish line wins!

GAME

First to 360°

> **Game Purpose**
> **To practice drawing angles of specific measures**
>
> **Materials**
> • Activity Masters 74–76: *First to 360°* Game Boards
> • Compass
> • Small counters
> • Protractor

How To Play The Game

1 This is a game for 2 players. Use Game Board 1. Each player uses a compass to draw a circle and draw in a radius.

2 Player 1 chooses an angle measurement on the game board and marks it with a counter. Then Player 1 uses the protractor to draw that angle in his or her circle.

3 Player 2 places a counter on any angle measurement on the game board that shares a side (not just a corner) with the one that is marked. Player 2 then draws the chosen angle in his or her circle.
• Keep a record of each player's running total.
• Sometimes a good strategy might be to put a counter on an angle measurement even if you cannot use it. That way, your opponent is blocked from using that measurement.

4 Take turns until one player's circle is completed. The angles must total exactly 360°. If they do, that player wins!

5 Play again using Game Board 2 and then Game Board 3.

CHALLENGE

Exterior Angles

Every polygon has interior angles—the type of angles you have been studying. Every polygon also has exterior angles. In this activity, you will explore exterior angles.

You'll need a protractor and a straightedge.

Exterior angles are formed by extending the sides of a polygon. A triangle has 3 exterior angles.

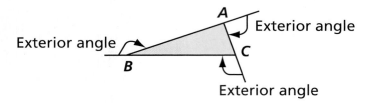

1 Use a protractor to measure the exterior angles at vertices *A*, *B*, and *C*.

m∠*A* = ■°.   m∠*B* = ■°.   m∠*C* = ■°.

2 Add the measures of the angles.
The measures of m∠*A* + m∠*B* + m∠*C* = ■°.

Now trace each of the four polygons below. Then use a straightedge to extend each side of the polygon. The first figure shows one exterior angle for you.

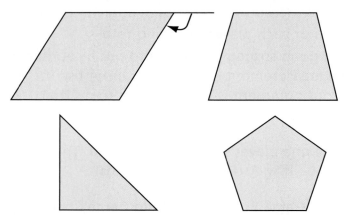

3 Measure the exterior angles of each figure and add them.

4 What pattern do you see in the sum of the exterior angles of each of the polygons?

10 Area and Perimeter

Dear Student,

In this chapter, "Area and Perimeter," you will measure flat, or two-dimensional, figures in two ways: by finding their perimeters and by finding their areas. Perimeter is the measurement of length around the outside of a figure, and area is the measurement of the space inside.

You already know how to find the area of a rectangle because you have used arrays of tiles to think about multiplication.

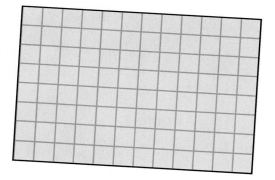

You will use this knowledge to help you figure out area formulas for parallelograms, triangles, and trapezoids. You will also figure out formulas for the perimeters of various figures.

Mathematically yours,
The authors of *Think Math!*

Up, Up, and Away!

Have you ever flown a kite? Flying kites is a popular pastime in many places around the world. Flat kites come in the familiar diamond shape, but they also come in squares, triangles, and in shapes like a fish or dragon. There are flat kites, box kites, train kites, and many other types of kites.

FACT·ACTIVITY 1

Figure 1

Use Figure 1 to answer questions for 1–2.

❶ Measure the perimeter of Figure 1. What is the perimeter?

❷ Based on the scale of Figure 1, what is the actual perimeter of the kite?

Scale:
1 in. = 1 ft

❸ What is the perimeter of the square kite? Explain how you found your answer.

❹ On a separate sheet of paper, draw a kite in the shape of a parallelogram. Measure the length of its sides to the nearest inch. Find its perimeter. If you built this kite using a scale of 1 in. = 1 ft, what would its perimeter actually be?

Square Kite

70 cm

In late March and early April, the sky on the National Mall in Washington D.C. is filled with colorful kites. People of all ages participate in the Smithsonian Kite Festival flying their handmade kites.

Vanessa has sketched a design for a kite. Use her design for Problems 1–4.

1 Identify the figures that make up the kite.

2 Find the perimeter and area of each figure you named in Problem 1.

3 About how much crepe paper does Vanessa need to make her kite?

4 Using your estimate from Problem 3, draw a kite design that has the same area but a different shape.

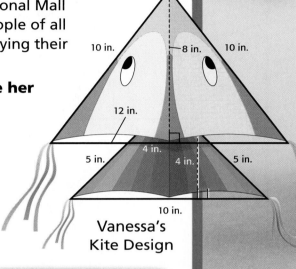

Vanessa's
Kite Design

CHAPTER PROJECT

- Design a kite that is a figure such as a triangle, rhombus, or a square.

- Make a sketch of your kite on grid paper. Decide on a scale for your drawing. Then, estimate the perimeter and area of your kite.

- Now, you are going to make a kite based on your drawing and the area of your kite. Gather all the materials you will need.

- Tape or tie a frame together. Measure and cut out your sail. Attach it to the frame with tape. Attach one end of the flying line to the frame and the other end to the reel wound with flying line. Make a tail and decorate your kite.

Kite Materials

- Frame (wooden sticks)
- Sail (newspaper, plastic, crepe paper, etc.)
- Flying line
- Tail (optional, makes it steadier against strong wind)
- Reel (cardboard, glue sticks, etc.)

ALMANAC

The area of the largest kite ever made was 630 square meters.

EXPLORE
Perimeter of Parallelograms

**The sides of these parallelograms are labeled to show
each length and which sides are equal in length.**

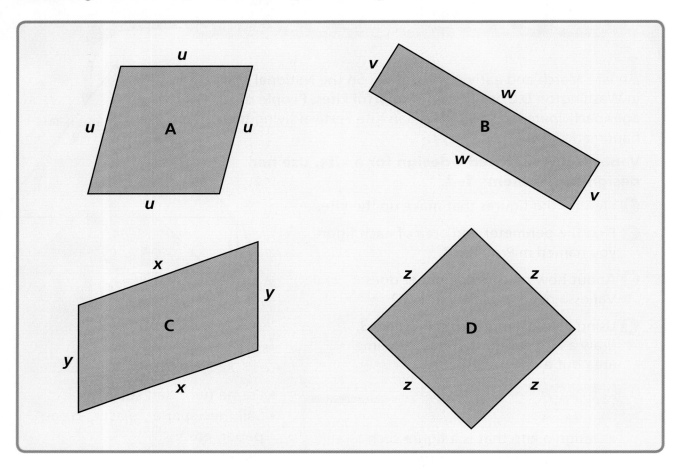

1 Find the perimeter of each figure.

_____

2 What can you say about the equality of side lengths in
any parallelogram?

_____

3 How can you find the perimeter of any parallelogram?

REVIEW MODEL
Finding Perimeter

Perimeter is the distance around a figure. You can find the perimeter of any polygon by adding the lengths of its sides.

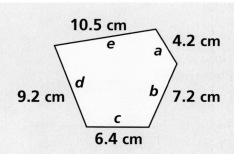

$$P = a + b + c + d + e$$

$$\downarrow \quad \downarrow \quad \downarrow \quad \downarrow \quad \downarrow$$

$$4.2 + 7.2 + 6.4 + 9.2 + 10.5 = 37.5$$

So, the perimeter is 37.5 centimeters.

You can use these formulas to find the perimeters of parallelograms.

Since a parallelogram has two pairs of congruent sides, you can use one of these formulas to find its perimeter.

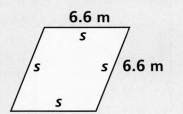

$P = 2 \times (l + s)$	$P = (2 \times l) + (2 \times s)$
$P = 2 \times (7 + 5)$	$P = (2 \times 7) + (2 \times 5)$
$P = 2 \times 12$	$P = 14 + 10$
$P = 24$	$P = 24$

So, the perimeter is 24 feet.

If all the sides of a parallelogram are congruent, you can use this formula to find its perimeter.

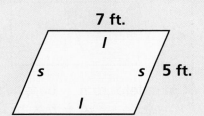

$P = 4 \times s$

$P = 4 \times 6.6$

$P = 26.4$

So, the perimeter is 26.4 meters.

✔ Check for Understanding

Find the perimeter of each polygon.

1
2.2 cm
2.6 cm

2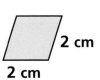
2 cm
2 cm

3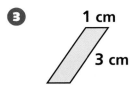
1 cm
3 cm

4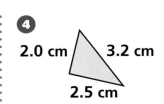
2.0 cm   3.2 cm
2.5 cm

REVIEW MODEL
Finding Area of a Parallelogram

Area is the amount of space inside a two-dimensional figure. You measure area in square units.

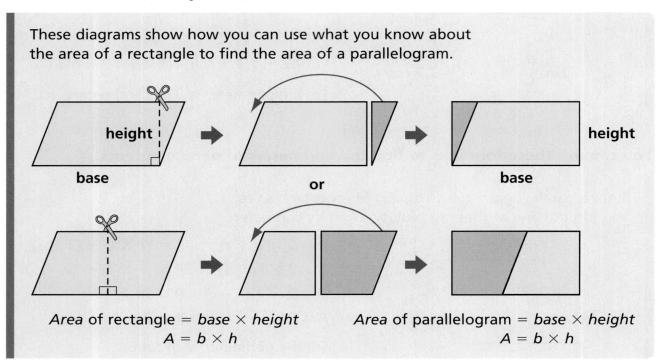

These diagrams show how you can use what you know about the area of a rectangle to find the area of a parallelogram.

Area of rectangle = base × height
$A = b \times h$

Area of parallelogram = base × height
$A = b \times h$

Example 1 Find the area.

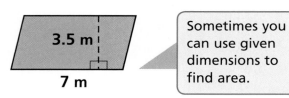

3.5 m

7 m

Sometimes you can use given dimensions to find area.

Area = base × height
7 m × 3.5 m
24.5 sq m

Example 2 Find the area.

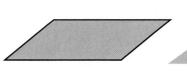

Area = base × height
3 cm × 1 cm
3 sq cm

Sometimes you need to first measure to find the lengths of the base and the height.
$b = 3$ cm
$h = 1$ cm
Then you can find the area.

✔ Check for Understanding

Find the area of each parallelogram. For 3 and 4, use a cm ruler to first find the base and height.

❶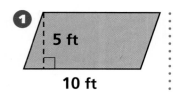
5 ft
10 ft

❷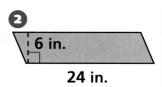
6 in.
24 in.

❸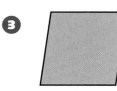

❹

EXPLORE
Area of Triangles

You will need scissors, tape, and an inch ruler.

1 Cut out the two triangles from Activity Master 92. Save the trapezoids for later.

2 Compare the two triangles. Do you think they are congruent? Why or why not?

3 Find at least two different ways to form a parallelogram with the two triangles. Choose one and tape the triangles together to make that parallelogram.

4 Use an inch ruler to measure the base and height of your parallelogram to the nearest half-inch. What is the area of the parallelogram?

5 Use the area of the parallelogram to find the area of each triangle.

- **How does the area of the triangle compare to the area of the parallelogram?**

- **How do the lengths of the sides of the triangle compare to the length of the base of the parallelogram?**

- **What part of the triangle has the same height as the height of the parallelogram?**

REVIEW MODEL
Finding Areas of Triangles and Trapezoids

These diagrams show how you can use what you know about finding the area of a parallelogram to find the area of a triangle or the area of a trapezoid.

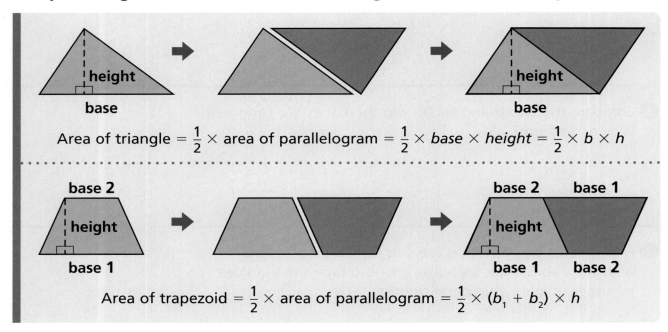

Area of triangle $= \frac{1}{2} \times$ area of parallelogram $= \frac{1}{2} \times base \times height = \frac{1}{2} \times b \times h$

Area of trapezoid $= \frac{1}{2} \times$ area of parallelogram $= \frac{1}{2} \times (b_1 + b_2) \times h$

Example 1 Find the area.

Area $= \frac{1}{2} \times b \times h = \frac{1}{2} \times 5 \times 4$

$= \frac{1}{2} \times 20 = 10$

So, the area is 10 sq ft.

Example 2 Find the area.

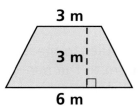

Area $= \frac{1}{2} \times (b_1 + b_2) \times h = \frac{1}{2} \times (3 + 6) \times 3$

$= \frac{1}{2} \times (9) \times 3 = 4.5 \times 3 = 13.5$

So, the area is 13.5 sq m

✔Check for Understanding

Find the area of each figure.

1

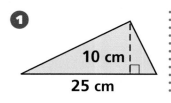

10 cm

25 cm

2

7 in.

4 in.

11 in.

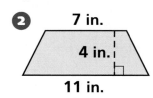

3

6 ft

15 ft

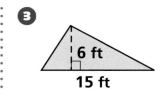

4

19 m

5 m

6 m

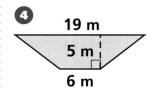

EXPLORE
Area and Perimeter of an Odd-Shaped Figure

Some of the people of Oddtown want to build a new playground on an odd-shaped piece of land. They will put a fence around it and cover the entire area of the playground with sand.

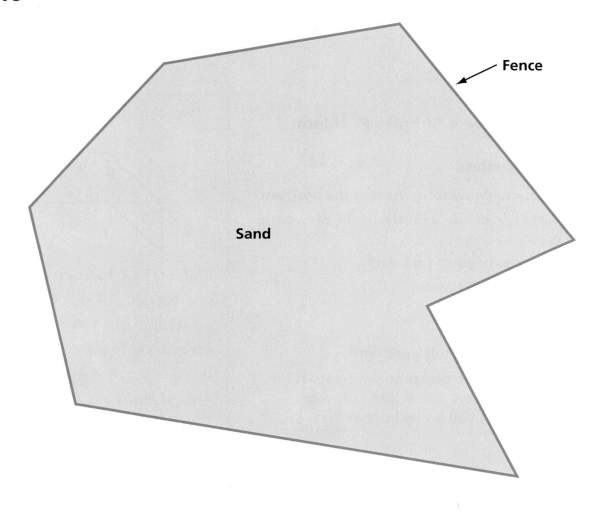

Fence

Sand

Use Activity Master 93 and tools such as scissors, a pencil, and a ruler to answer the questions below.

 You know how to find the area of a triangle. How could you figure out the area of the playground?

 How would you figure out how much fencing is needed?

REVIEW MODEL
Problem Solving Strategy
Solve a Simpler Problem

Charlotte drew this sketch to help her figure out how much carpet she needs to cover the floor of her playroom. What is the area of the playroom?

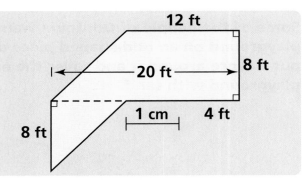

12 ft

20 ft

8 ft

1 cm

4 ft

8 ft

Strategy: Solve a Simpler Problem

 Read to Understand

What do you know from reading the problem?

Charlotte has drawn a sketch of the playroom she wants to carpet.

What do you need to find out?

the area of the playroom

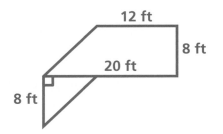 **Plan**

How can you solve this problem?

You can solve a simpler problem by splitting the odd-shaped playroom into polygons that have areas you know how to find.

 Solve

How can you split the sketch to help you solve a simpler problem?

You can split the figure into a trapezoid and a triangle (or into a rectangle and a parallelogram). Then you can use formulas to find the areas of the polygons.

 Check

Look back at the problem. Did you answer the question that was asked? Does the answer make sense?

Two of Many Possible Ways

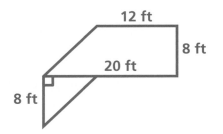

12 ft

8 ft

20 ft

8 ft

Area of the Trapezoid
$A = \frac{1}{2} \times (20 + 12) \times 8 =$
$\frac{1}{2} \times (32) \times 8 = 128$
Area of the Triangle
$A = \frac{1}{2} \times 8 \times 8 = \frac{1}{2} \times 64 = 32$
Area of Playroom:
128 sq ft + 32 sq ft = 160 sq ft

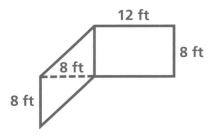

12 ft

8 ft

8 ft

8 ft

Area of the Rectangle
$A = 12 \times 8 = 96$
Area of the Parallelogram
$A = 8 \times 8 = 64$
Area of Playroom:
96 sq ft + 64 sq ft = 160 sq ft

Problem Solving Practice

Use the strategy *solve a simpler problem* to solve.

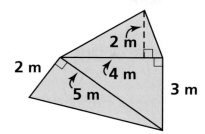

1 Erica drew this sketch of a pen she made for her pet rabbit. What is the area of the pen?

2 Doug earns $15 an hour. He worked 5.5 hours on Monday, 7 hours on Tuesday, 4.5 hours on Wednesday, and 3 hours on Thursday. How much did he earn those four days?

Problem Solving Strategies

✔ Act It Out
✔ Draw a Picture
✔ Guess and Check
✔ Look for a Pattern
✔ Make a Graph
✔ Make a Model
✔ Make an Organized List
✔ Make a Table
✔ **Solve a Simpler Problem**
✔ Use Logical Reasoning
✔ Work Backward
✔ Write an Equation

Mixed Strategy Practice

Use any strategy to solve. Explain.

3 Four children want to share three muffins equally. How much will each child get?

4 The sum of two numbers is 32. Their product is 240. What are the two numbers?

5 A pet store has 148 fish. There are the same number of fish in each of 8 aquariums and 12 fish in another aquarium. How many fish are in each of the 8 aquariums?

6 The total rainfall last week was 4.6 inches. For the first 3 days it did not rain at all. On the next three days it rained 0.6 inch each day. How much did it rain on the last day?

For 7–9, use the diagram.

7 What color is the part of the diagram where you would write 15?

8 There are two numbers in the blue section of the diagram. Name three other numbers you could write in the blue section?

9 Describe the numbers that belong in the green section of the diagram.

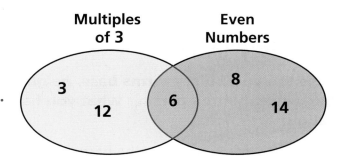

**Choose the best vocabulary term from Word List A
for each sentence.**

1 The measurement of space inside a plane figure
is called the ___?___.

2 A quadrilateral with exactly one pair of parallel sides
is a(n) ___?___.

3 A closed plane figure formed by three or more line segments
is called a(n) ___?___.

4 The distance from the base to the farthest point of a plane
figure is the ___?___ of the figure.

5 A(n) ___?___ has opposite sides that are both parallel and
congruent.

6 A rectangle with four sides of equal length is a(n) ___?___.

7 Two ___?___ lines intersect to form four right angles.

8 A quadrilateral with four equal sides is a(n) ___?___.

9 Sides of a polygon that have the same length are ___?___.

Word List A

area
base
congruent
height
parallel
parallelogram
perimeter
perpendicular
polygon
rectangle
rhombus
right angle
scale
square
trapezoid

Complete each analogy using the best term from Word List B.

10 Index card is to corner as rectangle is to ___?___.

11 Fence is to backyard as ___?___ is to polygon.

Word List B

area
parallel
perimeter
right angle

Talk Math

**Use the vocabulary terms *base*, *height*, and *perpendicular*
to discuss with a partner what you have just learned
about area.**

12 How can you measure the base and height of a parallelogram and
then use those measurements to find its area?

13 How can you measure the base and height of a triangle and then use
those measurements to find its area?

14 How can you measure the base and height of a trapezoid and then use
those measurements to find its area?

Word Definition Map

15 Create a word definition map for the word *perimeter.*

A What is it?

B What is it like?

C What are some examples?

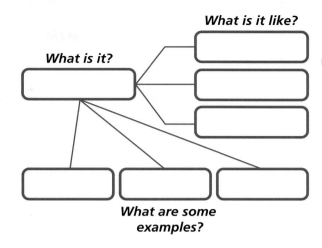

Concept Map

16 Create a concept map using the word *area.* Use what you know and what you have learned about area of a triangle, parallelogram, trapezoid, and irregular figures.

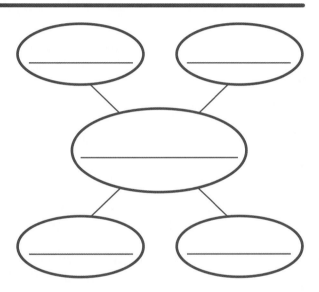

BASE This word has many meanings in the English language. It can be first, second, or third *base* in baseball. It can be the bottom part of a pillar, lamp, or platform. It can be a military camp or fort.

Base also has more than one meaning in mathematics. In the expression 4^3 (which means the product of three 4s, or $4 \times 4 \times 4$), the number 4 is the *base*, and 3 is the exponent. In geometry, the *base* is one side of a polygon. In a triangle, parallelogram, or trapezoid, the height and *base* are always perpendicular.

In all of the definitions, the *base* relates in some way to place or position.

Technology
Multimedia Math Glossary
www.harcourtschool.com/thinkmath

Perimeter Race

> **Game Purpose**
> **To practice finding perimeters of rectangular figures**
>
> **Materials**
> • Activity Master 88: *Directions Spinner*
> • Activity Master 89: *Centimeter Graph Paper*
> • Pencil and paper clip

How To Play The Game

1 This is a game for 2 players. Each player starts at one of the dots on the graph paper.

2 Take turns. Spin the spinner to find your direction.

• If the pointer lands on "Free," you choose the direction.

• If the pointer lands on "Free: 2 cm," you choose the direction, but you must extend your path 2 centimeters in that direction.

Start a path by drawing a line from the dot according to your spin. On your next turn, extend your path from where you left off.

3 You lose your turn if you cannot extend your path without retracing a path, crossing the boundary of a region, or leaving the grid.

If you cannot move in any direction, you may begin a new path from any point on your path so far.

Perimeter = 4 cm ← (not 5)

4 Draw your path until you close a region. Its perimeter is your score (even if the perimeter includes lines drawn by the other player). Write your initials in your completed figure for scoring and so you don't try to draw a path through it later.

5 After you have closed a region, continue your path from any point on your path so far that is not inside another region. Draw as many regions as possible. Add up all their perimeters as you go. You win if you have the greater total when time is called.

GAME

Area Race

Game Purpose
To practice finding areas of rectangular figures

Materials
- Activity Master 88: *Directions Spinner*
- Activity Master 89: *Centimeter Graph Paper*
- Pencil and paper clip

How To Play The Game

1 This is a game for 2 players. Each player starts at one of the dots on the graph paper. The goal is to get the greater sum of areas.

2 Take turns. Spin the spinner to find your direction.
- If the pointer lands on "Free," you choose the direction.
- If the pointer lands on "Free: 2 cm," you choose the direction, but you must extend your path 2 centimeters in that direction.

Start a path by drawing a line from the dot according to your spin. On your next turn, extend your path from where you left off.

3 You lose your turn if you cannot extend your path without retracing a path, crossing the boundary of a region, or leaving the grid.

If you cannot move in any direction, you may begin a new path from any point on your path so far.

4 Draw your path until you close a region. Its area is your score (even if the perimeter includes lines drawn by the other player). Write your initials inside for scoring and so you don't try to draw a path through it later.

5 After you have closed a region, continue your path from any point on your path so far that is not inside another region. Draw as many regions as possible. Add up all their areas as you go. You win if you have the greater total when time is called.

CHALLENGE

Area, Area, Area

Use what you have learned about area, division, and fractions to find the area of each part of the figure.

1 Area of the square = 64 sq in.

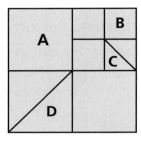

Area of **A** = ■   Area of **B** = ■   Area of **C** = ■   Area of **D** = ■

2 Area of the rectangle = 144 sq cm

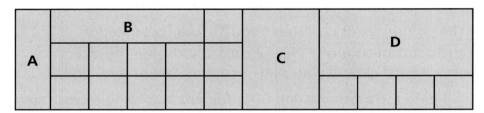

Area of **A** = ■   Area of **B** = ■   Area of **C** = ■   Area of **D** = ■

3 Area of the tangram puzzle = 24 sq in.

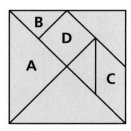

Area of **A** = ■   Area of **B** = ■   Area of **C** = ■   Area of **D** = ■

11 Fraction Computation

Dear Student,

In this chapter, "Fraction Computation," you will use what you already know about fractions to learn to add, subtract, and multiply them.

The fraction machines that you used earlier can help you answer questions such as, "How many eggs are in $\frac{2}{3}$ of a dozen eggs?"

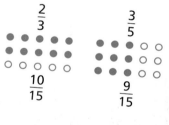

Multiplying $\frac{2}{3} \times 12$ is the same as finding $\frac{2}{3}$ of 12, so you already know something about multiplying with fractions! Also, "common sense" tells you that half of **two** thirds is **one** third. That is the same as saying $\frac{1}{2} \times \frac{2}{3} = \frac{1}{3}$ so there is something else you know about multiplying fractions.

You used **dot sketches** to help you find common denominators and compare fractions.

This process can also help you to add or subtract the fractions $\frac{2}{3}$ and $\frac{3}{5}$. Which is greater, $\frac{2}{3}$ or $\frac{3}{5}$? How much greater? What ideas do you have about how to add $\frac{2}{3}$ and $\frac{3}{5}$?

$$\frac{2}{3} \qquad \frac{3}{5}$$

$$\frac{10}{15} \qquad \frac{9}{15}$$

These examples show only a small fraction of the ideas you will learn as you begin to add, subtract, and multiply fractions!

Mathematically yours,
The authors of **Think Math!**

Joy Ride

A carousel, or merry-go-round, is a popular ride at fairs and carnivals. The carousel in Bushnell Park, in Hartford, Connecticut, was built in 1914. The hand-carved and hand-painted horses swirl around under a 24-sided pavilion. For $1.00, you can ride the carousel for $3\frac{1}{2}$ minutes.

FACT·ACTIVITY 1

Use the information in the table about carousel horses to answer the questions.

1 What fraction of all the horses are the chariot horses?

2 What fraction are the jumpers and the standers altogether?

3 If $\frac{31}{48}$ of the total number of horses are jumpers, what fraction of the horses are standers?

4 Suppose $\frac{21}{48}$ of the horses are on the outer row of the carousel. What fraction of the horses are on the inner rows?

5 If you go on the ride twice, how many minutes will you ride in all?

Carousel Horses	
Type of Horse	**Number of Horses**
chariot	2
jumper	■
stander	■
Total	**48**

Our fascination with horses does not stop with carousel horses. Real horses can be much greater in size and weight than carousel horses. There are more than 200 breeds of horses in the world. The chart compares average heights and weights of different adult horse breeds.

1 How much taller is the Thoroughbred than the American Miniature?

2 Suppose a young Arabian foal gained $\frac{3}{4}$ lb, $\frac{7}{8}$ lb, and $\frac{15}{16}$ lb in 3 consecutive days. Find the total weight gain in the 3 days.

3 Which horse is $\frac{1}{4}$ the weight of a Thoroughbred?

Average Size of Horse Breeds		
Clydesdale	6 ft	1,800 lb
Thoroughbred	$5\frac{1}{3}$ ft	1,000 lb
Arabian	5 ft	900 lb
American Miniature	$2\frac{5}{6}$ ft	250 lb

CHAPTER PROJECT

A horse's size is often measured in hands. To measure by hands, one hand is placed on the ground and the other directly above it. The process is repeated by moving upward to the horse's shoulders. Work with a partner. How many hands tall are you? Use hands to estimate your height.

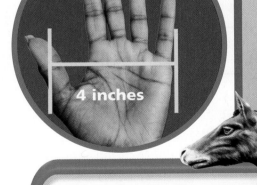

4 inches

- Have a partner trace your outline.

- Let your body length be equal to one unit. Use hands to measure the length of your body based on the outline.

- If your body length is about 14 hand-lengths long, then a hand represents $\frac{1}{14}$ of your body length.

- Use this measure to estimate body lengths of objects in the classroom. Display the results on a poster and share with your class.

ALMANAC Fact

Horses are thought to be related to a prehistoric animal called Hyracotherium that lived 50 million years ago and was about the size of a fox!

REVIEW MODEL
Adding and Subtracting Fractions with Like Denominators

When adding or subtracting fractions with like denominators, you add or subtract the numerators, and then write the sum over the denominator. Sometimes you can simplify your answer.

Add. $\frac{3}{7} + \frac{4}{7}$

Step ❶ Add the numerators.
$3 + 4 = 7$

Step ❷ Write the sum of the numerators over the denominator.
$\frac{3}{7} + \frac{4}{7} = \frac{7}{7}$

Step ❸ Write the fraction in simplest form.
$\frac{3}{7} + \frac{4}{7} = \frac{7}{7}$, or 1

Subtract. $\frac{5}{6} - \frac{1}{6}$

Step ❶ Subtract the numerators.
$5 - 1 = 4$

Step ❷ Write the difference of the numerators over the denominator.
$\frac{5}{6} - \frac{1}{6} = \frac{4}{6}$

Step ❸ Write the fraction in simplest form.
$\frac{5}{6} - \frac{1}{6} = \frac{4}{6}$, or $\frac{2}{3}$

Example A

Add the numerators.
$11 + 7 = 18$

Write $\frac{18}{15}$ as a mixed number.

$\frac{11}{15} + \frac{7}{15} = \frac{18}{15}$, or $1\frac{3}{15}$, or $1\frac{1}{5}$

Write in simplest form.

Example B

Subtract the whole-number parts. $6 - 2 = 4$

Subtract the numerators.
$7 - 1 = 6$

$6\frac{7}{9} - 2\frac{1}{9} = 4\frac{6}{9}$, or $4\frac{2}{3}$

Write in simplest form.

✔ Check for Understanding

Find the sum or difference.

❶ $\frac{3}{8} + \frac{3}{8}$

❷ $\frac{13}{18} - \frac{7}{18}$

❸ $\frac{8}{9} + \frac{7}{9}$

❹ $5\frac{2}{3} - 1\frac{1}{3}$

❺ $12\frac{3}{4} + 3\frac{1}{4}$

❻ $\frac{17}{15} - \frac{2}{15}$

❼ $4\frac{5}{6} + \frac{5}{6}$

❽ $3\frac{11}{12} - \frac{5}{12}$

EXPLORE
Fraction Stories

1

> After leaving home, Max drove $16\frac{7}{10}$ miles before stopping to buy gas. After driving another $14\frac{3}{10}$ miles, he got to his friend's home.

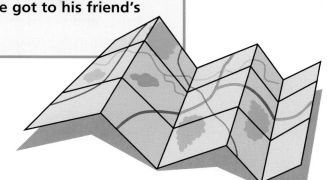

A How far did he travel from his home to his friend's home?

B What is the difference in distance between the two legs of the trip (before and after the gas station)?

2

> Kristy measured a small rectangular table and found that it was $26\frac{3}{8}$ inches long and $16\frac{7}{8}$ inches wide. She plans to make a tile border around the edge of the table.

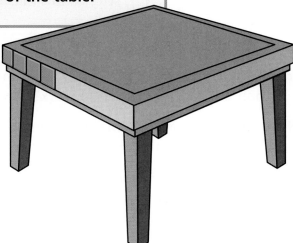

A What is the total distance around the edge of the table?

EXPLORE
Estimating Sums and Differences

❶

> Eduardo's pencil measures $4\frac{7}{8}$ inches long, and his friend Yori's pencil measures $6\frac{1}{4}$ inches long.

A Would you estimate the difference in lengths to be greater than 1 inch? Why?

B Would you estimate the difference in lengths to be greater than 2 inches? Why?

C About how much longer is Yori's pencil? How did you make your estimate?

---

❷

> Amy spent $1\frac{1}{2}$ hours on her reading homework and $1\frac{3}{4}$ hours on her science project.

A Would you estimate that she spent more than 2 hours on this schoolwork? Why?

B Would you estimate that she spent more than 3 hours on this schoolwork? Why?

C About how many hours would you say she spent on this schoolwork?

REVIEW MODEL
Adding and Subtracting Fractions with Unlike Denominators

When adding or subtracting fractions with unlike denominators, you first write the fractions with a common denominator. Then, you add or subtract the numerators. Sometimes you can simplify your answer.

Add. $\frac{1}{4} + \frac{2}{3}$

Step ❶ Find a common denominator of 4 and 3.

> You can use dot sketches to help you find a common denominator.

$\frac{1}{4} = \frac{2}{8} = \frac{3}{12}$ | $\frac{2}{3} = \frac{4}{6} = \frac{8}{12}$

So, a common denominator of 4 and 3 is 12.

Step ❷ Write equivalent fractions, using the common denominator.

$$\frac{1}{4} + \frac{2}{3} = \frac{3}{12} + \frac{8}{12}$$

Step ❸ Add the numerators. Write the sum over the denominator.

$$\frac{1}{4} + \frac{2}{3} = \frac{3}{12} + \frac{8}{12} = \frac{11}{12}$$

Subtract. $\frac{3}{5} - \frac{1}{3}$

Step ❶ Find a common denominator of 5 and 3.

$\frac{3}{5} = \frac{6}{10} = \frac{9}{15}$ | $\frac{1}{3} = \frac{2}{6} = \frac{3}{9} = \frac{4}{12} = \frac{5}{15}$

So, a common denominator of 5 and 3 is 15.

Step ❷ Write equivalent fractions, using the common denominator.

$$\frac{3}{5} - \frac{1}{3} = \frac{9}{15} - \frac{5}{15}$$

Step ❸ Subtract the numerators. Write the difference over the denominator.

$$\frac{3}{5} - \frac{1}{3} = \frac{9}{15} - \frac{5}{15} = \frac{4}{15}$$

Example A

$$1\frac{5}{6} + 2\frac{3}{4} = 1\frac{10}{12} - 2\frac{9}{12} = 3\frac{19}{12} \text{ or } 4\frac{7}{12}$$

Example B

$$5\frac{1}{2} - 1\frac{1}{3} = 5\frac{3}{6} - 1\frac{2}{6} = 4\frac{1}{6}$$

✔ Check for Understanding

Find the sum or difference.

❶ $\frac{1}{6} + \frac{2}{3}$

❷ $\frac{8}{9} - \frac{1}{2}$

❸ $3\frac{3}{4} + 2\frac{2}{3}$

❹ $5\frac{4}{5} - 1\frac{1}{3}$

EXPLORE
Combinations

1 Dillion used model to show different combinations of shirts and pants.

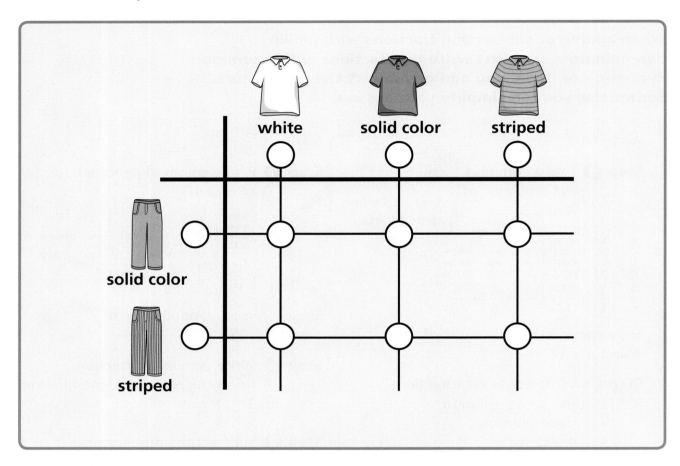

A Two-thirds of the shirts have no stripes.

B One-half of the pants have no stripes.

C What fraction of all possible outfits have no stripes?

---

2 Make a model to show the possible combinations of eye color (brown, blue, hazel, green, gray) and hair color (blond, black, brown).

Use your model to answer these questions:

A How many combinations have brown eyes, but not brown hair?

B What fraction of all possible combinations have brown eyes, but not brown hair?

REVIEW MODEL
Multiplying Fractions

To multiply fractions you can shade a rectangle or use dot sketches to help you find the product. Sometimes you can simplify your answer. Find $\frac{3}{4} \times \frac{2}{3}$.

One Way

Use a rectangle.

Step ❶ Draw a rectangle for $\frac{3}{4} \times \frac{2}{3}$.

Show fourths.

Show thirds.

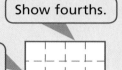

Step ❷ Shade an area that is $\frac{3}{4}$ by $\frac{2}{3}$.

Step ❸ $\frac{6}{12}$ of the rectangle is shaded.

So, $\frac{3}{4} \times \frac{2}{3} = \frac{6}{12}$, or $\frac{1}{2}$.

Write in simplest form.

Another Way

Use a dot sketch.

Step ❶ Draw a dot sketch for $\frac{3}{4} \times \frac{2}{3}$.

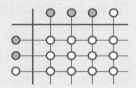

Step ❷ Shade the dots where the lines for the shaded dots intersect.

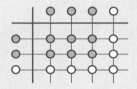

Step ❸ $\frac{6}{12}$ of the dots at the intersections are shaded.

So, $\frac{3}{4} \times \frac{2}{3} = \frac{6}{12}$, or $\frac{1}{2}$.

Write in simplest form.

A Third Way

Compute.

Multiply the numerators. $\frac{3}{4} \times \frac{2}{3} = \frac{3 \times 2}{} = \frac{6}{}$

Multiply the denominators. $\frac{3}{4} \times \frac{2}{3} = \frac{3 \times 2}{4 \times 3} = \frac{6}{12}$ or $\frac{1}{2}$

Write in simplest form.

✔ Check for Understanding

Find the product.

❶ $\frac{1}{4} \times \frac{2}{5}$

❷ $\frac{1}{2} \times \frac{3}{4}$

❸ $\frac{5}{6} \times \frac{3}{8}$

❹ $\frac{3}{10} \times \frac{1}{3}$

REVIEW MODEL
Problem Solving Strategy
Solve a Simpler problem

Heather and Dylan both moved into a new neighborhood in the past year. Heather has lived in her new house for $\frac{1}{6}$ of the year and Dylan has lived in his new house for $\frac{3}{4}$ of the year. How much longer has Dylan lived in his new neighborhood?

Strategy: Solve a Simpler Problem

 Read to Understand

What do you know from reading the problem?

Heather has lived in her new house for $\frac{1}{6}$ of the year. Dylan has lived in his new house for $\frac{3}{4}$ of the year.

What do you need to find out?

how much longer Dylan has lived in his new neighborhood

 Plan

How can you solve this problem?

You can *solve a simpler problem* by finding common denominators for the two fractions and then subtracting one from the other.

 Solve

How can you solve a simpler problem?

You can find a common denominator for $\frac{1}{6}$ and $\frac{3}{4}$. Both fractions have a common denominator of 12. $\frac{1}{6}$ is equivalent to $\frac{2}{12}$ and $\frac{3}{4}$ is equivalent to $\frac{9}{12}$. $\frac{9}{12} - \frac{2}{12} = \frac{7}{12}$

So, Dylan has lived in his new neighborhood for $\frac{7}{12}$ of a year longer than Heather.

 Check

Look back at the problem. Did you answer the question that was asked? Does the answer make sense?

Problem Solving Practice

Use the strategy *solve a simpler problem* to solve.

1 Christine measured the amount of rain that fell on the weekend. On Saturday, $\frac{2}{3}$ inch fell and on Sunday $\frac{1}{4}$ inch fell. What was the difference in the amount of rain that fell on Saturday and Sunday?

2 Taylor is preparing for a bicycle race. He rode his bike 14 miles each day for 21 days. How many total miles did he ride?

Problem Solving Strategies

✔ Act It Out
✔ Draw a Picture
✔ Guess and Check
✔ Look for a Pattern
✔ Make a Graph
✔ Make a Model
✔ Make an Organized List
✔ Make a Table
✔ **Solve a Simpler Problem**
✔ Use Logical Reasoning
✔ Work Backward
✔ Write an Equation

Mixed Strategy Practice

Use any strategy to solve. Explain.

3 Morgan wrote the following clues for a Mystery Number Puzzle. I am a 2-digit multiple of 3. I am even. The sum of my digits is a 2-digit number. I am less than 50. What number am I?

4 Patrick is making a display with some books. The first row has 1 book, the second row has 4 books, the third row has 9 books, and the fourth row has 16 books. If the pattern continues, how many books will be in the sixth row?

5 Austin has a collection of 36 baseball cards. He decided to give $\frac{1}{3}$ of them to his brother, Peter. He also gave $\frac{1}{4}$ of his cards to his sister, Deanna. Austin kept the rest. How many cards does each sibling have?

6 On Monday, Charmaine walked 8 blocks east from her house to go to school. After school she walked 4 blocks south to the library, and then 6 blocks west to the store. She walked 4 blocks north to her friend's house before she walked back home. How many blocks in all did Charmaine walk on Monday?

For 7–9, use the table.

7 Richard hands the cashier three $20 bills. How much change will he get back if he buys a helmet and a set of 4 wheels?

8 How much does it cost to buy the skateboard and the skateboard ramp?

9 Stephanie is saving $20 a week to buy a skateboard and elbow pads. How many weeks will she need to save before she can buy the items?

Skateboard Items for Sale	
Item	**Cost**
Skateboard	$49.99
Skateboard ramp	$39.95
Elbow pads	$19.99
Helmet	$29.95
Set of 4 wheels	$17.50

Choose the best vocabulary term from Word List A for each sentence.

1 If several fractions represent length in inches, they have a(n) __?__.

2 The product of two fractions is called a(n) __?__.

3 Two fractions that have the same denominator are fractions with a(n) __?__.

4 A number that has a whole number and a fraction is a(n) __?__.

5 If a fraction is greater than 1, it is called a(n) __?__.

6 Two fractions that have the same value are __?__.

7 The number below the bar of a fraction is the __?__.

8 The number above the bar of a fraction is the __?__.

9 The places where two lines cross in a dot sketch are called the __?__.

10 A(n) __?__ is a rectangle in which the lengths of the sides represent the factors in a multiplication problem.

Word List A

area model
common denominator
common unit
denominator
dot sketch
equivalent fractions
fraction of a fraction
fraction of a set
improper fraction
intersections
least common denominator
mixed number
numerator
unlike denominators

Complete each analogy using the best term from Word List B.

11 Less than one is to proper fraction as greater than one is to __?__.

12 North America is to the equator as __?__ is to the fraction bar.

Word List B

area model
denominator
mixed number
numerator

⬭Talk Math

Discuss with a partner what you have just learned about fractions. Use the vocabulary terms *numerator*, *denominator*, and *fraction*.

13 How can you add two fractions with unlike denominators?

14 How can you subtract mixed numbers with like denominators?

Word Definition Map

15 Create a word definition map for the word *mixed number.*

  A What is it?

  B What is it like?

  C What are some examples?

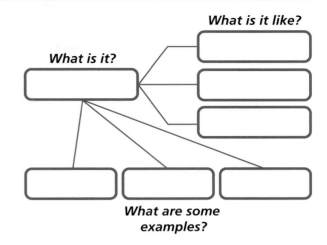

What is it?

What is it like?

What are some examples?

Tree Diagram

16 Create a tree diagram for the concept of *multiplying fractions.* Use what you know and what you have learned about multiplication and fractions.

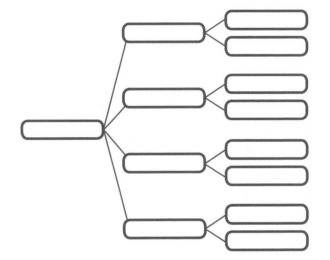

What's in a Word?

INTERSECTIONS *Intersections* are crossroads. A crossroad is the point where two or more roads cross each other. When you stand in a crossroad, you are standing on two roads at the same time. Line *intersections* are used to model multiplication of whole numbers and of fractions. The point where the lines cross—the *intersection*—is the solution to the problem. The solution is part of both lines, in much the same way as a person standing in a crossroad is part of both roads.

GO ONLINE
Technology
Multimedia Math Glossary
www.harcourtschool.com/thinkmath

Fraction Sums and Differences

Game Purpose
To practice adding and subtracting fractions with like denominators

Materials
- Activity Masters 95–96: Fraction Bars 1–2
- Activity Master 97: *Fraction Sums and Differences* Game Board
- Scissors, Index cards

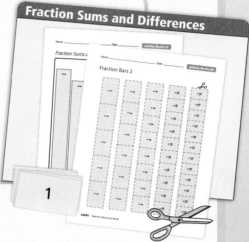

How To Play The Game

1 Play this game with a partner. Each player will need cut-out fraction bars from Activity Masters 95 and 96. Use the index cards to make two sets of number cards, 1 to 12. The object of the game is to match the sums and differences of two fractions to the different fractions on your game board.

2 Mix up the number cards, and place them face-down in a stack. Decide who will go first, and then take turns.

3 Pick three number cards. Choose one of the numbers—but not 1—to be the denominator of two fractions. The other numbers will be the numerators.

- Add or subtract the two fractions. Try to make one of the fractions represented by a bar on your game board.

- If you can make one of the fractions shown on the game board, explain how you can add or subtract to make that fraction. Then use the fraction bar pieces to check whether the sum or difference matches the length of the bar on the game board. (You might need to share fraction tiles with your partner.)

- If your match is successful, trace the pieces onto the game board bar as a visual record. Put a check mark in the box to the left of the bar on the game board. Write the number sentence on the bar.

- Once a bar is used, it may not be used again.

4 Play until the number cards run out. The one with more check marks wins.

GAME

Close or Closer

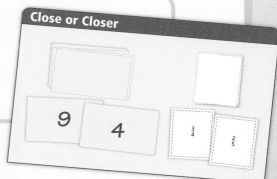

Game Purpose
To practice finding fractions of a set

Materials
- Activity Master 27: Fraction Cards 1
- Index Cards, Scissors

How To Play The Game

1 This is a game for 2 players. Make a set of 1–9 number cards. Mix them up, and put them face down in a stack. Cut out the Fraction Cards. Mix them up, and put them face down in another stack. Each fraction card refers to that fraction of 120. So, for example, the $\frac{3}{4}$ card means $\frac{3}{4}$ of 120, or 90.

2 Take turns being the dealer. The dealer turns over two number cards to make a 2-digit target number. Then the dealer turns over two fraction cards and leaves them on the table.

3 Take turns choosing one of the face-up fraction cards. The player who is **not** the dealer goes first. Each time you remove a fraction card from the table, replace it with another fraction card from the stack. There are always 2 face-up fraction cards on the table.

- You may have only 1 or 2 fraction cards in your hand at any time. Before choosing a third fraction card, discard one of your others.

- Find the number that the fraction of 120 on your fraction cards equals so you can find how close you are to the target number. You can add or subtract the two fractions and find that part of 120. Or you can find the two individual fraction parts of 120 first and then add or subtract those amounts.

- If you are happy with your fraction cards, you may pass and not choose another card. However, if you pass, you may not choose another fraction card for the rest of the game.

4 Play until both players have passed or until there are no more fraction cards left in the stack. Whoever has the number closer to the target number wins!

CHALLENGE

Fractions of Areas

Use the figure below. It has an area of 1 square unit.

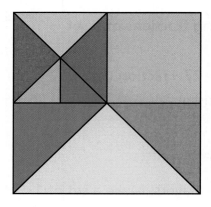

1 Use logical reasoning and what you know about geometric figures to write the fraction of the figure represented by each color.

2 What fraction of the figure does each of the following represent?

A Light Blue + Red

B Orange + Green

C Light Blue + Orange

D Red + Blue + Green

E Orange + Green + Yellow

3 Suppose the figure were a piece of metal that was worth exactly $500. What would be the value of each of the following?

A Yellow

B Light Blue

C Orange + Green

4 Suppose the figure had an area of 2 square units. Which answers above, if any, would change? Explain your reasoning.

Chapter

12 Three-Dimensional Geometry

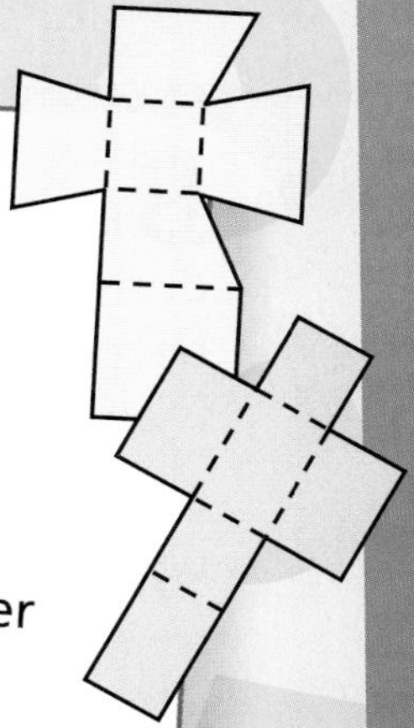

Dear Student,

When you were studying geometry in two dimensions, you learned that you could cut apart a figure, rearrange its pieces, and make a new figure with the same area.

You may already know how to find the volume of a three-dimensional figure that is shaped like a brick. In this chapter you will use the cutting-and-rearranging idea to identify rules for finding the volumes of other three-dimensional figures. As in earlier grades, you will use two-dimensional nets to make three-dimensional figures. You will see some new nets as well as some familiar ones, and you will sometimes compare three-dimensional figures by comparing their nets. Which of the two nets shown above looks like it would fold up into a brick-shaped object?

Here's another problem you will learn to solve. Imagine that you want to figure out how much paper it would take to wrap a box. How might you do this?

To solve problems like these, you will use the knowledge that you already have about finding the areas of two-dimensional figures such as parallelograms, triangles, and trapezoids. Onward, into the third dimension!

Mathematically yours,
The authors of *Think Math!*

Building a Birdhouse

Birdhouses in backyards or parks attract birds, usually during nesting season. In southern states, February is the best time to put up a birdhouse. In northern states, March is an appropriate time.

Birdhouses come in all shapes and sizes depending on the type of bird it is meant to attract.

Birdhouse A

Birdhouse B

Birdhouse C

Birdhouse D

FACT·ACTIVITY 1

Look at the birdhouses and answer the questions.

1. What two-dimensional figures can you identify in Birdhouses A, B, and C?

2. Which of the two-dimensional figures in Problem 1 appear to have congruent sides? Explain.

3. What three-dimensional figures do you see in the birdhouses? Identify the birdhouse and the figure.

4. Compare the roofs of Birdhouse B and Birdhouse C. Write the number of faces, vertices, and edges for each birdhouse.

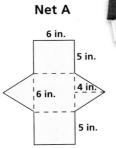

Shanti and Todd are building different model birdhouses using cardboard. Both designs have the same rectangular prism for the bottom of the birdhouse.

Net A

6 in.

5 in.

6 in. | 4 in.

5 in.

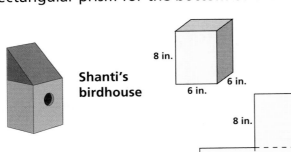

Shanti's birdhouse

8 in.

6 in.

6 in.

Todd's birdhouse

Net B

8 in.

6 in. | 6 in.

8 in. | 8 in. | 6 in.

8 in.

6 in.

Net C

7.8 in.

6 in. | 7.8 in.

5 in. | 5 in.

5 in.

6 in.

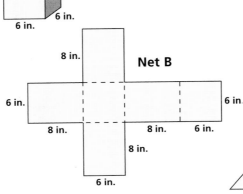

Look at the birdhouses and answer the questions.

1 Which net matches the roof of Shanti's birdhouse? of Todd's bird house? What does the other net show?

2 What is the total surface area of Shanti's birdhouse? of Todd's birdhouse? Remember to include the base and use only the outside dimensions.

3 Find the volume of Todd's birdhouse.

CHAPTER PROJECT

You are going to design a birdhouse and then make a model which is half its actual size.

- Sketch a three-dimensional model and label its sides with measurements. Then draw a net with each side half of the given dimensions in the drawing.

- Trace the net on manila cardboard, cut it out, then fold and tape the sides together. Decorate your model.

- Find the surface area of the model.

ALMANAC
Fact

Cowbirds, sometimes known as lazy birds, neither nest nor take care of their young. Instead, the female cowbird lays her eggs in other birds' nests and lets the other birds take care of her young!

EXPLORE
Three-Dimensional Figure Search

Find as many three-dimensional figures as possible from your class collection that appear to match each set of attributes.

Group 1

 Same number of faces as vertices

 Either all faces are triangles, or at most one is not

 No parallel faces

 All faces but one share a vertex

Group 2

 Fewer faces than vertices

 Two faces that are parallel, but not congruent

 Other faces are not parallelograms or triangles

Group 3

 More faces than vertices

 One pair of congruent faces that appear parallel, but are twisted in relation to each other

 All other faces are triangles

Group 4

 Fewer faces than vertices

 Two congruent, parallel polygonal faces

 All other faces are parallelograms

REVIEW MODEL
Faces, Vertices, and Edges

Figures pictured here have faces, edges, and vertices.

Faces are the flat surfaces that "surround" the insides of a three-dimensional figure.

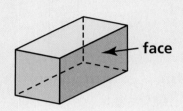

face

Edges are the seams where the faces meet.

edge

Vertices are the places where more than two faces meet at a point.

vertex

You can count the number of faces, vertices, and edges on these three-dimensional figures.

Example 1

How many faces, vertices, and edges does this three-dimensional figure have?

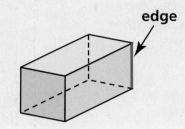

It has 5 faces, 6 vertices, 9 edges.

Example 2

How many faces, vertices, and edges does this three-dimensional figure have?

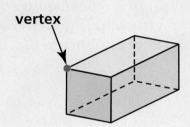

It has 5 faces, 5 vertices, 8 edges.

✔Check for Understanding

Copy and complete the table.

	Three-Dimensional Figure	Number of Faces	Number of Vertices	Number of Edges
1	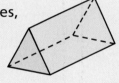	■	■	■
2		■	■	■
3	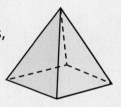	■	■	■
4		■	■	■

REVIEW MODEL
Classifying Three-Dimensional Figures

A three-dimensional figure with flat faces that are polygons is a *polyhedron*. Polyhedra are named by the polygons that form their bases.

A *prism* is a polyhedron that has two congruent polygons as bases. All other faces of a prism are parallelograms.

rectangular prism   triangular prism

A *pyramid* is a polyhedron with one face that can be any polygon. All other faces are triangles that meet at the same vertex.

square pyramids

There are *other polyhedra* that are not prisms and not pyramids. Some have parallel bases that are not congruent, some look twisted, and others have flat faces that are not parallelograms or triangles.

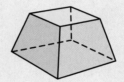

other polyhedra

A three-dimensional figure with a curved face is *not* a polyhedron.

cylinder   cone   sphere

✔ Check for Understanding

Classify each three-dimensional figure. Write *prism, pyramid, other polyhedron,* or *not a polyhedron.*

EXPLORE
Measuring Three-Dimensional Structures

Build this structure with inch cubes.

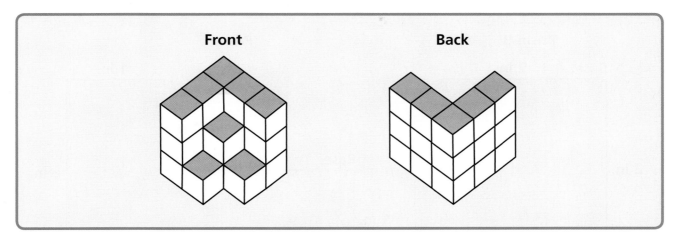

Front   Back

1 How many inch cubes does it take to build the structure?

---

2 How many layers, of floors, does the structure have?

---

3 How many cubes are in the bottom layer?
Sketch the shape of this floor.

---

4 How many cubes are in the second layer?
Sketch the shape of this floor.

---

5 How many cubes are in the top layer?
Sketch the shape of this floor.

EXPLORE
Volume of Prisms

Use the information in each diagram to predict how many inch cubes you will need to build the prism. Build each with cubes and record the volume.

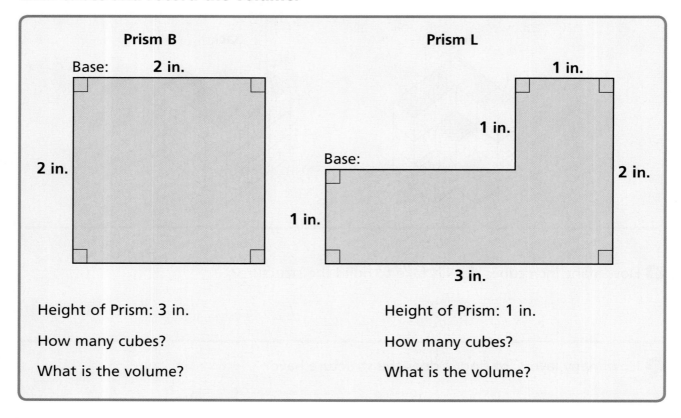

Prism B

Base: **2 in.**

2 in.

Height of Prism: 3 in.

How many cubes?

What is the volume?

Prism L

1 in.

1 in.

Base:

2 in.

1 in.

3 in.

Height of Prism: 1 in.

How many cubes?

What is the volume?

Use the information in the diagram or Figures O and S from the class collection.

How might you find the volume of a triangular prism?

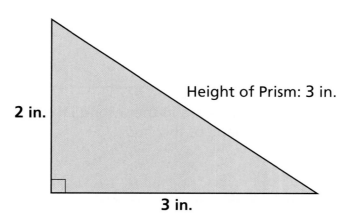

2 in.

Height of Prism: 3 in.

3 in.

REVIEW MODEL
Volume of a Prism

Volume is the measure of space a three-dimensional figure occupies.

Volume is measured in cubic units, such as cubic inches (cu in.), cubic centimeters (cu cm), cubic feet (cu ft), or cubic kilometers (cu km).

You can find the volume of a prism by multiplying its base area by its height.

Rectangular Prism	Triangular Prism
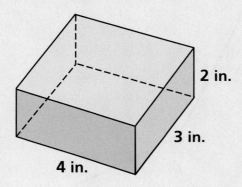	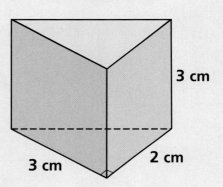
The area of the rectangular base is *base length × width*, or 4 × 3 = 12; 12 sq in.	The area of the base of the prism is $\frac{1}{2}$ × *base length × height*, or $\frac{1}{2}$ × 3 × 2 = 3; 3 sq cm.
The volume of the prism is *base area × height*, or 12 × 2 = 24; 24 cu in.	The volume of the prism is *base area × height*, or 3 × 3 = 9; 9 cu cm.

✔ Check for Understanding

Find the volume of each rectangular prism.

Three of the faces of these triangular prisms are rectangles. Find the volume of each prism.

1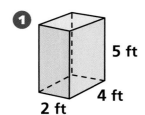
5 ft
4 ft
2 ft

2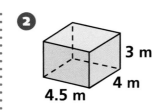
3 m
4 m
4.5 m

3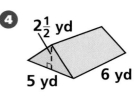
2 cm
3 cm
3 cm

4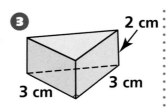
$2\frac{1}{2}$ yd
5 yd
6 yd

Look at Figure C in your class collection. Use the net to help you figure out how much paper was used to make that polyhedron.

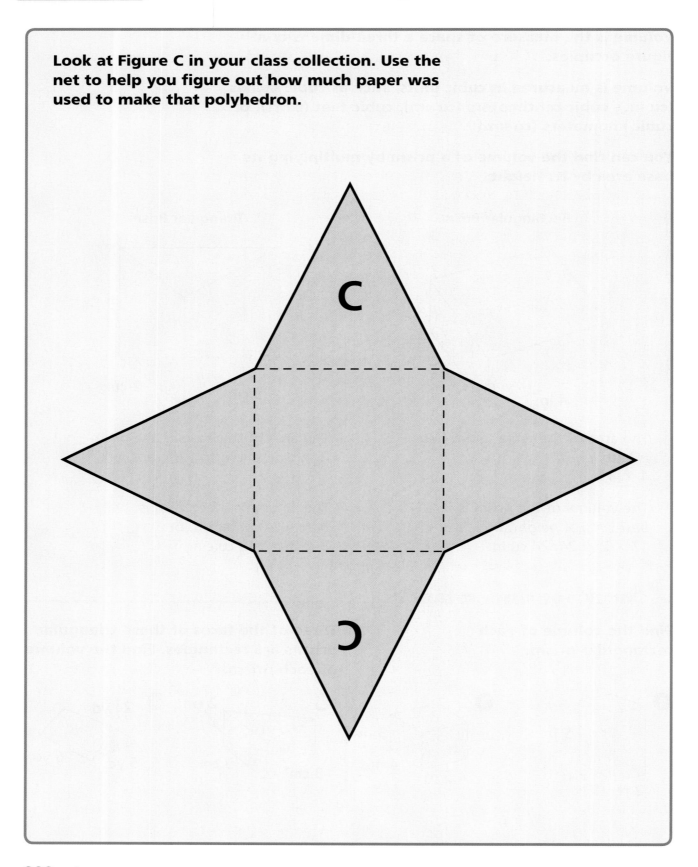

REVIEW MODEL
Surface Area

Surface area is the amount of area on the surface of a three-dimensional figure.

Surface Area, like all area, is measured in square units, such as square inches (sq in.), square centimeters (sq cm), square feet (sq ft), or square kilometers (sq km).

You can find the surface area of a polyhedron by finding the area of each face of the polyhedron and then finding the sum of the areas. You can use a net of the three-dimensional figure to help you find the area of each face.

Rectangular Prism

There are 4 large congruent rectangles and 2 congruent squares, so the surface area of the prism is $(4 \times 6) + (2 \times 4)$; 32 sq in.

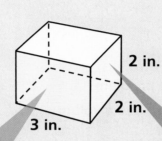

The area of each of the larger rectangular faces is *length* × *width*, or $2 \times 3 = 6$; 6 sq in.

The area of each square face is *length* × *width*, or $2 \times 2 = 4$; 4 sq in.

✔Check for Understanding

Find the surface area of each three-dimensional figure.

1 rectangular prism

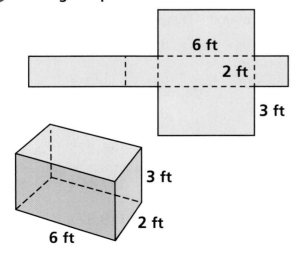

2 square pyramid

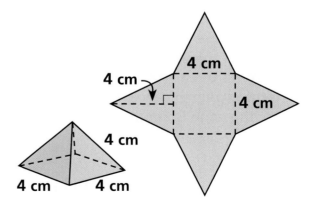

REVIEW MODEL
Problem Solving Strategy
Guess and Check

William wants a cube-shaped box that has a volume of about 150 cubic inches to hold his marble collection. About how many inches long should each edge of the box be?

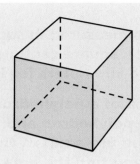

Strategy: Guess and Check

Read to Understand

What do you know from reading the problem?

William wants a cube-shaped box that has a volume of about **150** cubic inches.

What do you need to find out?

the edge length of a cube-shaped box that has a volume of **150** cubic inches

Plan

How can you solve this problem?

I can *guess and check* by trying different numbers for the length.

Solve

How might you *guess and check* to solve the problem?

Try an edge length and multiply it by itself three times. If the volume is less than the target volume, increase the guess. If the volume is greater than the target volume, decrease the guess.
So, the edge is about 5.3 inches.

Edge n	Volume n^3	< or > target
3	27	< 150
5	125	< 150
6	216	> 150
5.5	166.375	> 150
5.4	157.464	> 150
5.3	148.877	< 150

Check

Look back at the problem. Did you answer the questions that were asked? Does the answer make sense?

Problem Solving Practice

Use the strategy *guess and check* to solve.

1 Jeanne wants to build a square patio with an area of about 30 square meters. To the nearest tenth of a meter, how long should she make each side of the patio?

2 Tickets for the concert cost $14.50 for one child and one adult. The adult's ticket costs $3.00 more than the child's ticket. What is the cost of each ticket?

Problem Solving Strategies

✔ Act It Out
✔ Draw a Picture
✔ **Guess and Check**
✔ Look for a Pattern
✔ Make a Graph
✔ Make a Model
✔ Make an Organized List
✔ Make a Table
✔ Solve a Simpler Problem
✔ Use Logical Reasoning
✔ Work Backward
✔ Write an Equation

Mixed Strategy Practice

Use any strategy to solve. Explain.

3 Emily bought three items at the grocery store. After paying $4.20, $6.75, and $9.40 for the items, she had $2.50 left. How much money did she start with?

4 Marti joined an exercise club. On the first day she exercised for 5 minutes, on the second day for 10 minutes, and on the third day for 15 minutes. If this pattern continued, for how many minutes did she exercise on the tenth day?

5 A train has 9 cars, each seating 56 people. What is the total number of people who can be seated on the train?

6 Hal has 3 more baseball cards than Abby. Kristen has 5 more cards than Abby. If Hal has 12 cards, how many cards does Kristen have?

For 7–8, use the diagram.

Ms. Blackstone has a collection of number cubes in her classroom. She found a box and measured its dimensions. For 7 and 8, use the diagram of her box.

7 If she has 50 number cubes that are each 1 cubic inch, will they all fit in the box? How do you know?

8 If she decides to put wrapping paper on all the faces of the box, how much paper will she need?

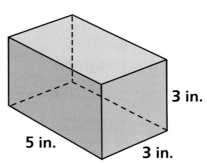

5 in.　3 in.　3 in.

Choose the best vocabulary term from Word List A for each definition.

1 A(n) __?__ is a three-dimensional figure that has two congruent polygon-shaped bases and other faces that are all rectangles.

2 The __?__ is the sum of the areas of all the surfaces of a three-dimensional figure.

3 Area is measured using __?__.

4 The __?__ of a three-dimensional figure are line segments formed when two faces meet.

5 The polygons that are flat surfaces of a three-dimensional figure are its __?__.

6 The __?__ of a three-dimensional figure are the points where three or more of its edges intersect.

7 A three-dimensional figure with flat faces that are polygons is called a(n) __?__.

8 A(n) __?__ is a three-dimensional figure with a polygon base and faces that are triangles that meet at a common vertex.

Complete each analogy using the best term from Word List B.

9 Cylinder is to __?__ as prism is to pyramid.

10 Banana is to banana peel as __?__ is to surface area.

Word List A

base
congruent
cubic units
edges
faces
height
length
parallel faces
perpendicular
polyhedron
prism
pyramid
square units
surface area
vertices
volume
width

Word List B

base
cone
sphere
volume

☐ Talk Math

Discuss with a partner what you have learned about three-dimensional figures. Use the vocabulary terms *base*, *faces*, and *height*.

11 How can you tell the difference between a cone and a cylinder?

12 How can you find the volume of a triangular prism?

13 How can you find the surface area of a prism?

Word Web

14 Create a word web for the term *base.*

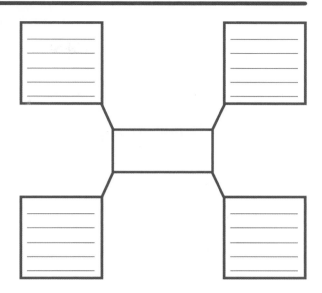

Tree Diagram

15 Create a tree diagram using the terms *cone, cylinder, prism,* and *pyramid.* Use what you know and what you have learned about solid figures.

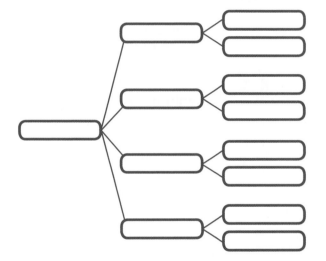

What's in a Word?

?

VOLUME In daily life, *volume* has many meanings. It is the level of loudness of music or other sounds. An encyclopedia *volume* is one book from a set. The sales *volume* of a store is how many items were sold. Some stores offer *volume* discounts—which means you pay less if you buy a lot of something. But in math, *volume* is a measure. It is the amount of space taken up by a three-dimensional figure. It is determined by the number of unit cubes—whole or part—that fit inside a space.

GO ONLINE Technology
Multimedia Math Glossary
www.harcourtschool.com/thinkmath

GAME

Volume Builder

Game Purpose
To practice estimating and finding volume of a rectangular prism

Materials
- Cubes
- Coin

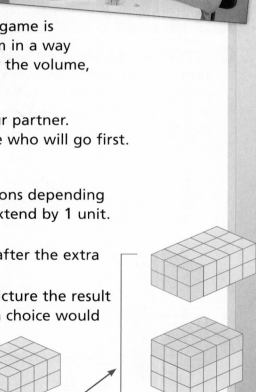

Volume Builder

heads = 1
tails = 2

How To Play The Game

1 This is a game for 2 players. The object of the game is to extend the dimension of a rectangular prism in a way that will give the greatest volume. The greater the volume, the more points you score.

2 Start with a cube placed between you and your partner. The volume of this prism is 1 cubic unit. Decide who will go first. Then take turns.

3 Toss the coin. Extend one of the three dimensions depending on the result of your coin toss. Heads means extend by 1 unit. Tails means extend by 2 units.

- The figure must remain a rectangular prism after the extra cubes have been added.

- Decide which dimension to increase. Try to picture the result and estimate the new volumes. Decide which choice would result in a prism of the greatest volume.

   Example: You get heads, and this is the prism so far.

   Heads means you add 1 to any dimension. You could extend the prism in one of three ways:

- Calculate the new volume. Record that number as your point score for that round.

4 Play until one player reaches or goes past 200 points.

GAME

Surface Area Builder

Game Purpose
To practice estimating and finding surface area of a rectangular prism

Materials
- Cubes
- Coin

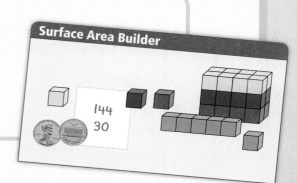

How To Play The Game

1 This is a game for 2 players. The object of the game is to extend the dimension of a rectangular prism in a way that will give the greatest surface area. The greater the surface area, the more points you score.

2 Start with a cube placed between you and your partner. The surface area of this prism is 6 square units. Decide who will go first. Then take turns.

3 Toss the coin. Extend one of the three dimensions depending on the result of your coin toss. Heads means extend 1 unit. Tails means extend 2 units.

- The figure must remain a rectangular prism after the extra cubes have been added.
- Decide which dimension to increase. Try to picture the result and estimate the new surface areas. Decide which choice would result in a prism with the greatest surface area.

  Example: You get heads, and this is the prism so far.

  Heads means you add 1 to any dimension. You could extend the prism in one of three ways:
- Calculate the new surface area. Record that number as your point score for that round.

4 Play until one player reaches or goes past 200 points. That player wins.

CHALLENGE

The Ever Changing Volume

You can experiment to see how volume changes as dimensions change.

You will need: 6 sheets of centimeter grid paper cut into squares that are 20 squares by 20 squares, scissors, tape

Directions

1 Cut out a 1 × 1 square from each corner of one sheet of the centimeter grid paper. Fold the edges and tape the corners to make an open box. What is the volume of the box in cubic units?

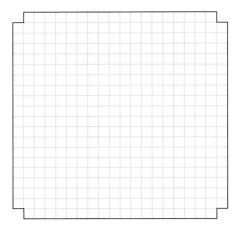 

2 Use a new sheet of grid paper. Cut out a 2 × 2 square from each corner, and make a box. What is the volume?

3 Use a new sheet of grid paper. Cut out a 3 × 3 square from each corner, and make a box. What is the volume?

4 Use a new sheet of grid paper. Cut out a 4 × 4 square from each corner, and make a box. What is the volume?

5 Use a new sheet of grid paper. Cut out a 5 × 5 square from each corner, and make a box. What is the volume?

6 Use a new sheet of grid paper. Cut out a 6 × 6 square from each corner, and make a box. What is the volume?

7 For which size cut-out corner is the volume of the box the greatest? How do you know?

Dear Student,

In this chapter, you'll start by exploring mobiles. Look at the mobile below. Can you use the key of shape weights at the right to figure out the mobile's total weight?

Total Weight: ?

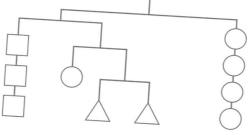

What if you only knew a mobile's total weight, but not the weight of each different shape? How might knowing that the mobile is balanced help you to find the weight of each shape?

In this chapter, you'll solve mobile puzzles as well as other types of puzzles. Whatever the puzzle may be, you'll find that there are lots of ways to describe and solve it. We hope you enjoy the puzzles!

Mathematically yours,

The authors of *Think Math!*

△ = 3
□ = 4
○ = 6

Balancing Act

Tightrope walking acts have been performed in front of crowds for centuries. Some of the first tightrope walkers were in ancient Egypt and China. The act was called "rope dancing" and the performers walked over knives. In modern circuses, tightrope walkers have a net under them for safety and use a balancing pole to help them perform fantastic tricks. The longer and heavier the pole, the steadier the tightrope walker will be.

FACT·ACTIVITY 1

3 ounces

A balancing pole can weigh up to 31 pounds and be as long as 39 feet. A clown is putting items in the baskets on his pole to help him balance.

Use the items to the right to answer the questions.

1 In his first act, the clown walks across the tightrope with 2 juggling balls in each basket. What is the total weight of the balls in both baskets?

2 During the second act, the clown replaces the left basket with 2 top hats and 1 juggling ball. How many more juggling balls are needed in the right basket to make his shoulder pole balanced?

7 ounces

3 What other combination of objects can the clown put in the left and right baskets so that his shoulder pole is balanced?

4 An equation which describes the items in the clown's shoulder pole in Problem 3 is $2b + c = c + h$. What does the b represent?

6 ounces

What happens if the weights of the baskets are not the same? This clown knows physics too! To stay balanced on the rope, the clown moves the pole so that one basket is closer to his body than the other. In other words, the body acts as a balance point.

The pictures show 3 ways the clown balances the pole on the tightrope. Use these pictures to answer the questions.

1. Write an equation using only variables to represent the objects and distances shown. Explain what each variable represents.

2. Suppose the clown has 3 hats in the left basket and 3 juggling balls in the right basket. Where should the clown balance the 6-ft pole? Explain.

3. Suppose the clown has 2 juggling balls in the left basket and 2 hats in the right basket. Where should the clown balance the 6-ft pole? Explain.

1 ft   5 ft

15 oz   3 oz

$15 \times 1 = 3 \times 5$

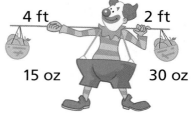

3 ft   3 ft

15 oz   15 oz

$15 \times 3 = 15 \times 3$

4 ft   2 ft

15 oz   30 oz

$15 \times 4 = 30 \times 2$

CHAPTER PROJECT

Materials: straws, paper clips, construction paper

Make your own mobile and experiment with balancing its different layers.

Slide 3 paper clips over a horizontal straw as shown in the model, one on each end and one in the middle. Repeat the first step to extend your mobile to 2 or more layers. Cut out 3 or 4 shapes from construction paper. Then trace and cut out 15 copies of each shape. Each layer of your mobile will only use 1 type of paper shape. Clip the shapes to the paper clips. You will need to add or subtract paper clips to balance your mobile.

• Describe how you balanced your mobile.

ALMANAC
Fact

Jean François Gravelet walked across a tightrope over Niagara Falls between Canada and the United States in 1895. Later, he cooked and ate an omelette while crossing.

EXPLORE
Balancing Mobiles

Martina makes mobiles that balance perfectly! Her secret is to make sure that every arm has the same total weight on each end.

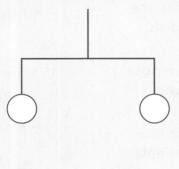

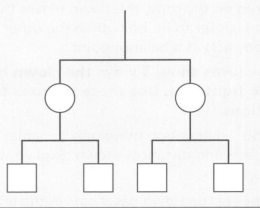

The different shapes she uses each weigh different amounts. That makes it trickier to balance mobiles that combine different shapes, but Martina is an expert. She made these balanced mobiles.

A   Total Weight: 20

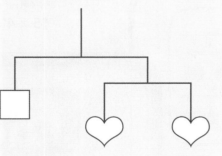

B   Total Weight: 24

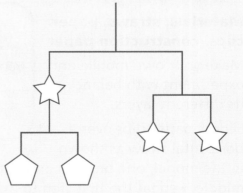

Find the weight of each shape in the two mobiles above.

REVIEW MODEL
Writing an Equation for a Mobile

The shapes on the two sides of an arm of a mobile must have the same weight to balance.

You can use words and you can use equations to describe relationships shown on the mobile.

Total Weight: 48

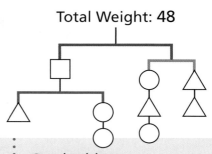

On the red arm—
• 1 triangle weighs the same as 2 circles.

$$1t = 2c$$

On the green arm—
• 2 circles and 1 triangle weigh the same as 2 triangles.

$$2c + 1t = 2t$$

On the blue arm—
• 1 square, 1 triangle, and 2 circles weigh the same as 2 circles and 3 triangles.

$$1s + 1t + 2c = 2c + 3t$$

To find the weight of each shape, you can write the halved numbers at each side of an arm and the weights inside or near each shape.

$\triangle = 6$
$\bigcirc = 3$
$\square = 12$

Total Weight: 48

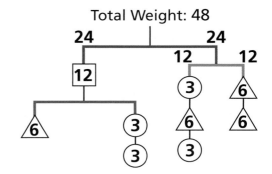

✔ Check for Understanding

Write two equations to agree with each mobile. Find the weight of each shape.

1 Total Weight: 48

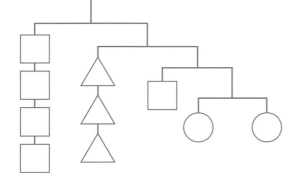

2 Total Weight: 24

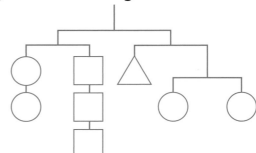

EXPLORE
Exploring Balance Puzzles

Brenda had two kinds of blocks. She put some on a balance scale and the two sides weighed exactly the same.

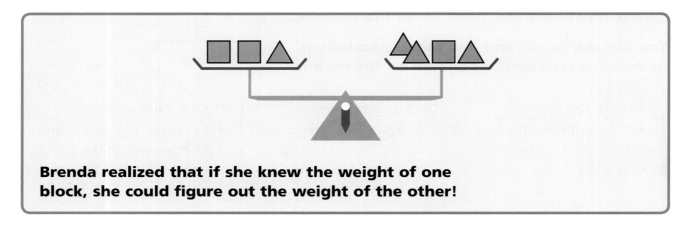

Brenda realized that if she knew the weight of one block, she could figure out the weight of the other!

1 If a ▲ weighs 3 ounces, how much does a ■ weigh?

Explain your answer.

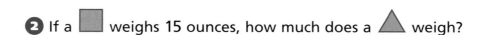

2 If a ■ weighs 15 ounces, how much does a ▲ weigh?

REVIEW MODEL
Balancing Weights

For a balance scale to balance, the two pans must each have the same total weight. If you add the same weights or take away the same weights from both pans, the pans remain balanced.

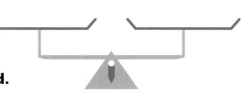

You can use equations to describe relationships shown on balance scales.

Write an equation for the balance scale.

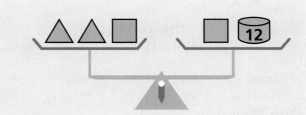

Step ❶ Record what you see on the pans.

$$\triangle + \triangle + \square = \square + 12$$

or

$$t + t + s = s + 12$$

or

$$2t + s = s + 12$$

2 $\triangle$ and 1 $\square$ on the left weigh the same as 1 $\square$ and 12 on the right.

Step ❷ Simplify.

Remove 1 $\square$ from each pan.

2 $\triangle$ on the left weigh the same as 12 on the right.

$$\triangle + \triangle = 12$$

or

$$t + t = 12$$

or

$$2t = 12$$

So, 1 $\triangle$ = 6, or $t = 6$

Example

Write an equation for the balance scale.

$c + t + 6 = 2c + t + 4$, or

$6 = c + 4$, or

$2 = c$

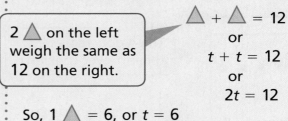

✔ Check for Understanding

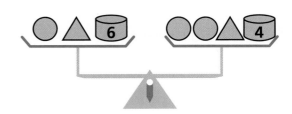

Write an equation for each balance scale.

❶

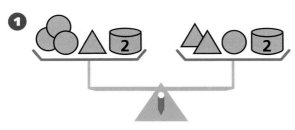

❷

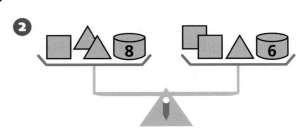

REVIEW MODEL
Drawing a Diagram for a Situation

Sometimes you can use diagrams to describe situations and help you find unknown numbers. You have to be flexible with these diagrams. You cannot rely on sizes and lengths to help you figure out the unknowns.

Situation:

Sophia baked some cookies. She put them on a platter in 3 rows with the same number of cookies in each row. She had 4 cookies left over.

Draw a diagram to show the number of cookies she had.

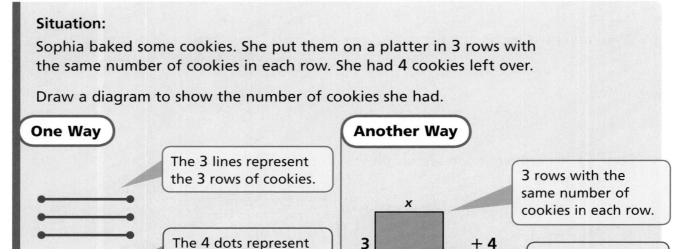

One Way

The 3 lines represent the 3 rows of cookies.

The 4 dots represent the left over cookies.

Another Way

3 rows with the same number of cookies in each row.

plus 4 cookies left over

Example Ramon has 3 more baseball cards than Mark. Mark has twice as many cards as Paulo.

Draw a diagram to show all the baseball cards.

This is a possible diagram.

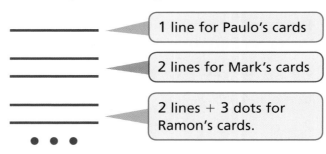

1 line for Paulo's cards

2 lines for Mark's cards

2 lines + 3 dots for Ramon's cards.

✔Check for Understanding

Draw a diagram to describe each situation.

❶ Alex lined up his 8 toy cars end-to-end. Then Troy added his cars to the line.

Draw a diagram to show all the cars.

❷ Julia has 4 more books than Lisa. Lisa has 3 times as many books as Rachel.

Draw a diagram to show how many books Julia has.

REVIEW MODEL
Writing an Equation for a Situation

You can write an equation to describe a situation.

Jason earns the same amount of money each day for walking his neighbor's dog. He earns an extra $10 once each week for giving the dog a bath. Write an equation to describe the total amount Jason earns in one week.

Step ❶ Choose a letter to stand for the amount Jason earns each time he walks the dog.

> Use *w* to stand for "**w**alks".

Choose a different letter for the total amount he earns each week.

> Use *t* to stand for "**t**otal amount".

Step ❷ Use words to describe a rule for the situation. The total amount Jason earns in one week **is** 7 times the amount he earns each day walking the dog **plus** $10 for giving the dog a bath.

Step ❸ Use an equation to describe a rule for the situation. $t = 7w + 10$

Example Natalie bought some salads and some small pizzas at the snack bar. The salads cost $5 each and the pizzas cost $3 each. Describe the total amount Natalie spent.

Use words to describe the situation. The total amount is $5 times the number of salads she bought plus $3 times the number of pizzas she bought.

Use an equation to describe the situation. $t = 5s + 3p$

> Use *t* to stand for the total cost, *s* to stand for the number of salads, and *p* to stand for the number of pizzas.

✔Check for Understanding

Use words to describe a rule for each situation. Then write an equation for the situation.

❶ Marcus bought some markers for $2 each and some notebooks for $6 each. Describe the total amount he spent. Use *m* for the number of markers, *n* for the number of notebooks, and *t* for the total amount he spent.

❷ Tami has 3 pockets with the same number of dimes in each pocket. She also has 8 dimes in her hand. Describe the total number of dimes she has. Use *p* for the number of dimes in each pocket and *t* for the total number of dimes.

REVIEW MODEL
Problem Solving Strategy
Work Backward

Drew played a number trick with his friend, Amy. He told Amy to choose a number, add 4, and multiply the result by 6. Then he told her to subtract 8 and divide that number by 2. Amy said the result was 20. Drew told Amy her starting number. What was Amy's starting number?

Strategy: Work Backward

Read to Understand

What do you know from reading the problem?

Amy chose a mystery number, performed operations on the number, and had a result of 20.

What do you need to find out?

the starting number

Plan

How can you solve this problem?

You can work backward by starting with the resulting number, 20.

Solve

How can you work backward to solve the problem?

You can work backward through the list of steps and undo the operations. First, multiply 20 by 2, add 8, divide the result by 6, and subtract 4.

So, Amy's starting number was 4.

Check

Look back at the problem. Did you answer the question that was asked? Does the answer make sense?

Problem Solving Practice

Use the strategy *work backward* to solve.

1 Ryan has three younger sisters. His sister, Jen, is half the age of their sister, Ashley. Ashley is 10 years older than their sister, Amanda. Amanda is half Ryan's age. If Ryan is 24 years old, how old are his sisters?

2 Mrs. McCarthy bought tickets for her family to go to the art museum. She bought two adult tickets and two student tickets for a total of $42.50. If the adult tickets were $12.50 each, how much was each student ticket?

Problem Solving Strategies

✔ Act It Out
✔ Draw a Picture
✔ Guess and Check
✔ Look for a Pattern
✔ Make a Graph
✔ Make a Model
✔ Make an Organized List
✔ Make a Table
✔ Solve a Simpler Problem
✔ Use Logical Reasoning
✔ **Work Backward**
✔ Write an Equation

Mixed Strategy Practice

Use any strategy to solve. Explain.

3 104 students showed up to participate in an after-school sports program. There can be up to 10 teams and there can be no more than 15 students on a team. If all teams have the same number of students and no students are left over after the teams are made, how many teams will there be? How many students will be on each team?

4 Mr. Dawson bought deli meat for the class picnic. One package of turkey weighed 2.75 pounds. A package of ham weighed 1.85 pounds, and a package of roast beef weighed 0.94 pound. Did he buy more turkey than the ham and roast beef together? Explain.

5 Kayla has 14 pages of stamps in her collection. There are 24 stamps on each page. How many stamps does Kayla have in her collection?

6 Samantha counted 46 tiles around the walls in her kitchen. The tiles go in a pattern of blue, yellow, green, and white. If the first tile is blue, what color is the 46th tile?

For 7–8, use the table.

7 How much time did Cody spend in the computer lab on Monday and Tuesday?

8 How much longer did Cody spend in the computer lab on Tuesday than on Friday?

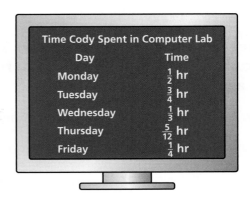

Time Cody Spent in Computer Lab	
Day	Time
Monday	$\frac{1}{2}$ hr
Tuesday	$\frac{3}{4}$ hr
Wednesday	$\frac{1}{3}$ hr
Thursday	$\frac{5}{12}$ hr
Friday	$\frac{1}{4}$ hr

Choose the best vocabulary term from Word List A for each definition.

Word List A

balance

balance scale

describing situations with diagrams

describing situations with equations

equation

mobile

variable

1. Art with hanging parts that move easily is called a(n) __?__.

2. To __?__ a mobile, both sides of an arm must have the same weight.

3. An algebraic or numerical sentence that shows two quantities are equal is a(n) __?__.

4. A(n) __?__ has two pans and pivots freely on a fulcrum to compare weights.

5. A letter or symbol that stands for one or more values is called a(n) __?__.

6. When you use algebra to represent word problems, you are __?__.

7. When you use pictures to solve word problems, you are __?__.

Complete each analogy using the best term from Word List B.

Word List B

balance scale

equation

mobile

variable

8. Seat is to seesaw as pan is to __?__.

9. Word is to sentence as __?__ is to equation.

Talk Math

Use the vocabulary terms *equation, balance,* and *variable* to discuss with a partner what you have just learned about algebra.

10. How are a mobile and an equation alike?

11. How are a balance scale and an equation alike?

12. How can you write an equation from a diagram?

Concept Map

13 Create a concept map for the term *balance*. Include the words *mobile*, *balance scale*, and *equation*.

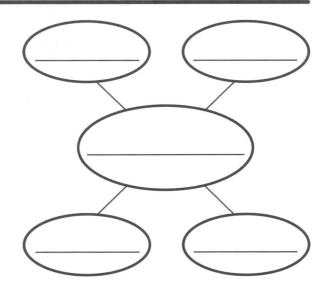

Word Web

14 Create a word web using the word *variable*.

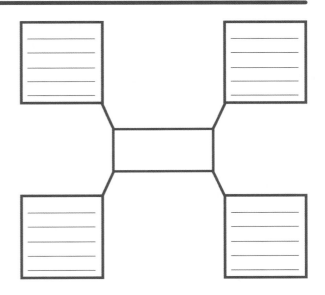

What's in a Word?

BALANCE *Balance* comes from a Latin word that means "a scale having two pans." An object was placed in one pan. Weights of known measure were placed in the other pan until the pans *balanced.* The weight of the object was the sum of the weights. Today, we use *balance* in many other ways as well. You *balance* your checkbook to know how much money you have in the bank. You *balance* yourself by standing without wobbling. You might use a *balance* beam in gym class. A *balanced* meal has just the right number of elements.

GO ONLINE Technology
Multimedia Math Glossary
www.harcourtschool.com/thinkmath

GAME

The Balance Puzzle

> ### Game Purpose
> **To practice relating balance puzzles to equations and solving the puzzles**
>
> ### Materials
> • Activity Master 137: *The Balance Puzzle* Scale and Spinner
> • Activity Master 138: *The Balance Puzzle* Game Pieces
> • Paper clip

How To Play The Game

1 This is a game for 2 players. Cut out all the game pieces. To use the spinner, put a pencil through the paper clip. Put the pencil point on the center of the spinner. Then spin the paper clip around the pencil. Decide who will be the Puzzler and who will be the Solver.

The Balance Puzzle

2 The Puzzler secretly picks two numbers from 4 to 9 to be the weights of the blocks. Record the weights. Show which is for the square and which is for the triangle.

3 The Solver spins and puts that many game pieces in the left pan of the scale.

4 The Puzzler fills the right pan with game pieces—using the secret weights—until the pans balance. Use as few pieces as possible.

5 The Solver guesses the weight of the square or the triangle.
• A correct guess earns as many points as the number of pieces in the right pan.
• An incorrect guess means use the same weights on your next turn. Record this puzzle so you can use it again. If your next spin gives the same pieces for the left pan, spin again.

6 Trade roles. Play until someone gets 6 points and wins the game!

GAME

Picture Puzzler

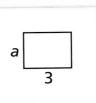

How To Play The Game

1 This is a game for 2 players. Decide which color cube will represent tens and which will represent ones. Each player will need 20 counters. Choose your colors. Roll one number cube to see who goes first. Then take turns.

2 Toss the cubes. Make your target number according to the colors.

3 Find a diagram that can represent your target number. Any counting number can be used for **a**.

4 Name the value for **a** so your partner can be sure that your diagram represents your target number
- If your diagram is correct, put a counter in the square.
- If your diagram is not correct, try one more time.

Example: Your target number is 63.

You choose this square and say that **a** = 21.

$21 \times 3 = 63$, so you can put a counter on the square.

5 The winner is the first player to fill a 2-by-2 block of squares.

Variation: You can choose which of the rolls to use for the tens and ones each time you toss the cubes.

CHALLENGE

Balance Please!

For each mobile:
- Find the weight of each shape for the total weight given.
- Choose a new total weight so that it is possible to balance the mobile with weights that are still whole numbers.
- Determine the new weight of each shape so that the mobile balances for the new total weight. Remember, in any one mobile, the same shape always has the same weight.

1 Total Weight = 72

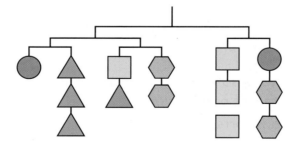

2 Total Weight = 48

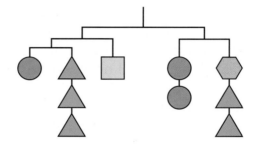

3 Total Weight = 28

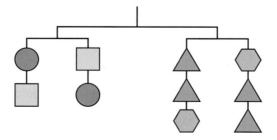

14 Data and Probability

Dear Student,

In this chapter you will be studying probability. You will be conducting experiments, gathering data, and using probability to make predictions.

Probability is a measure of how "surprising" an event is. Chances are you have flipped a coin to decide who will go first when playing a game. Would you use this method if you did not believe that it was fair? The reason you trust this method is that you expect the chance of a coin landing on heads or landing on tails to be equal.

Sometimes we are surprised even when probability says that we should not be. If you were to flip a coin 4 times and get 4 heads, what is the probability that it will land on heads with the next flip? Is the probability the same as always, or is it higher or lower? Because 4 heads in a row is surprising, you might expect that the next flip will be tails. Still, the probability that the next flip will turn up heads is still exactly $\frac{1}{2}$. After all, the coin does not remember what happened the last 4 times! Probability helps us decide what should or should not be expected.

Chances are you will soon learn lots more about probability. And chances are it is time to get started!

Mathematically yours,
The authors of *Think Math!*

Probability and Data

Games using spinners, cards, number cubes, or other instruments of probability have been in existence for about 4,000 years. There are games that are based on strategy and others that are based on racing. You can learn how to play strategy games better by knowing probability.

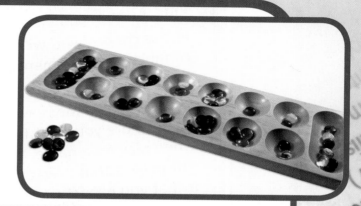

FACT·ACTIVITY 1

Afia is playing a spinner game using the spinner below. Use the spinner for 1–4.

1. Write a fraction to describe the probability of spinning a *P*; a *B*; an *E*.

2. Write a fraction to describe the probability of the spinner landing on a vowel. (Do not include *Y* as a vowel.)

3. Write a fraction to describe the probability of the spinner landing on a consonant.

4. Write a number sentence expressing the probability of the spinner landing on a vowel or the letter *B*.

The first crossword puzzle, originally known as a "word-cross," was written by Englishman Arthur Wynne. What word games do you know?

FACT·ACTIVITY 2

Suppose a word game used two 10-sided decahedra labeled with letters instead of numbers. The letters on each decahedron are shown below.

Decahedron 1:	A	B	C	D	E	F	G	H	I	K
Decahedron 2:	L	M	N	O	P	R	S	T	U	V

1 List all possible outcomes for rolling a vowel on decahedron 1 and a vowel on decahedron 2.

2 There are 100 possible outcomes for rolling the two decahedra. Copy and complete the table to the right. Write as a fraction the theoretical probability for rolling two vowels.

		Decahedron 2	
		vowel	consonant
Decahedron 1	vowel		$\frac{24}{100}$
	consonant	$\frac{14}{100}$	$\frac{56}{100}$

3 Is it possible to roll your 2 initials? Explain why or why not. What is the probability of rolling your initials?

4 Write each fraction in the table as a decimal and as a percent.

CHAPTER PROJECT

Working in small groups, determine a question you would like your classmates to answer such as, "What is your favorite board game?" Other acceptable survey topics include word games or sports games.

Survey 20 people and make a poster to present your results. Use a circle graph to display the data. Using your results, write questions for other students to answer. Then make a prediction about the favorite game of a larger group of students (such as all 5th graders).

ALMANAC Fact

At the Elliott Avedon Museum and Archives of Games in Waterloo, Canada, visitors not only see exhibits about board games, but they also get to sit down and play the games. There are more than 5,000 objects and documents at the museum.

EXPLORE
A Probability Experiment

Imagine playing a game in which the chances of various outcomes were not all the same. You can be sure that certain outcomes are more likely than others, but HOW MUCH more likely? Here is a way to find out by doing an experiment.

1 Use Activity Master 142: Colors Spinner. Color, cut out, and assemble the spinner.

2 Make a table that lists the possible outcomes.

3 Spin the paper clip on your spinner 20 times. Record the result of each spin using tally marks.

4 How likely is each outcome?

REVIEW MODEL
Finding Probability

Probability is the measure of the likelihood of a particular event. The probability of an event is a number from 0 to 1, where 0 means the event is never expected to occur and 1 means the event is always expected.

Probability is a comparison of the number of outcomes that are part of the event (sometimes called favorable outcomes) to the total number of possible, equally likely outcomes.

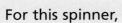

For this spinner,

- There are 8 possible *outcomes.* Each section of the spinner is a possible outcome.

- There are 4 possible *events:* red, green, yellow, blue.

The probability of the pointer landing on blue is $\frac{1}{8}$.

> number of blue sections
> total number of sections

The probability of the pointer landing on red is $\frac{3}{8}$.

> number of red sections
> total number of sections

The probability of the pointer landing on green OR yellow is $\frac{4}{8}$.

> number of green OR yellow sections
> total number of sections

Example

Erin made this set of cards.

3	6	9	12	15
18	21	24	27	30

She drew one card at random from the deck. Describe the probability for each event.

- Number is 12 $\frac{1}{10}$
- Number is less than 12 $\frac{3}{10}$
- Number is greater than 12 $\frac{6}{10}$, or $\frac{3}{5}$
- Number is less than 32 $\frac{10}{10}$, or 1

✔ Check for Understanding

Use a fraction to describe the probability of each event.

1 yellow

2 not blue

3 red OR green

4 2 or 3

5 less than 4

6 more than 5

0	1	2	3	4

EXPLORE
A Sampling Experiment

**The bag contains red, blue, and green cubes.
The total number of cubes and the number of
each color are secrets. Don't peek!**

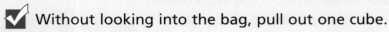

Follow these steps to perform an experiment.

✔️ Without looking into the bag, pull out one cube.

✔️ Record the color and put the cube back into the bag.

✔️ Shake the bag a bit to mix up the contents.

✔️ Repeat this process until you have recorded 20 pulls.

① Summarize your experiment by assigning a fraction for each
color that represents the number of pulls of that color out of
the total number of pulls.

② Explain why this does not help you know the total number of
cubes in the bag.

REVIEW MODEL
Understanding Percent

Percent means "per hundred." A percent is a part of 100 and can be written as a fraction with 100 as the denominator.

Fifty percent, or 50%, means 50 per 100 and can be written as $\frac{50}{100}$.

- 75 of the 100 squares are green.

- 75 of 100 is $\frac{75}{100}$.

- So, 75% of the grid is green.

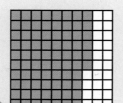

> It's easy to write percents for fractions with 100 as a denominator.

- 10 of the 25 squares are blue.

- 10 of 25 is $\frac{10}{25}$, or $\frac{40}{100}$.

- So, 40% of the grid is blue.

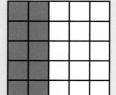

> If the denominator is NOT 100, write an equivalent fraction with 100 as the denominator.

Examples

The Eagles won 16 of the 20 games they played. What percent of the games did they win?

They won $\frac{16}{20}$ of the games. $\frac{16}{20} = \frac{80}{100}$

So, they won 80% of the games.

Joanna got 78% of the 50 problems correct on her math quiz. How many problems did Joanna get correct?

$78\% = \frac{78}{100}$ $\frac{78}{100} = \frac{39}{50}$

So, Joanna got 39 problems correct.

✔ Check for Understanding

Write a percent for the blue part of each diagram.

1

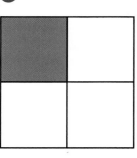

2

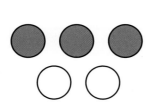

3

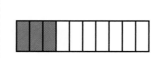

4

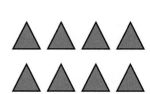

---

5 Jake spelled 46 of the 50 words on the spelling test correctly. What percent of the words were spelled correctly?

6 $\frac{1}{4}$ of the students in the fifth-grade class bought pizza for lunch. What percent of the students bought pizza?

EXPLORE
A Circle Graph

The students at the Hilltop School voted for new school colors. This graph shows the results.

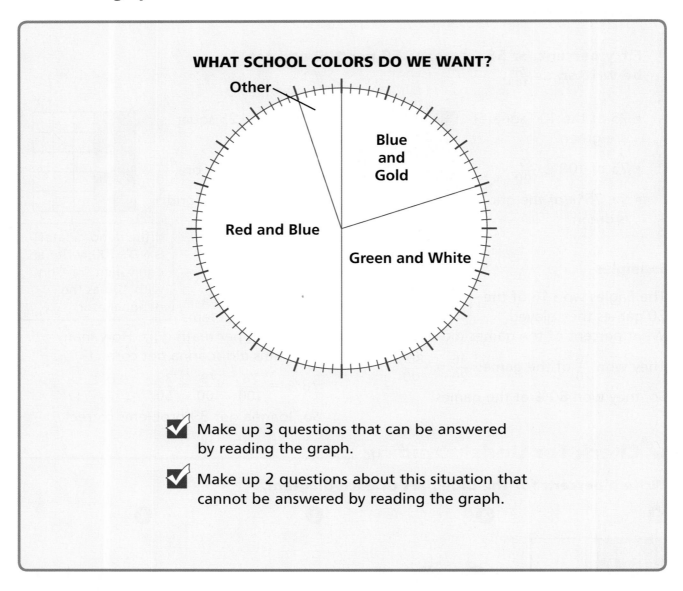

WHAT SCHOOL COLORS DO WE WANT?

Other

Blue and Gold

Red and Blue

Green and White

✓ Make up 3 questions that can be answered by reading the graph.

✓ Make up 2 questions about this situation that cannot be answered by reading the graph.

REVIEW MODEL
Making Circle Graphs

A circle graph is an appropriate graph to use when you want to show how the parts relate to the whole.

If you think of a complete circle as 100%, you can express parts of a circle graph, as percents.

The table shows the results of a survey of fifth-grade students.

In all, 50 students were surveyed.

10 + 8 + 18 + 6 + 8 = 50

OUR FAVORITE SPORTS				
Baseball	Golf	Soccer	Tennis	Other
10	8	18	6	8

The steps below show a way to make a circle graph of the data.

Step ❶ Write the data as fractions or decimals. Then write the data as percents.

OUR FAVORITE SPORTS				
Baseball	Golf	Soccer	Tennis	Other
10	8	18	6	8
$\frac{10}{50}$, or 0.20	$\frac{8}{50}$, or 0.16	$\frac{18}{50}$, or 0.36	$\frac{6}{50}$, or 0.12	$\frac{8}{50}$, or 0.16
20%	16%	36%	12%	16%

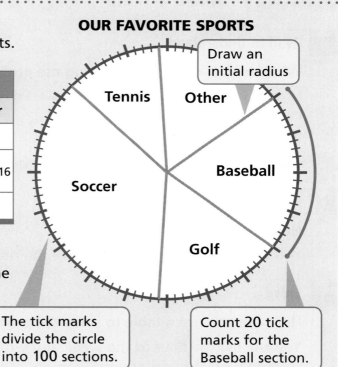

OUR FAVORITE SPORTS

Draw an initial radius

The tick marks divide the circle into 100 sections.

Count 20 tick marks for the Baseball section.

Step ❷ Use a ruler to draw an initial radius from the center to the edge of the circle. Use the tick marks to help you draw a radius to show each section.

Step ❸ Label the sections and write a title for the graph.

✔Check for Understanding

The table shows the results of a survey of fifth-grade students. Use the data in this table to make a circle graph.

OUR FAVORITE VACATIONS				
Beach	Famous City	National Park	Camping	Other
8	4	3	5	5

REVIEW MODEL
Problem Solving Strategy
Make a Table

Below is a list of the **18** students in Ms. Sweetland's class.
They each told their busiest school day of the week.

Jon	Mon	Patrick	Thu	Isacc	Thu	Drew	Mon	Lauren	Wed	Emily	Thu
Colin	Fri	Sierra	Mon	Kirin	Mon	Hassan	Thu	Mike	Mon	Weston	Thu
Ray	Wed	Amy	Tue	Jasmine	Wed	Sammy	Fri	Judy	Tue	Grant	Mon

What fraction of the class has their busiest school day on Monday?

Strategy: Make a Table

Read to Understand

What do you know from reading the problem?

I know which school day is the busiest day for each of the **18** students
in Ms. Sweetland's class.

What do you need to find out?

the fraction of the class that has their busiest school day on Monday

Plan

How can you solve this problem?

You can make a table to help solve the problem.

Solve

How can you use a table to solve the problem?

You can list the days of the week and write a tally mark for each
student who chose that day. Then, count the number of tally marks
for Monday. Write that number as a fraction of **18**.

So, the fraction of Ms. Sweetland's class that has their busiest school
day on Monday is $\frac{6}{18}$, or $\frac{1}{3}$.

Check

Look back at the problem. Did you answer the question that was
asked? Does the answer make sense?

Problem Solving Practice

Problem Solving Strategies

- ✔ Act It Out
- ✔ Draw a Picture
- ✔ Guess and Check
- ✔ Look for a Pattern
- ✔ Make a Graph
- ✔ Make a Model
- ✔ Make an Organized List
- ✔ **Make a Table**
- ✔ Solve a Simpler Problem
- ✔ Use Logical Reasoning
- ✔ Work Backward
- ✔ Write an Equation

Use the strategy *make a table* to solve.

Below is a list of the students in the math club and their ages.

Wilson	9	Alexandra	11	Paul	11	Alison	10
Julie	10	Miles	10	Kristin	9	Lynn	8
Matthew	9	Bradley	8	Haley	10	Avi	11
Brooke	11	Corey	10	Mike	10	Brenda	9
Ryan	10	Kaitlin	9	Adele	8	Faith	10

1 What fraction of the students in the math club are 9 years old?

2 What age are the most students in the math club?

Mixed Strategy Practice

Use any strategy to solve. Explain.

3 Scott has 1 cup of milk in his refrigerator. He uses $\frac{1}{3}$ cup for some pancakes and drinks $\frac{1}{2}$ cup. How much milk is left?

4 Mr. Silva's class can go to the Book Fair on Monday, Tuesday, Wednesday, or Friday. They can go in the morning or afternoon. How many choices do they have?

5 Lily is at a football game. On the first play her team moved the ball forward 12 yards from the 20 yard line. On the second play, they lost 6 yards. On the third play, they gained 5 yards. What yard line were they on after the third play?

6 A science camp had a total of 350 campers during the summer. The camp had two sessions. If the second session had 10 more campers than the first session, how many campers were at each session?

For 7–8, use the diagram of the playground.

7 What is the perimeter of the playground?

8 What is the area of the playground?

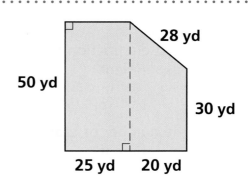

Choose the best vocabulary term from Word List A for each sentence.

Word List A

probability
outcome
event
certain
probable
improbable
sampling
population
random
sample
percent

1 A set of outcomes is called a(n) __?__.

2 A(n) __?__ outcome is one that is sure to happen.

3 A possible result of an experiment is called a(n) __?__.

4 A(n) __?__ outcome is an unlikely outcome.

5 A(n) __?__ experiment is an experiment used to make predictions about a population.

6 The __?__ is the likelihood that an event will happen.

7 The __?__ is the full set in a sampling experiment.

8 To tell the number of hundredths, you can use a(n) __?__.

9 A(n) __?__ is a part of a population.

10 Every member of a population has equal chance of being selected in a(n) __?__ selection.

Complete each analogy using the best term from Word List B.

Word List B

certain
event
sample

11 Part is to whole as __?__ is to population.

12 Yes is to no as __?__ is to impossible.

Talk Math

Discuss with a partner what you have learned about probability. Use the vocabulary terms *outcome* and *probability*.

13 How can you use a fraction to describe the results of a probability experiment?

14 How can you use an experiment to make a prediction?

15 How does the number of trials affect the results of a probability experiment?

Word Web

16 Create a word web for the
term *event*.

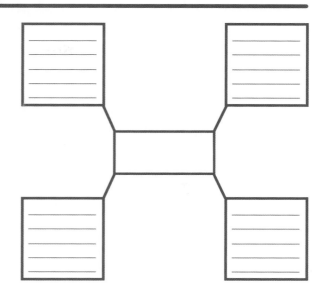

Word Line

17 Create a word line using the
terms *certain, impossible,
improbable,* and *probable.*

Words:

Sequence:

_____

What's in a Word?

SECTOR *Sector* comes from a Latin word, *secare.* It means
"to cut." You can see that if you cut something, you might end
up with a section of it. In math, a *sector* is a section of a circle.
It is shaped like a slice of pie.

In everyday life, a *sector* can be a section of other things as well.
It can be a section of the population, such as the public *sector* or
the urban *sector.* It can be a section of a town, such as the business
sector. It can even be a section of a track on a computer disk.
But even though a computer disk
is in the shape of a circle, its *sector*
is not shaped like a slice of pie.

Technology
Multimedia Math Glossary
www.harcourtschool.com/thinkmath

Number Pyramid

> **Game Purpose**
> **To practice categorizing numbers while generating a random data set**
>
> **Materials**
> • Activity Master 143: Blank Cards
> • Activity Master 144: *Number Pyramid Game* Board
> • scissors

How To Play The Game

1 This is a game for 2 players.

• Each player will need a set of blank cards. Write the numbers 1 through 12 on the blank cards. Cut them out. Combine both sets of cards. Mix them up. Place them face down in a stack.

• Each player will need a game board. Label the one empty square in the pyramid with any category that includes at least one of the numbers on the cards. For example, you could write "Not 2 or 3" or "Less than 9."

• Decide who will go first, and then take turns.

2 Pick a number card. Record the number in a blank box at the top of your game board. Decide whether the number matches any of the categories on the pyramid.

• If the number matches a category, put a check mark in the box for that category.

• If the number matches more than one category, choose one of them. Put a check mark next to that category.

• If the number does not match a category, that is the end of your turn.

Put the card back in the stack. Mix up the cards again.

3 When you have matched at least one number to each category, you have completed your pyramid. You win!

GAME

Matching Quantities

Game Purpose
To practice converting between fractions, decimals, and percents

Materials
- Activity Masters 149–150: *Matching Quantities Cards*
- scissors

How To Play The Game

1 This is a game for 2 players. Cut out all the *Matching Quantities* Cards. Mix them up. Place them face down in a stack. Each player takes 4 cards from the top of the stack. Then put 4 more cards face up on the table. Decide who will go first, and then take turns. The goal is to collect more cards than the other player.

2 Look at your cards. Decide whether any of them has an expression that is equivalent to an expression on a card on the table.

- If you have a matching card, place it on top of its match so the other player can see the match. Then take both cards, and put them aside in your own stack. Take a new card so that you will have 4 cards in your hand and place a new card on the table.

- If you do not have a matching card, put one of your cards at the bottom of the face down stack. Pick another card from the top. You must wait until your next turn to use that card.

3 When all of the cards in the face down stack are gone, you can still try to match cards on the table with cards in your hand. The game ends when all of the cards in the face down stack are gone and no matches can be made with the cards on the table. Whoever has more cards in his or her stack wins.

CHALLENGE

Theoretical and Experimental Probabilities

Try a probability experiment.

PART 1: Count the number of boys and girls in your class, including yourself. Tear a sheet of paper into the same number of pieces as the number of boys and girls. On each small piece of paper, write a B for each boy or a G for each girl in your class. Put the pieces into a bag.

- If you pick one paper, is it more likely to have a *B* or *G* on it?
- What is the probability that you will pick *B*? a *G*?

That is the theoretical probability. You know the number of boys and girls, and each paper has a fair chance of being chosen, so you can find this probability mathematically.

PART 2: Now pick 20 times. Record B or G for each pick. Put the paper back in the bag after each pick. Copy the table below. Keep a tally of your results.

Boy/Girl	Number of Picks	Totals
B		
G		

Write these two fractions.

$$\frac{\text{number of boys picked}}{\text{total number of picks}} \quad \text{and} \quad \frac{\text{number of girls picked}}{\text{total number of picks}}$$

Those are experimental probabilities.

- Do you think the experimental probabilities are close to the theoretical probabilities?

PART 3: Work in a group of 4 students. Each student should do the experiment 30 more times. Then, combine your results. Write the new experimental probabilities. The denominator of each fraction will be 200. That includes the 20 original trials plus the 30 more.

- How do the group's results compare to the theoretical probabilities?
- Did the experimental probabilities with 200 trials come closer to the theoretical probabilities than the experiment with 20 trials?

If you did 2,000 trials, the results would be very close to the theoretical probabilities. The greater the number of trials, the closer you will get.

15 Graphing

Dear Student,

In this chapter you will be using graphs to solve problems that involve measurement. To graph, you will be using points' coordinates, similar to the way you did in Chapter 6. For example, what are the coordinates of Point *C*?

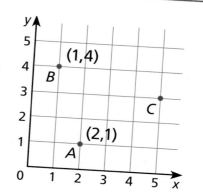

Suppose the horizontal axis of this graph was labeled "seconds" and the vertical axis was labeled "feet," and I told you that Sam walks 4 feet per second. Which point shows how far Sam walked after 1 second? In this chapter you will see how you can extend a graph to figure out, for example, how far Sam has gone after ten, one hundred, or even one thousand seconds.

Now it is time to start because you need to finish one lesson per math class and class has already begun!

Mathematically yours,
The authors of *Think Math!*

Indy 500: Vroom!

The Indianapolis Motor Speedway was built in 1909 as a testing facility for the automobile industry. In 1911, track owners made the race 500 miles. This race is known today as the Indy 500.

FACT·ACTIVITY 1

The graph shows the time it takes one driver to complete a 500 mile race. If you look at the time and the distance, you can determine that the average speed of Driver A is 200 mph.

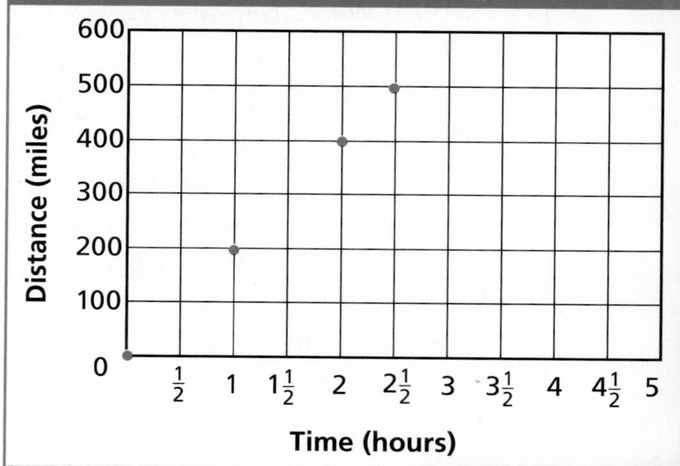

1 How many miles has Driver A driven in the first hour?

2 How much time does it take to drive 400 miles? 500 miles?

3 Copy the graph on grid paper. Connect the points. What is the distance Driver A traveled after $\frac{1}{2}$ hour? after $1\frac{1}{2}$ hours?

4 The table shows the time and distance driven by Driver B. Include Driver B's data on the graph you made for Problem 3.

DRIVER A'S TIME AND DISTANCE IN A RACE

Distance (miles) vs Time (hours)

DRIVER B'S TIME AND DISTANCE IN A RACE	
Time (hours)	Distance (miles)
0	0
1	125
2	250
3	375
4	500

FACT·ACTIVITY 2

The drivers in a race do not drive at a constant speed. In a long race like the Indy 500, drivers usually stop for 1 to 3 "pit stops" for refueling, repairs, and tire changes.

Use the Race Story graph for 1–4.

❶ How long does it take the driver to finish the race?

❷ The driver went ■ miles in the first 60 minutes, so his speed was ■ miles per hour.

❸ When did the driver make pit stops? How can you tell from the graph?

❹ Between the first and second pit stops, the driver drove ■ miles in ■ minutes. Did he drive faster or slower than he did in the first part of the race? Explain.

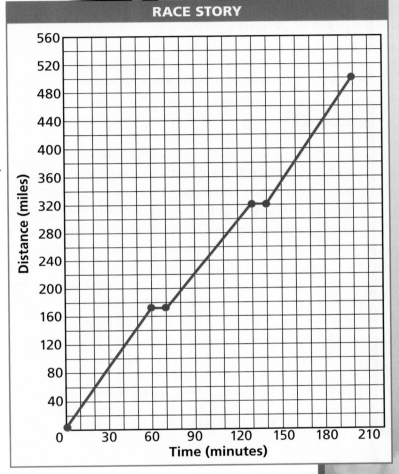

RACE STORY

CHAPTER PROJECT

Research three different kinds of cars. Find each car's gas mileage for highway and city driving, and its fuel tank capacity. The gas mileage is the average number of miles the vehicle travels on a gallon of gas. The higher the gas mileage, the less you will spend on gas.

- Compare the gas mileage of the cars you chose. Draw a graph to display the results! Use 10 data points. You may put all three cars on the same graph.

ALMANAC

The winner of the 2006 Indy 500 race reached a speed of 221 miles per hour. After crossing the finish line, the winner drove the car down Victory Lane and drank a glass of milk!

REVIEW MODEL
Making a Straight-Line Graph

You can complete an input-output table and make a graph to show how some measurement units are related.

In 1 pint there are 2 cups.

Complete the input-output table to show how pints and cups are related.

input →	Pints	1	4	2	3
output →	Cups	2	8	4	6

Follow these steps to make a graph.

Step ❶

For each pair of numbers in the table, use the input as the first coordinate of a point, and use the output as the second.

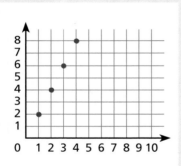

Step ❷

Write labels on the graph's axes to tell what each coordinate stands for. Write a title for the graph.

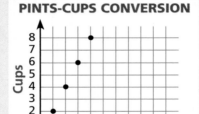

Step ❸

Connect the points, and see if they make a line. The coordinates of each point on this line show the same capacity in pints and in cups.

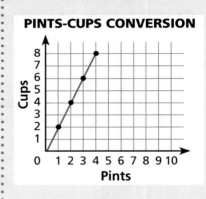

✔Check for Understanding

Copy and complete each table. Then use Activity Master 154: Conversion Graph I to make a graph for each table. (Note: You will need to change the labels on the graph on the activity master for each problem.)

❶ In 1 quart there are 4 cups.

Quarts	1	4	■	5
Cups	4	■	8	■

❷ In 1 yard there are 3 feet.

Yards	1	6	■	4
Feet	■	■	0	■

EXPLORE
Fitting the Graph on the Page

Beth is writing an article for the school newspaper. She wants to include a graph showing how to convert inches to feet.

Use Activity Master 157: Conversion Graph III to make a graph with inches on one axis and feet on the other. Your graph must include at least 6 grid points.

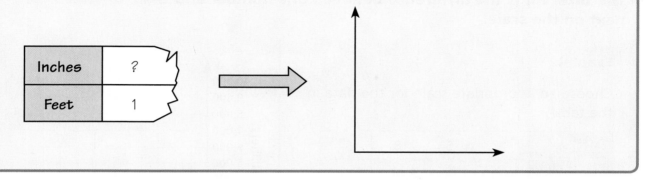

| Inches | ? |
| Feet | 1 |

1 Make a table showing the conversions from inches to feet.

2 Make a graph of the points in the table.

REVIEW MODEL
Choosing an Appropriate Scale

When you make a graph, you need to choose a reasonable scale for the axes.

- The **scale** is the set of numbers that are placed at equal distances along the axes. Sometimes the two axes are labeled with the same scale, and sometimes different scales are used. You should choose a scale that allows you to show all the numbers in the data you are graphing.

- The **interval** is the difference between one number and the next on the scale.

Example

Choose an appropriate scale for the data in the table.

Liters	1	5	8	$6\frac{1}{2}$
Milliliters	1,000	5,000	8,000	6,500

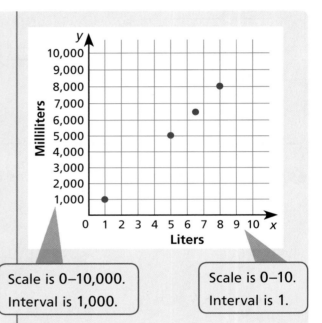

- The greatest number in the row for liters is 8. So for the x-axis, a scale of 0–10 with an interval of 1 is good.

- The greatest number in the row for milliliters is 8,000. So, for the y-axis, a scale of 0–10,000 with an interval of 1,000 is good.

Scale is 0–10,000.
Interval is 1,000.

Scale is 0–10.
Interval is 1.

✔Check for Understanding

Copy and complete each table. For each table, choose an appropriate scale for the data and use Activity Master 157: Conversion Graph III to make a graph.

1

Meters	3	6	1	2	0
Millimeters	■	■	1,000	■	■

2

Years	2	5	1	6	0
Months	■	■	12	■	■

Getting Home on Time

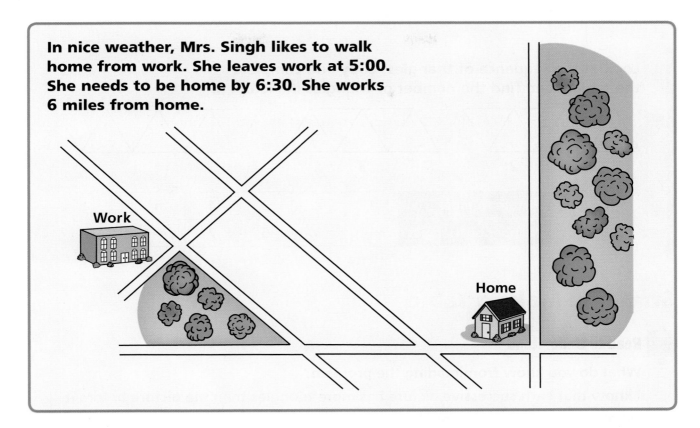

In nice weather, Mrs. Singh likes to walk home from work. She leaves work at 5:00. She needs to be home by 6:30. She works 6 miles from home.

Work

Home

❶ If it takes her 30 minutes to walk 1 mile, how long will it take her to get home? Will she be home in time?

❷ If she can walk fast and jog a bit so that she covers 5 miles in 1 hour, how long will it take her to get home? Will she be home in time?

❸ What is the slowest speed at which she could walk and still make it home by 6:30?

REVIEW MODEL
Problem Solving Strategy
Make a Table

Look at the sequence of triangles. Copy and complete the table. Then find the number of triangles in Picture *n*.

 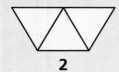 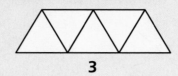 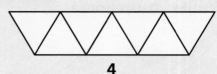

Picture Number	1	2	3	4	n
Number of Triangles	1	3	5	7	2n−1

Strategy: Make a Table

 Read to Understand

What do you know from reading the problem?

I know that each successive picture has more triangles than the picture before it.

What do you need to find out?

the number of triangles in Picture *n* in this sequence

 Plan

How can you solve this problem?

You can make a table and look for a pattern in the number of triangles.

 Solve

How can you use a table to solve the problem?

You can look for patterns in the way the number of triangles increases in each successive picture in this sequence.

What pattern do you notice?

There are two more triangles in each successive picture. There is only 1 triangle in the first picture. For all the other pictures, the number of triangles is 2 times the Picture Number in the sequence, less 1 triangle.

So, the *n*th picture will have $2n - 1$ triangles.

 Check

Look back at the problem. Did you answer the question that was asked?

Problem Solving Practice

Use the strategy *make a table* to solve.

Problem Solving Strategies

✔ Act It Out
✔ Draw a Picture
✔ Guess and Check
✔ Look for a Pattern
✔ Make a Graph
✔ Make a Model
✔ Make an Organized List
✔ **Make a Table**
✔ Solve a Simpler Problem
✔ Use Logical Reasoning
✔ Work Backward
✔ Write an Equation

1 Based on the sequence below, how many circles are in Picture *n*?

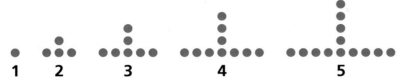

2 Below is a list of students in the chorus and the grade they are in.

Miranda	4	Shawn	5	Amanda	5	Ryan	4	Adele	3
Lindsey	5	Faith	4	Kevin	5	Jody	5	Sabrina	5
Jarrell	3	Ellen	4	Eva	5	Sarah	5	John	4
Heather	5	Kendall	5	Jordan	5	Ashley	4	Lauren	5

What fraction of the students are in fifth grade?

Mixed Strategy Practice

Use any strategy to solve. Explain.

3 Shelby bought $\frac{3}{4}$ yard fabric. She used $\frac{1}{6}$ yard of the fabric for a collar. How much fabric is left?

4 There are 186 people going on a field trip on buses. Each bus can seat 38 people. How many buses will be needed for the field trip?

5 On Friday, Rashad received a check. He deposited $75.50 into his savings account. Before he deposited the money, he used $12.75 from the check to buy a gift and he deposited $15.00 into his checking account. He kept $20.00 in cash. How much was Rashad's check?

6 Caitlin drew this triangle. She then reflected it over the vertical dashed line and translated it down 2 spaces. What are the new vertices of the triangle?

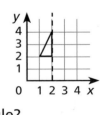

For 7–8, use the graph.

7 What is the median score? What is the range?

8 Jody scored better than the mean score, but less than the mode. What was her score?

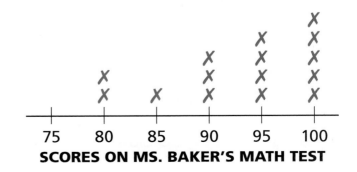

SCORES ON MS. BAKER'S MATH TEST

Chapter 15 Vocabulary

Choose the best vocabulary term from Word List A for each sentence.

Word List A

conversion graph
conversion rule
converting measurements
coordinate grid
interval
miles per hour
rate
scale
slope
speed
steepness

1. How one quantity changes in comparison to the change of another quantity is called ___?___.

2. The incline of a graphed line with respect to the axes is its ___?___.

3. The difference between one number and the next on the scale of a graph is a(n) ___?___.

4. A common rate that compares distance over time is ___?___.

5. The numbers placed at fixed distances on the axes of a graph form the ___?___.

6. The distance an object travels divided by the time it takes to travel the distance is the ___?___.

7. The operation or operations needed to convert one unit to another related unit is called a(n) ___?___.

8. A diagram that shows the relationship between two measures is called a(n) ___?___.

9. Changing kilograms to pounds is called ___?___.

Complete each analogy using the best term from Word List B.

Word List B

coordinate grid
interval
scale
slope
speed

10. Latitude and longitude are to a map as horizontal and vertical lines are to a ___?___.

11. Inches is to length as miles per hour is to ___?___.

Talk Math

Discuss with a partner what you have learned about tables and graphs of measurement relationships. Use the vocabulary terms *conversion rule* and *rate*.

12. How can you tell whether the graph of three or more points will lie along a straight line?

13. Suppose you know how much the temperature has changed in degrees Fahrenheit. How can you find out how much it changed in degrees Celsius?

Word Definition Map

14 Create a word definition map for the term *coordinate grid.*

A What is it?

B What is it like?

C What are some examples?

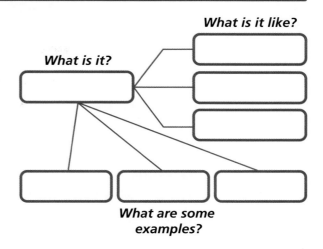

Degrees of Meaning Grid

15 Create a degrees of meaning grid using the terms *conversion rule* and *rate.* Use what you know and what you have learned about comparing units.

General	Less General	Specific	More Specific

What's in a Word?

SCALE In math, *scale* refers to the numbers set at fixed distances that label a graph. In music, a *scale* is a group of tones that go up or down in pitch with each tone relating to the others in a specific way. In daily life, a *scale* is a machine that measures the weight of something. A climber *scales* a cliff.

Scale has to do with intervals. A graph *scale* has intervals depending on what it measures. The tones in a musical *scale* are set at definite intervals. A weight *scale* has intervals in pounds or grams. A climber moves hands and feet at intervals in order to go forward.

GO ONLINE Technology
Multimedia Math Glossary
www.harcourtschool.com/thinkmath

GAME

Graphing Tic-Tac-Toe

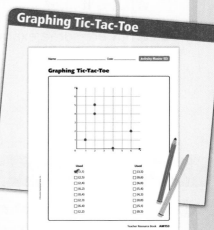

Game Purpose
To recognize when points on a coordinate grid lie along a straight line

Materials
- Activity Master 153: *Graphing Tic-Tac-Toe*
- Color pencils
- Straightedge

How To Play The Game

1 This is a game for 2 players. You will both use the same *Graphing Tic-Tac-Toe* game and straightedge. You will each need a different color pencil. The object of the game is to mark 3 points that lie along a straight line. Remember, there might be more than one way to make a straight line using given points.

2 Decide who will go first, and then take turns.
- Choose an ordered pair from the list. Mark the point with those coordinates in your color on the grid.
- Put a check mark in the box to show that the ordered pair has been used. Once an ordered pair has been used, it may not be used again.

3 The first player to mark 3 points that lie along a straight line wins. Be sure to check the points with the straightedge if you are unsure whether a straight line has been made.

Example: Jai went first. He is using orange. Kari is using blue. After 6 turns each, Kari wins.

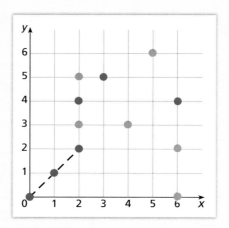

GAME

The Great Race

Game Purpose
To practice plotting points to show time and the related distance traveled

Materials
- Activity Masters 160–162: *The Great Race* Game Board, Time Cards, and Distance Cards
- Color pencils • Scissors • Straightedge

The Great Race

How To Play The Game

1 This is game for 2 players. Use the same game board. Start at (0,0). The goal is to cross the finish line in less time. It does not matter how many turns you take. Choose your color pencil.

2 Cut out all the cards. Mix them together. Place them face down in a stack. Decide who will go first. Then take turns. Start by taking 4 cards in turn. Be sure to have 4 cards in your hand at all times.

3 Choose one of your cards. Place it face up on the table.
- If the card is a Time card, the other player must play a Distance card.
- If the card is a Distance card, the other player must play a Time card.
- If the other player does not have the right type of card, he or she must discard and take a new card until the right type of card can be played.

4 The cards show your time and distance for this part of the trip. On your first turn, start at (0,0). Calculate the time and distance. Mark the point on the grid. Draw a line segment between the two points. On the rest of your turns, start at your last point.

5 If you run out of cards, re-mix the discard stack. Both players must cross the finish line. But whoever took less time wins.

CHALLENGE

Lots of Conversions

Copy and complete each conversion table. Draw a graph on grid paper to show each conversion. Then use the table and graph to answer the questions. You might need to extend the table or the graph to answer some of the questions.

1 Convert kilograms to pounds. 1 kilogram is about 2.2 pounds.

Kilograms	1	2	3	4	5
Pounds	2.2	■	■	■	■

A About how many pounds are equivalent to 1.5 kilograms?

B About how many kilograms are equivalent to 7 pounds?

C About how many kilograms are equivalent to 0.5 pound?

D About how many kilograms are equivalent to 10 pounds?

2 Convert gallons to liters. 1 gallon is about 3.8 liters.

Gallons	1	2	3	4	5
Liters	3.8	■	■	■	■

A About how many liters are equivalent to 2.5 gallons?

B About how many gallons are equivalent to 10 liters?

C About how many gallons are equivalent to 4.5 liters?

D About how many gallons are equivalent to 25 liters?

3 Convert kilometers to miles. 1 kilometer is about 0.6 mile.

Kilometers	1	2	3	4	5
Miles	0.6	■	■	■	■

A About how many miles are equivalent to 3.4 kilometers?

B About how many kilometers are equivalent to 4 miles?

C About how many kilometers are equivalent to 1.5 miles?

D About how many kilometers are equivalent to 9 miles?

Table of Measures................................. **264**

All the important measures used in this book are in this table. If you've forgotten exactly how many feet are in a mile, this table will help you.

Glossary.. **266**

This glossary will help you speak and write the language of mathematics. Use the glossary to check the definitions of important terms.

Index... **278**

Use the index when you want to review a topic. It lists the page numbers where the topic is taught.

Table of Measures

METRIC	CUSTOMARY
LENGTH	
1 centimeter (cm) = 10 millimeters (mm) 1 meter (m) = 1,000 centimeters 1 meter = 100 centimeters (cm) 1 meter = 10 decimeters (dm) 1 kilometer (km) = 1,000 meters	1 foot (ft) = 12 inches (in.) 1 yard (yd) = 3 feet, or 36 inches 1 mile (mi) = 1,760 yards, or 5,280 feet
CAPACITY	
1 liter (L) = 1,000 milliliters (mL) 1 metric cup = 250 milliliters 1 liter = 4 metric cups 1 kiloliter (kL) = 1,000 liters	1 tablespoon (tbsp) = 3 teaspoons (tsp) 1 cup (c) = 8 fluid ounces (fl oz) 1 pint (pt) = 2 cups 1 quart (qt) = 2 pints 1 quart = 4 cups 1 gallon (gal) = 4 quarts
MASS/WEIGHT	
1 gram (g) = 1,000 milligrams (mg) 1 kilogram (kg) = 1,000 grams	1 pound (lb) = 16 ounces (oz) 1 ton (T) = 2,000 pounds

TIME

1 minute (min) = 60 seconds (sec)
1 hour (hr) = 60 minutes
1 day = 24 hours
1 week = 7 days
1 year (yr) = 12 months (mo),
or about 52 weeks
1 year = 365 days
1 leap year = 366 days
1 decade = 10 years
1 century = 100 years
1 millennium = 1,000 years

=	is equal to		$\perp$	is perpendicular to
$\neq$	is not equal to		$\parallel$	is parallel to
>	is greater than		$\overleftrightarrow{AB}$	line AB
<	is less than		$\overrightarrow{AB}$	ray AB
2^3	the third power of 2		$\overline{AB}$	line segment AB
10^2	ten squared		$\angle ABC$	angle ABC
10^3	ten cubed		$\triangle ABC$	triangle ABC
10^4	the fourth power of 10		°	degree
(2,3)	ordered pair (x, y)		°C	degrees Celsius
%	percent		°F	degrees Fahrenheit

FORMULAS

PERIMETER

Polygon	$P =$ sum of the lengths of the sides
Parallelogram	$P = (2 \times l) + (2 \times s)$, or $P = 2 \times (l + s)$
Rhombus	$P = 4 \times s$

AREA

Rectangle	$A = l \times w$
Square	$A = s^2$
Parallelogram	$A = b \times h$
Triangle	$A = \frac{1}{2} \times b \times h$
Trapezoid	$A = \frac{1}{2} \times (b_1 + b_2) \times h$

VOLUME

Prism $V =$ base area $\times h$

PRONUNCIATION KEY

a	add, map	f	fit, half	n	nice, tin	p	pit, stop	yōō	fuse, few
ā	ace, rate	g	go, log	ng	ring, song	r	run, poor	v	vain, eve
â(r)	care, air	h	hope, hate	o	odd, hot	s	see, pass	w	win, away
ä	palm, father	i	it, give	ō	open, so	sh	sure, rush	y	yet, yearn
b	bat, rub	ī	ice, write	ô	order, jaw	t	talk, sit	z	zest, muse
ch	check, catch	j	joy, ledge	oi	oil, boy	th	thin, both	zh	vision,
d	dog, rod	k	cool, take	ou	pout, now	th	this, bathe		pleasure
e	end, pet	l	look, rule	ŏŏ	took, full	u	up, done		
ē	equal, tree	m	move, seem	ōō	pool, food	û(r)	burn, term		

ə the schwa, an unstressed vowel representing the sound spelled *a* in above, *e* in sicken, *i* in possible, *o* in melon, *u* in circus

Other symbols:
• separates words into syllables
′ indicates stress on a syllable

acute angle [ə•kyōōt′ ang′gəl] An angle that has a measure less than a right angle (less than 90°)

Example:

addends [ad′endz] Numbers that are added in an addition problem

adding products [′ad•ing prä′•dəkts] The process of adding partial products to find the total product

algebra [′al•jə•brə] Mathematics that deals with the relationship between numbers

algebraic expression [′al•jə•brā•ik ik•′spre•shən] An incomplete number sentence where some of the variables are replaced with letters or symbols that represent numbers

Example: $x + 3$ $10 - x$ $x + 5$
            are all algebraic expressions

algebraic notation [′al•jə•brā•ik nō•′tā•shən] Mathematical shorthand used to express numerical properties, patterns, and relationships

angle [ang′gəl] A figure formed by two rays that meet at a common endpoint

Example:

approximation [əprok′səmā′shən] An estimation

area [âr′ē•ə] The measurement of two-dimensional space inside a plane figure

area model [âr′ē•ə mö′dəl] A rectangular diagram used to model multiplication and division of whole numbers and multiplication of fractions

Example: To find the product of 84 × 12, the area model becomes:

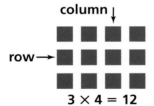

	80	4
10	800	40
2	160	8

area of a net [âr′ē•ə əf ′ā net] The total area of all the faces of a net

array [ə•rā′] An arrangement of objects in rows and columns

Example:

column ↓

row →

3 × 4 = 12

average [av′rij] See *mean*

axis [ak′səs] The horizontal or vertical number line used in a graph or coordinate plane

balance [′ba•lən(t)s] *verb* To equalize in weight or number

balance scale [′ba•lən(t)s skāl] An instrument used to weigh objects and to compare the weights of objects

Multimedia Math Glossary   www.harcourtschool.com/thinkmath

base [bās] A two-dimensional figure's side or a three-dimensional figure's face by which the figure is measured or named

Example:

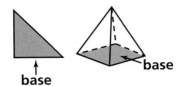

benchmark fraction [bench'märk frak'shən] A familiar fraction used as a point of reference

billion [bil'yən] One thousand million; written as 1,000,000,000

break ['brāk] To separate a number into smaller numbers that total the given number

certain [sur'tən] Sure to happen; will always happen

column ['kä•ləm] A vertical line in an array

Example:

combination [kam•bə•nā'•shən]] A choice in which the order of items does not matter

combined partial products ['käm•bind 'pär•shŭl prä•dəkts] A combination of any of the partial products (but not the final product) of a multiplication problem

common denominator [kä'mən di•nä'mə•nā•tòr] A number that may be evenly divided by each of the denominators of a given group of fractions

Example: 6, 12, and 18 are all common denominators of $\frac{1}{3}$ and $\frac{1}{2}$

common factor [kä'mən fak'tər] A number that is a factor of two or more numbers

common multiple [kä'mən mul'tə•pəl] A number that is a multiple of two or more numbers

common unit [kä'mən 'yü•nət] A unit that quantities have in common so that a calculation can be performed on them

comparing [kəm•'pār•ing] Describing whether two or more numbers are equal to, less than, or greater than each other

compatible numbers [kəm•pa'tə•bəl num'bərz] Numbers that are easy to compute mentally and are chosen to simplify the calculation of an estimate

composite [käm•pä'zət] A number having more than two factors

Example: 6 is a composite number, since its factors are 1, 2, 3, and 6.

concave [kän•'kāv] Used to describe a polygon with at least one angle measuring more than 180°; one or more line segments that are outside the polygon can always be drawn between two vertices

cone [kōn] A three-dimensional figure that has a flat, circular base and one apex

Example:

congruent [kən•grōō'ənt] Having the same size and shape

congruent figures [kən•grōō'ənt fi•'gûrz] Figures that have the same size and shape

Example:

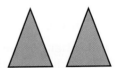

The triangles are congruent

constant speed ['kän(t)•stənt 'spēd] The assumption that speed stays the same throughout each interval of distance or time

conversion graph [kən•'vər•zhən 'graf] A graph that shows how to convert between measurements

conversion rule [kən•'vər•zhən 'rül] A rule that describes how to convert between measurements

converting measurements [kən•'vərt•ing 'me•zhar•mənts] Changing measurements from one unit to another

convex [kän•'veks] Used to describe a polygon with all interior angles measuring less than 180°; all diagonals are inside the polygon

coordinate grid [kō•ôr′də•nət grid] A grid formed by two intersecting and perpendicular number lines called axes

Example:

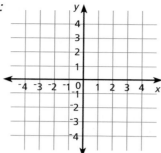

coordinates [kō•ôr′də•nəts] The numbers in an ordered pair

cubic unit [kyōō′bik yōō′nət] A unit of volume with dimensions 1 unit × 1 unit × 1 unit

cylinder [si′lən•dər] A three-dimensional figure that has two parallel bases that are congruent circles

Example:

decimal [de′sə•məl] A number with one or more digits to the right of the decimal point

decimal part of a number [de′sə•məl pärt ′əf ′ā num•′bər] The digit or digits to the right of a decimal point that represent a fraction whose denominator is either 10 or a power of 10 (10; 100; 1,000; and so on)

Example: 3.27 2 and 7 are the decimal parts

denominator [di•nä′mə•nā•tər] The number below the bar in a fraction that tells how many equal parts are in the whole

Example: $\frac{3}{4}$ ← denominator

describing situations with diagrams [di•′skrīb•ing ′si•chə•′wā•shəns ′with ′dī•ə•grams] Drawing pictures or diagrams to help describe and solve problems

describing situations with equations [di•′skrīb•ing ′si•chə•′wā•shəns with i•′kwā•zhəns] Using equations to help describe and solve problems

difference [dif′ər•əns] The result of subtracting two numbers

digit [di′jit] Any one of the ten symbols 0, 1, 2, 3, 4, 5, 6, 7, 8, 9 used to write numbers

digits in the same place-value position [di′jits ′in the ′sām plās val•′yōō pə•′zi•shən] Digits with like place value in two numbers and are used to compare numbers

dividend [di′və•dend] The number being divided in a division problem

Example: 36 ÷ 6; 6)̄36

The dividend is 36.

divisibility [də•′vi•zə•′bi•lə•tē] The capacity of being divided, without a remainder

divisible [də•vi′zi•bəl] A number is divisible by another number if the quotient is a whole number and the remainder is zero.

Example: 21 is *divisible* by 3.

divisible by [də•vi′zə•bəl ′bī] Can be divided without a remainder

Example: Numbers divisible by 12 are 12, 24, 36. . .

division [də•vi′zhən] The process of sharing or grouping a number into equal parts; the operation that is the inverse of multiplication

divisor [də•vi′zər] The number that divides the dividend

Example: 15 ÷ 3; 3)̄15

The divisor is 3.

dot sketch [′dät ′skech] An array of small circles that is used to represent a fraction, to find equivalent fractions, to multiply fractions, and to show combinations

Example:

○○○○○
●○○○○
●○○○○ $\frac{1}{5}$
●○○○○

double [′de•bəl] When both addends are the same number

doubling products [ˈdə•b(ə-)ling prä•dəkts]
The process of finding the product of two numbers if one factor is even, by multiplying by half of the even number and then multiplying the result by 2.

Example: 6 × 15 = (3 × 15) × 2

edge [ej] The line segment where two or more faces of a three-dimensional figure meet

Example: 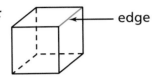 edge

endpoint [endˈpoint] The point marking the end of a line segment

equalize [ˈē•kwə•ˈlīz] Redistributing amounts so that everyone gets the same amount

equal to [ˈē•kwəl tōō] Having the same value

equals [ˈē•kwəlz] The statement when two variables are equivalent

equation [i•kwāˈzhən] An algebraic or numerical sentence that shows that two quantities are equal

equilateral triangle [ē•kwə•laˈtə•rəl trīˈang•gəl]
A triangle with three congruent sides

Example:
3 in. 3 in. 3 in.

equivalent [ē-•kwivˈə•lənt] Having the same value

equivalent decimals [ē•kwivˈə•lənt deˈsə•məlz]
Decimals that name the same number or amount

Example: 0.4 = 0.40 = 0.400

equivalent fractions [ē•kwivˈə•lənt frakˈshən]
Fractions that name the same number or amount

equivalent mixed number [ē•kwivˈə•lənt mikst numˈbər] Two or more mixed numbers that have the same value

Example: $2\frac{13}{8}$, $3\frac{5}{8}$, and $3\frac{10}{16}$ are all equivalent mixed numbers.

estimate [esˈtə•mət] *noun* A number close to an exact amount

estimate [esˈtə•māt] *verb* To find a number that is close to an exact amount

estimating [ˈes•ti•māt•ing] Finding a number that is close to an exact amount

estimation [ˈes•tə•ˈmā•shən] An educated guess at an answer

even [ˈē•vən] A whole number that is divisible by 2

Examples: 2, 4, 6, 8, 10, 12, 14, 16, . . .

event [i•ventˈ] One outcome or a set of outcomes in an experiment

expanded notation [ik•ˈspand•id nō•ˈtā-shən] A way to write numbers by showing the value of each digit

Examples: 635 = 600 + 30 + 5
1,479 = 1,000 + 400 + 70 + 9

expanded form [ik•spandˈid fôrm] A way to write numbers by showing the value of each digit

Example: 832 = 800 + 30 + 2

exponent [ekˈspō•nənt] A number that shows how many times the base is used as a factor

Example: 10^3 = 10 × 10 × 10; 3 is the exponent.

face [fās] A polygon that is a flat surface of a three-dimensional figure

Example: 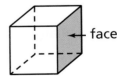 face

factor [fakˈtər] A number multiplied by another number to find a product

factoring [fakˈtər•ing] The process of finding factors of a number

flip [•flip] A movement of a figure to a new position by flipping the figure over a line; a reflection

Example:

fraction of a fraction [frak'shən əf 'ā frak'shən] A smaller part of a fraction, where the larger fraction represents the whole

Example: **One third of a *half* mile is one sixth of the *whole* mile.**

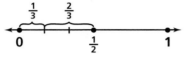

fraction of a set [frak'shən əf ' ā 'set] A fraction of a group

fractions that add to 1 [frak'shəns 'that 'ad 'too 'wən] Two or more fractions that have a sum equal to 1

Example: $\frac{1}{8} + \frac{7}{8} = 1$

fractions that name tenths and hundredths [frak'shəns 'that 'nām tenths 'and hun'drədths] Fractions that can be directly written in decimal form

Example: = $\frac{3}{10}$ can be written as 0.3 and $\frac{17}{100}$ can be written as 0.17

function [funk'shən] A relationship between two quantities in which one quantity depends on the other

greater [grā'tər] Having a larger value

greater than (>) [grā'tər than] A symbol used to compare two numbers, with the greater number given first

Example: 6 > 4

height [hīt] The distance from the base to the farthest point of a two- or three-dimensional figure

Example:

horizontal axis [hôr•ə•'zän•tul] The horizontal number line on a coordinate plane

Example:

horizontal coordinate [hôr•ə•'zän•tul kō•ôr'də•nəts] In a coordinate pair, the value that is represented by *x*, which shows the horizontal location

Example: = In the coordinate pair (4,3) the horizontal coordinate is 4.

horizontal line [hôr•ə•'zän•tul līn] A line parallel to the horizon

hundredth [hun'drədth] One of one hundred equal parts

Examples: 0.56   fifty-six hundredths
$\frac{45}{100}$ forty-five hundredths

improbable [im•'prä•bə•bəl] Not likely to happen

improper fraction [im•'prä•pər frak 'shən] A fraction where the numerator is larger than the denominator

Example: = $\frac{4}{3}$ is an improper fraction.

input [in'•poot] The number that is the start of a process and then acted on

intersections [in•tər•'sek•shən] The places where lines cross in dot sketches used to show combinations

Example:

interval [in'tər•vəl] The difference between one number and the next on the scale of a graph

inverse [in'vərs] Operations that undo each other, like addition and subtraction or multiplication and division

isosceles triangle [ī•sä'sə•lēz trī'ang•gəl] A triangle with at least two congruent sides

Example:

10 in. /\ 10 in.

7 in.

kite ['kīt] A quadrilateral with no parallel sides, two pairs of congruent sides, two lines of symmetry, and all vertices are convex

Example:

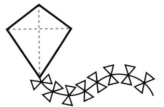

largest product ['lär•jest prä•dəkt] The product with the greatest value when multiple products are compared

least common denominator (LCD) [lēst kä'mən di•nä'mə•nā•tər] The least common multiple of two or more denominators

Example: The LCD for $\frac{1}{4}$ and $\frac{5}{6}$ is 12.

length ['lenkth] The measure of a side of a figure

less [less] Having a smaller value

less than (<) [less than] A symbol used to compare two numbers, with the lesser number given first

Example: 4 < 6

like denominators ['līk di•nä•mə•tər] Two or more denominators that are the same number

like place values ['līk plās val'yoo] The same place-value position in two or more numbers

Example: 18.7

3.9

204.16

The digits that share a *like place value* with 8 are 3 and 4.

line [līn] A straight path in a plane, extending in both directions with no endpoints

Example: ◄─────►

line segment [līn seg'mənt] A part of a line between two endpoints

Example: ●────●

line of symmetry [līn of si'mə•trē] Line that separates a figure into two congruent parts

maximum ['mak•sə•məm] The largest possible quantity or number

mean [mēn] The average of a set of numbers, found by dividing the sum of the set by the number of addends

measurements ['me•zhər•mənts] The sizes, quantities, or amounts, found by measuring

measuring height of a parallelogram ['me•zhə•ring 'hīt əf 'ā pâ•rə•lel'ə•gram] To measure the perpendicular difference from a base to the opposite side

Example:

Height of a parallelogram

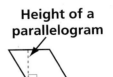

median [mē'dē•ən] The middle number in a set of data that are arranged in order

miles per hour ['miəl] A measurement of speed that shows the number of miles traveled for each hour (60 mins.)

million [mil'yən] One thousand thousands; written as 1,000,000

minimum ['mi·nə·məm] The smallest possible quantity or number

mixed number [mikst num'bər] A number that is made up of a whole number and a fraction

Example: $1\frac{5}{8}$

mobile ['mō·'bēl] A structure that is balanced from a point; a representation of a balanced equation

Example:

mode [mōd] The number or item that occurs most often in a set of data

multiple [mul'tə·pəl] The product of a given whole number and another whole number

Example: 3 × 9 = 27, so 27 is a multiple of 3 and 9.

negative [ne'gə·tiv] Any integer less than zero

Examples: ⁻4, ⁻5, and ⁻6 are negative integers.

neighbor numbers ['nā·bər 'nem·bərz] Consecutive numbers one less and one greater than a certain number

Example: Neighbor numbers of 16 are 15 and 17

numerator [noo'mə·rā·tər] The number above the bar in a fraction that tells how many equal parts of the whole are being considered

Example: $\frac{3}{4}$ ← numerator

obtuse angle [äb·toos' ang'gəl] An angle that has a measure is greater than 90° and less than 180°

Example:

odd ['äd] A whole number that is not divisible by 2

Example: 27   95   3

operation ['ä-pə·'rä·shən] The process of changing one number to another according to a rule

Example: operation signs: +, −, ÷, ×

opposite angles ['ä·pə·zət ang'gel] Angles that touch only at their vertex and share the same lines as sides

Example:

These two angles are *opposite angles.*

ordered pair [ôr'dərd pâr] A pair of numbers used to locate a point on a grid. The first number tells the left-right position and the second number tells the up-down position.

ordering ['ôr·dər·ing] Arranging according to size, amount, or value

organized list [ôr·ga·nīzəd] One way to organize data in order to solve a problem

origin [ôr'ə·jən] The point where the two axes of a coordinate plane intersect, (0,0)

outcome [out'kum] A possible result of an experiment

outlier [out'li·ər] A value separated from most of the rest in a set of data

output [out·pŏt] A number that is the result of some actions on an input

parallel [′par•ə•lel] Lines or figures in a plane that never intersect

Example:

parallel faces [′par•ə•lel ′fās•əs] Faces in a three-dimensional figure that are parallel to each other

parallelogram [′pâ•rə•lel′ə•gram] A quadrilateral with two pairs of parallel sides

Example:

part of a whole [′pärt əf ā hōl] One or more equal sections of one unit

Example: A quarter hour is $\frac{1}{4}$ of an hour, and an hour has 4 such parts in it.

partial product [′pär•shəl prä′dəkts] The product of parts (usually parts of different place values) of each factor

Example:
```
   24
 ×  3
   12  ← Multiply the ones: 3 × 4 = 12
 + 60  ← Multiply the tens: 3 × 20 = 60
   72
```

partition [pär′ti•shən] To break a number into smaller numbers that total the given number

percent [pər•sent′] A fraction expressed in hundredths

Example: $\frac{1}{10} = \frac{10}{100} = 10\%$

perimeter [pə•rim′ə•tər] The distance around a closed two-dimensional figure

perpendicular lines [pər•pen•dik′yə•lər līns] Two lines that intersect to form right angles

Example:

perpendicular faces [pər•pen•dik′yə•lər fās•əs] Faces in a three-dimensional figure that are perpendicular to each other

place value [plās val′yōō] A system of writing numbers so that as you move to the left, the value of each place is 10 times greater than the value of the place at its right

place-value position [plās val′yōō pə•′zi•shən] The place that a digit has in a number

polygon [pol′•i•gon] A closed two-dimensional figure formed by three or more line segments

Examples:

polyhedron [pol•i•hē′drən] A three-dimensional figure with faces that are polygons

Examples:

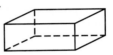

population [pä•pyə•lā′shən] The entire group of objects or individuals considered for a survey

positive [pä′zə•tiv] Any integer greater than zero

powers of 10 [paw•ərs ′əf tən] A number that results when 10 is used as a base with an exponent

Example: $10^1 = 10$; $10^2 = 10 \times 10 = 100$;
$10^3 = 10 \times 10 \times 10 = 1,000$;
and so on

prime [prīm] A number that has exactly two factors: 1 and itself

Examples: 5, 7, 11, 13, 17, and 19 are prime numbers.

prime factorization [prīm fak•tə•rə•′zā•shən] A number written as the product of all its prime factors

Examples:

 $40 = 5 \times 2 \times 2 \times 2$

prism [priz′əm] A three-dimensional figure that has two congruent, polygon-shaped bases, and other faces that are all rectangles

Examples:

rectangular prism   **triangular prism**

probability [prä·bə·bil′ə·tē] The likelihood that an event will happen

probable [prä·bə·bəl] Likely to happen

product [prä′dəkt] The result of multiplying two or more numbers

pyramid [pir′ə·mid] A three-dimensional figure with a polygon base and all other faces triangles that meet at a common vertex

Example:

 Q

quadrants [kwä·drənts] The four sections of the coordinate plane formed by the *x*-axis

Example:

quadrilateral [kwäd·rə·lat′ə·rəl] A polygon with four sides

Example:

quotient [kwō′shənt] The number, not including the remainder, that results from dividing

Example: 8 ÷ 4 = 2. The quotient is 2.

 R

random sample [ran′dəm sam′pəl] A sample in which each member of the population has an equal chance of being chosen

range [rānj] The difference between the greatest number and the least number in a set of data

Example: 2, 2, 3, 5, 7, 7, 8, 9
        The range is 9 − 2 = 7.

rate [rāt] How one quantity changes in comparison to the change of another quantity

reasonable [rēz·nə·bəl] Logical; sensible

rectangle [rek′tang·gəl] A parallelogram with four right angles

Example:

rectangular prism [rek·tang′gyə·lər pri′zəm] A prism in which all six faces are rectangles

Example:

reflection [ri·flek′shən] A movement of a figure to a new position by flipping it over a line; a flip

Example:

remainder [ri·′mān·dər] The number that is left over when a divisor does not divide a dividend equally

Example:

$$5\overline{)19} \quad \underline{3} \text{ r4} \leftarrow \text{remainder}$$
$$\underline{15}$$
$$4$$

rhombus [räm′bəs] A parallelogram with four congruent sides

Example:

right angle [rit ang′gəl] A special angle formed by perpendicular lines and with a measure of 90°

Example:

90°

rotation [rō·tā′shən] A movement of a figure to a new position by turning it around a vertex or point of rotation; a turn

Example:

rounding [round′ing] Replacing a number with one that tells about how many or how much

rounding up the quotient [round'ing 'əp t͟hə kwō 'shənt] A way of interpreting a remainder in which the quotient is rounded up to the next whole number

row ['rō] A horizontal line in an array

Example: **row →**

rule ['rool] The number that changes the input of an input-output table or algebraic equation

S

sample [sam'pəl] A part of a population

sampling ['sam•pəling] Surveying a part of a population to reach conclusions about the entire population

scale [skāl] A set of numbers placed at fixed distances along an axis to help label the graph

scale drawing [skāl drô'ing] A reduced or enlarged drawing whose shape is the same as an actual object and whose size is determined by the scale; a comparison of two sets of measurements

Example: 1 cm:5 mi

scatter plot ['ska•tər 'plät] A graph with points plotted to show a relationship between two variables

scalene triangle [skā'lēn trī'ang•gəl] A triangle with no congruent sides

Example:

30 cm
13 cm
18 cm

sector ['sek•tər] A section of a circle graph

Example: sector

separate ['se•pə•rāt] To break a number into smaller numbers that total the given number

shorthand ['shôrt•hand] A way of writing the output of an algebraic expression. See algebraic notation

similar [si'mə•lər] Having the same shape, but not necessarily the same size

Example:

simplest form [sim'pləst fôrm] The form for a fraction when the numerator and denominator have only 1 as their common factor.

slide ['slīd] A movement of a figure to a new position without turning or flipping it; a translation

Example:

slope [slōp] A line's incline with respect to the axes

speed [spēd] The distance traveled divided by the time it takes

sphere [sfir] A round object whose curved surface is the same distance from the center to all its points

Example:

split ['split] To break a number into smaller numbers that total the given number

square [skwâr] A polygon with four congruent sides

square number [skwâr num'bər] The product of a number and itself

Example: $4^2 = 16$; 16 is a square number.

square unit [skwâr yoo'nət] A unit of area with dimensions 1 unit × 1 unit

steepness [stēp•nes] In a graph, how quickly the *y*-values change as the *x*-values increase

steps away ['steps ə•'wā] The difference in two numbers; the distance between two numbers on a number line

straight angle ['strāt ang'gəl] An angle that has a measure of 180 degrees

sum [sum] The result of adding two or more numbers

surface area [sûr′fəs âr′ē•ə] The sum of the areas of all the faces, or surfaces, of a three-dimensional figure

tenth [tenth] One of ten equal parts

Example: 0.7 = seven tenths

thousandth [thou′zəndth] One of one thousand equal parts

Example: 0.006 = six thousandths

transformation [trans•fər•mā′shən] A movement of a figure to a new position by a translation, reflection, or rotation

translation [trans•lā′shən] A movement of a figure to a new position along a straight line; a slide

Example:

trapezoid [tra′pə•zoid] A quadrilateral with exactly one pair of parallel sides

Example:

triangular prism [trī•′ang•gyə•lər priz′əm] A prism in which two parallel faces are triangles

Example:

trillion [′tril-yən] One thousand billion, or 1,000,000,000,000

turn [′tərn] A movement of a figure to a new position by rotating the figure around a point

Example:

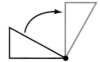

unlike denominators [ən•lik′ di•nä′mə•nā•tər] Two or more denominators that are not the same

unlike things [un•lik′] Two or more quantities that do not have a common unit

variable [vâr′ē•ə•bəl] A letter or symbol that stands for a value that can change

vertex [vûr′teks] The point where two or more rays meet; the point of intersection of two sides of a polygon; the point of intersection of three or more edges of a three-dimensional figure; the plural of vertex is vertices

Example:

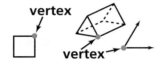

vertical axis [vər•ti•kəl ak′səs] The vertical number line on a coordinate plane

Example:

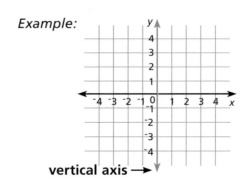

vertical coordinate [vər•ti•kəl kō•ôr′də•nət] In a coordinate pair, the value that is represented by y, which shows the vertical location

Example: In the coordinate pair (4,3), the vertical coordinate is 3.

vertical line [vər•ti•kəl lin] A line at a right angle to the horizon

vertical record [vər•ti•kəl ′re•kərd] A way to write partial products and the total product when multiplying two large numbers

Example:

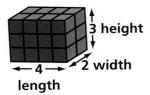

```
    53
   ×26
  1000
   300
    60
    18
  1378
```

volume [väl′yəm] The measure of the amount of space a three-dimensional figure occupies

Example:

3 height
2 width
4
length

The volume of this figure is 24 cubic units.

width [′width] A measure of a side of a figure

x-axis [eks•ak′səs] The horizontal number line on a coordinate plane

y-axis [wi•ak′səs] The vertical number line on a coordinate plane

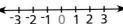

zero [zē•rō] The number (0) between the set of all negative numbers and the set of all positive numbers

Example:

-3 -2 -1 0 1 2 3

Index

A

Act It Out, 102–103, 122–123

Acute triangle, 152

Addition
Cross Number Puzzle, 5
decimals, 118
fraction, 186–189

Algebra
Cross Number Puzzle, 5
draw diagram for situations, 224
equations for balance puzzles, 222–223
equations for balancing mobile, 220–221
find a rule for input-output machines, 6–8, 10
Student Letter, 1, 217
write equation for situation, 225

Angles
formed by intersecting lines, 155
measuring, 151, 156

Area
of net, 208
odd-shaped figure, 175
parallelogram, 172
Student Letter, 167
surface area, 209
trapezoids, 174
triangles, 173–174

Area models
division, 134
splitting for multiplication, 22–23

B

Balance puzzles, 222–223

Balancing mobile, 220–221

C

Challenge, 18, 36, 52, 70, 84, 108, 128, 146, 166, 182, 198, 216, 232, 248, 262

Circle graph, 240–241

Classify
quadrilaterals, 158
three-dimensional figures, 204
triangles, 152

Coins
combinations of, 4

Compare
decimals, 113
fractions, 61

Compatible numbers
estimating by, 27

Composite numbers
defined, 44

Cone
classify, 204

Conversion
graphing, 252

Cross Number Puzzle
addition, 5
multiplying, 11
subtraction, 5

Cups
graphing conversion, 252

D

Data
circle graph, 240–241
describing, 101
line plots, 98
mean, 100
median, 99, 101
mode, 99, 101
percent, 239
range, 99, 101
sampling experiment, 238
scatter plot, 98
Student Letter, 233
survey, 97

Decimals
adding, 118
compare, 113

Page Placement Key: (t) top, (b) bottom, (c) center, (l) left, (r) right, (bg) background, (i) insert.

CHAPTER 1: 2 (bg) Corel; (tr) Mark Thomas/Jupiter Images; 3 (tr) Greg Epperson/Jupiter Images

CHAPTER 2: 20 (bg) Scott B. Rosen/Bill Smith Studio; (tr) Getty Images

CHAPTER 3: 38 (b) AP Photo/Ric Francis; 39 (bg) AP Photo/Bill Janscha; (r) AP Photo/Gene J. Puskar

CHAPTER 4: 54 (tr) Denis Scott/CORBIS; (br) SeaPics; (bl) SeaPics; (bg) Aqua Image/Alamy; 55 (br) SeaPics; (tr) CORBIS

CHAPTER 5: 72 (bl) John Delapp/AlaskaStock; (bg) Corel

CHAPTER 6: 86 (bl) Alexis Rosenfeld/Science Photo Library; (tr) Tony Kwan/Alamy; (bg) Jeff Rotman/Photo Researchers; 87 (tr) Index Stock Imagery/NewsCom; (cr) Alexis Rosenfeld/Photo Researchers

CHAPTER 7: 110 (bg) Christoph Wilhelm/Getty Images; (tr) Alamy; (cr) James L. Amos/CORBIS; 111 (tr) AP Photo/Dan Loh; (cr) Alamy; (br) Getty Images

CHAPTER 8: 130 (bg) Bob Daemmrich/The Image Works; (l) Jupiter Images; (tr) Alamy; (cr) Kelly-Mooney Photography/CORBIS; 131 (tr) Jupiter Images; (c) Alamy; (cr) Alamy

CHAPTER 9: 148 (bg) Jon Arnold Images/Alamy; (t) The Art Archive/Dagli Orti; 149 (t) Getty Images; (b) Art Resource, NY

CHAPTER 10: 168 (bg) John Neubauer/PhotoEdit; (tr) Jack Fields/CORBIS; (c) AFP/Getty Images; (br) Smithsonian Associates; 169 (t) AFP/Getty Images

CHAPTER 11: 184 (b) Angelo Cavalli/SuperStock; (tr) Age Fotostock/SuperStock; 185 (t) Robert Dowling/CORBIS; (t) Kit Houghton/CORBIS; (t) William Hamilton/SuperStock; (t) Alamy; (c) Masterfile; (br) Tierbild Okapia/Photo Researchers

CHAPTER 12: 200 (bg) Sarah Leen/Getty Images; (tr) Frank Lukasseck/Age Fotostock

CHAPTER 13: 218 (tl) ArenaPal/Topham/The Image Works; (cr) Alamy; (b) Index Stock Imagery; (br) Masterfile; 219 (b) Niagara Falls Public Library

CHAPTER 14: 234 (bg) Darren Matthews/Alamy; (bl) Alamy; (tr) iStockphoto; 235 (tr) Darren Matthews/Alamy; (cr) Alamy; (bg) Darren Matthews/Alamy

CHAPTER 15: 250 (bg) William Manning/CORBIS; (cr) Reuters/CORBIS; 251 (tr) George Tiedemann/ GT Images/CORBIS

All other photos © Harcourt School Publishers. Harcourt photos provided by the Harcourt Index, Harcourt IPR, and Harcourt photographers: Weronica Ankarorn, Eric Camden, Doug Dukane, Ken Kinzie, April Riehm, and Steve Williams.